Consumer Behaviour in Sport and Events: Marketing Action

Daniel C. Funk

Griffith Business School,
Department of Tourisim, Leisure,
Hotel and Sport Management,
Griffith University, PMB,
Gold Coast, Queensland,
Australia

ELSEVIER

AMSTERDAM • BOSTON • HEIDELBERG • LONDON • NEW YORK • OXFORD
PARIS • SAN DIEGO • SAN FRANCISCO • SINGAPORE • SYDNEY • TOKYO

Butterworth-Heinemann is an imprint of Elsevier

Butterworth-Heinemann is an imprint of Elsevier
Linacre House, Jordan Hill, Oxford OX2 8DP, UK
30 Corporate Drive, Suite 400, Burlington, MA 01803, USA

First edition 2008

Notice
No responsibility is assumed by the publisher for any injury and/or damage to
persons or property as a matter of products liability, negligence or otherwise, or from any
use or operation of any methods, products, instructions or ideas contained in the material
herein. Because of rapid advances in the medical sciences, in particular, independent
verification of diagnoses and drug dosages should be made

British Library Cataloguing in Publication Data
A catalogue record for this book is available from the British Library

Library of Congress Cataloging-in-Publication Data
A catalog record for this book is available from the Library of Congress

ISBN–13: 978-0-7506-8666-2

Typeset by Charon Tec Ltd., A Macmillan Company.
(www.macmillansolutions.com)

Printed and bound in Hungary

08 09 10 11 12   10 9 8 7 6 5 4 3 2 1

For information on all Butterworth-Heinemann publications
visit our website at elsevierdirect.com

Contents

Sport Marketing Series Preface   *vii*

Acknowledgements   *ix*

About the Author   *xi*

Series Editor Information   *xiii*

Introduction   *xv*

Part 1   **Provides the reader with an introduction to sport and event consumer behaviour followed by a comprehensive understanding of motivation, decision-making and a discussion of sportmarketing activities**   **1**

Chapter 1:   Introduction to Sport and Event Consumer Behaviour   3

Chapter 2:   Sport and Event Consumer Motivation   15

Chapter 3:   Consumer Decision-Making in Sport and Events   29

Chapter 4:   Marketing Action for Sport and Events   57

Part 2   **Provides the reader with a comprehensive understanding of Awareness, Attraction, Attachment, and Allegiance with marketing strategies to promote sport consumption within each stage and concludes with a discussion of perceived constraints that modify or inhibit behaviour**   **85**

Chapter 5:   Consumer Awareness of Sport and Events   87

Chapter 6:   Consumer Attraction to Sport and Events   109

Chapter 7:   Consumer Attachment to Sport and Events   137

Chapter 8:   Consumer Allegiance to Sport and Events   167

Chapter 9:   Constraints to Sport and Event
             Consumption   187

**Part 3   Provides an "Event Management Checklist: A
            Functional Guide to Preparation and Success" to
            help understand marketing actions related to the
            development, promotion and delivery of a
            sport event   201**

Chapter 10: Administrative Services   203

Chapter 11: Facilities and Support Services   221

Chapter 12: Special Events and Services   237

Index   *243*

Sport Marketing Series Preface

The *Sport Marketing Series* provides a superb range of texts for students and practitioners covering all aspects of marketing within sports. Structured in three tiers the series addresses:

- Sub-disciplines within sports marketing: for example, branding, marketing communications, consumer behaviour.
- Sports and sporting properties to which marketing is applied: for example, the marketing of football, the marketing of motor sports, marketing of the Olympic Games.
- Philosophy, methods and research in sports marketing: for example, research methods for sports marketing students, theoretical perspectives in sports marketing, undertaking successful research in sports marketing.

International in scope, they provide essential resources for academics, students and managers alike. Written by renowned experts worldwide and supported by excellent case studies and pedagogic tools to accelerate learning, the texts available in the series provide:

- a high quality, accessible and affordable portfolio of titles which match development needs through various stages;
- cutting-edge research and important developments in key areas of importance;
- a portfolio of both practical and stimulating texts in all areas of sport marketing.

The *Sport Marketing Series* is the first of its kind, and as such is recognised as being of consistent high quality and will quickly become the series of first choice for academics, students and managers.

Acknowledgements

There are a number of people and institutions that I would like to acknowledge for their support and inspiration during the writing of *Consumer Behaviour in Sport and Events: Marketing Action*. This book represents the culmination of a seven-month journey around the world collecting examples and new experiences. Without the support and inspiration of many, this book would have been difficult to complete.

I would like to acknowledge my partner Marcela Corona for her support and encouragement. I would like to thank the team at Butterworth-Heinemann/Elsevier for assistance and help during the development of the chapters and production process. I am grateful to Mark Pritchard at Central Washington University for his input in the development of this book and continued work on projects during my journey. Thanks mate! I appreciate the support from Griffith University for allowing me the opportunity to travel the world while writing this book.

During my journey, I would like to thank Makoto Nakazawa from Tskuba University for providing me a great start to this journey and a unique opportunity to experience many parts of Japan. Thanks to Kostas Alexandris at Aristotle University of Thessaloniki, Greece for the long coffee breaks and discussions on life, work and international affairs. I am grateful to Carl Cater and the Cater family for the experience of English countryside in Aldermaston. My thanks go out to my family and especially Jeff and Agnes for their hospitality in Darmstadt, Germany and later in San Marcos, California. I appreciate the support of Brock University in St. Catherines, Canada and Cheri Bradish. A special thanks to Laura Cousens for your hospitality, friendship and the use of the bike to ride to campus. I am grateful to Steve Sprinkle in Austin, Texas for your generous hospitality and week tour of Austin's iconic destinations. Thanks for the memories.

I would like to thank Besty Barber and the faculty members at Temple University for their hospitality and opportunity to live in Philadelphia and be a part of the Temple family. I appreciate the opportunity to visit my cousin Mary Jo for an enjoyable time skiing in the Colorado Mountains while working on this book. Special thanks to the Corona family for the chance to visit and experience the "real" Mexico. I am grateful to Larry Neal from Queensland University of Technology for your hospitality in Brisbane while working on final stages of this book. Finally, I would like to thank two graduate students Kevin Filo and Anthony Beaton for their continued work on the Psychological Continuum Model. Their ideas and work are well represented in this book. I would also like to thank the following students for their contributions: Amanda Ayling, Tennille Bruun, and Anne Eastgate.

To the countless other people who offered their time and support during this project and journey I thank you.

Sincerely
Daniel C Funk

About the Author

Daniel C. Funk, Ph.D. is a professor of Sport Management with the Griffith Business School, Gold Coast, Australia. He has established an international reputation in the area of Sport Marketing with and emphasis in Sport Consumer Behaviour. His research examines personal, psychological and environmental factors that shape consumer behaviour in sport, event and tourism. This research examines Awareness, Attraction, Attachment and Allegiance through the use of the Psychological Continuum Model; a framework to identify processes and stages that shape the development of attitudes and behaviours among sport consumers. The application of this research provides marketing and management solutions to sport, business, community and government organisations dedicated to the delivery of sport, tourism, event and recreation services and products.

Dr. Funk received his Ph.D. from Ohio State University, Columbus, Ohio. He has worked on the faculties at the University of Louisville and The University of Texas at Austin. Prior to academia, he spent 5 years working as a sport marketing professional developing, implementing, and promoting recreational sport programs and special events in the United States. He has published scholarly work in scientific journals including Journal of Sport Management, Journal of Business Research, Leisure Sciences, European Journal of Marketing, Tourism Management, Sport Management Review, Sport Marketing Quarterly, Perceptual & Motor Skills, European Sport Management Quarterly, International Journal of Sports Marketing and Sponsorship, and International Journal of Sport Management.

Dr. Funk has worked on various international projects examining marketing practices for professional sport teams and sporting events. He has given invited presentations at international conferences and seminars in Australia, Canada, Greece, Japan, New Zealand, Scotland, South Korea and United States. In 2007, he formed the Sport Tourism, Event Research Network STERN a collaborative research network of academics working to enhance the economic, social and environmental sustainability of the sport industry and related sectors. He is a co-author of the 3rd Edition of the premier Australian Sport Marketing text *Strategic Sport Marketing* and published in the 2005 Focus on Exercise and Health Research that examined the effect of modest exercise on perception of exertion for leisure and daily living activities. In 2005, Dr. Funk was selected for inclusion in the Academic Keys Who's Who, an authoritative online source of information available on leading and influential experts and scientists in the field of higher education. He served as co-editor for a special issue on "Sport Consumer Behavior" in the journal Sport Marketing Quarterly. In 2007, Dr Funk was recognized as a Research Fellow by the North American Society for Sport Management for his achievement in sport-related scholarship areas of Sport Marketing and Consumer Behaviour.

Series Editor Information

Simon is a Director of the Birkbeck Sport Business Centre, and Programme Director for the MSc Sport Management and the Business of Football at the University of London. His research interests are based around sport marketing, in particular sponsorship, advertising and marketing communications, relationship marketing, branding, fan behaviour and segmentation strategies. He has published extensively in various areas of sport marketing and sport management, and has worked with various organisations across sport. Simon has also served as a consultant to sport businesses on projects relating to sponsorship management, spectator behaviour, service quality in sport, the international development of sports markets and the use of the internet.

Amongst Simon's other responsibilities, he is Editor of the International Journal of Sports Marketing and Sponsorship, and is an Editorial Board member for Sport Marketing Europe, the International Journal of Sports Marketing and Management, the Journal of Leisure, Sport and Tourism Education, the International Journal of Sport Management, the Journal of Coaching Science and the Journal of Sport and Tourism. He also serves as a national correspondent for the European Association of Sport Management and Sport Marketing Quarterly.

Simon is the founder and Chair of both the Academy of Marketing's Sport Marketing Special Interest Group and the European Sport Marketing Network, is a lead examiner for and a contributor to the Chartered Institute of Marketing's Sports Marketing Certificate programme and is an external examiner at a number of other UK universities. He is an Associate Member of faculty at IESE (University of Navarra) in Madrid, an Honorary Research Fellow of Coventry Business School, and a member of the Advisory Panel for Sport and Markt's European Sport Sponsorship award.

Simon is co-editor of the following books: *The Business of Sport Management*, *The Marketing of Sports and The Business of Tourism Management* (all Financial Times Prentice Hall). He has also contributed chapters to books on football marketing, commercial sport, sport management and sport tourism.

Introduction

Consumer Behaviour in Sport and Events: Marketing Action is a book that emphasises the role of consumer behaviour in developing strategic marketing activities for sport and related events. The book provides a detailed understanding of personal, psychological and environmental factors that influence sport event consumption. This understanding allows for the development of marketing actions useful in matching needs and wants of consumers to build and sustain volume. The book seeks to inform industry professionals and advance students interested in the delivery of sport and event related products and services in business, community and government sectors.

The context of this book approaches the study of consumers by examining attitudes and behaviours relative to sport and related products. This examination covers a wide range of determinants that influence sport consumption but has a specific focus on both active and passive forms of behaviour (i.e., participants and spectators) as well as the event related context of sport events. Given the social, economic and environmental benefits of sports and events, the challenge for marketers is to understand the complexity of participation to develop marketing communication, enhance the consumption experience, and identify key elements of the decision-making process.

Consumer Behaviour in Sports and Events: Marketing Action utilises a theoretical and applied approach to explain the relevant concepts of sport consumer behaviour and its application to marketing activities. The book has three parts. An overview of the chapters that comprise each part is next.

Part 1 provides the reader with an introduction to sport consumer behaviour followed by a comprehensive understanding of motivation decision-making and sport marketing action. Chapter 1 introduces the reader to the study of sport consumer behaviour, its development as an inter-disciplinary field and provides a discussion for its application to business, community and government sectors dedicated to the delivery of sport, tourism, event and recreation services and products. This chapter concludes with an overview of the book. Chapter 2 presents a basic consumer motivation model that leads to a simplified decision-making model to provide a fundamental understanding of the psychology behind consumer behaviour. The final section introduces the notion of SportWay to discuss the numerous pathways individuals take to receive benefits and satisfy needs through sport directed behaviour.

Chapter 3 provides a discussion of the sport decision-making sequence that occurs within three major phases: inputs, internal processing and outputs. This chapter introduces the Psychological Continuum Model (PCM) framework and explains how the stage-based development of Awareness, Attraction, Attachment and Allegiance to sport and sport event participation occurs. Chapter 4 provides a 4-Step Sport Marketing Action process to guide informed decisions developing marketing activities designed to increase participation. This chapter also provides an innovative PCM staging tool that allows for quick and simple segmentation of consumers into stages to aid marketing actions. Chapter 4 concludes with a concise 7-step formula on how to prepare and write marketing reports for an organisation.

Part 2 provides a detailed discussion for personal, psychological and environmental determinants that contribute to the development of Awareness, Attraction, Attachment and Allegiance within the PCM framework and offers marketing recommendations designed to facilitate sport consumption within each stage. Chapter 5 provides an in-depth examination of Awareness and the socialisation processes that influence a person's introduction to sport and related events. The chapter concludes with recommendations for marketing activities designed to facilitate Awareness. Chapter 6 offers a comprehensive understanding of how Awareness leads to Attraction through the realisation that a sport or event satisfies needs and provides attractive benefits. Chapter 6 concludes with marketing recommendations designed to increase Attraction through strategic marketing actions. Chapter 7 provides a discussion for how Attraction leads to Attachment as the individual places emotional, symbolic and functional meaning on the sport or event. This chapter concludes with a discussion of marketing activities designed to reinforce existing attitudes and behaviours to enhance Attachment.

Chapter 8 presents a discussion of how Attachment leads to Allegiance as the psychological connection between an individual and sport object becomes more persistent, resistant, while influencing thinking and guiding behaviour. The chapter concludes with marketing recommendations to increase and sustain Allegiance. Chapter 9 introduces the reader to environmental, personal and psychological constraints that limit and alter the development of sport consumption. The chapter concludes with marketing recommendations to overcome constraints.

Part 3 includes an *Event Management Checklist: A Functional Guide to Preparation and Success*. The checklist provides a comprehensive understanding of marketing actions related to the development, promotion and delivery of an event. This checklist is as a generic tool for planning various types of events and divided into three areas: (1) *Administrative Services*, (2) *Facilities and Support Services*, and (3) *Special Events and Services*. The scope of the checklist is broad enough to touch on many of the areas and covers a number of topics from A to Z to provide assistance in preparing your next event.

PART 1

Provides the reader with an introduction to sport and event consumer behaviour followed by a comprehensive understanding of motivation, decision-making and a discussion of sport marketing activities

Introduction to Sport and Event Consumer Behaviour

Sport consumer behaviour is about the journey not the destination.

The phrase, "Sport consumer behaviour is about the journey not the destination", describes the essence of sport and event consumer behaviour. Sport consumer behaviour whether, it is watching or participating in a sport event, is about the experience. A desire to seek out a consumption experience reflects a desire to satisfy internal needs and receive benefits through acquisition. Even consumption activities that support this behaviour (e.g., retail and services) often attempt to enhance or reactivate the meaning of the sport experience. The amount of time and money individuals devotes to sport and events represent behavioural outcomes of some experiential journey. This journey corresponds to the specific sport or event pathway an individual travels to seek out experiences that provide positive outcomes. From this perspective, sport consumer behaviour and consumption activities that occur at sport event destinations signify the completion of the journey. As a result, the actions of sport marketing professionals should help individuals navigate and enjoy the journey.

Few experiences or settings in society have as much importance or record greater public exposure than sport (Eitzen & Sage, 2003). Statistics in several countries from the years 2002–2004 reveal the importance of sport. In England, 75% of adults took part in some form of sport, game, or physical activity during the previous year. In the United States, 72.1 million adults (35%) attended a sporting event. In addition, 61.8 million (30%) played a sport while 113.3 million (55%) participated in an exercise program. In Australia, over 44% or 7.1 million attended at least one sporting event. In Canada, 55% of the population is annually involved in sport. In Japan, 72% of the population engages in a recreational sport activity. The statistics highlight the importance of sport as well as the sport event context.

Sport and sport events have considerable social impact. Social impacts are consequences to human populations of any public action that alters the ways in which people live, work, play, relate to one another, organise to meet their needs, and generally cope as members of society (Institute for Environmental Studies, 1995). Participation in sport, whether this behavioural action is active, passive, indirect, individual, or event context related, has become an attractive strategy for local, regional, and national governments to provide social benefits for community residents (Johnson & Whitehead, 2000). Sport events play a significant role in a community's marketing and branding strategy (Higham &

Hinch, 2003) as event organisers can attract spectators and participants through the staging of sport events. The type of sport events can vary in terms of focus (e.g., participant or spectator, competitive, single purpose, multiple sport or festival, single day, weekly, monthly, or annual).

In general, sport events fall within four categories. Mega sport events target the international tourism market. The size and scope of their attendance, target market, public financial involvement, political effects, television coverage, facilities, economic and social impact are enormous (Olympics, FIFA World Cup). Hallmark events are linked with a particular destination or location resulting in increased status for that specific place (e.g., Tour De France, London Marathon, Melbourne Cup). Major events are not destination specific but provide significant economic benefits, media coverage and number of visitors based on their size and scope (e.g., Rugby World Cup, UEFA Cup, NFL Superbowl). Local events generally do not meet the criteria of mega, hallmark and major event types and are more regionally based (Triathlon Series, Premier League match).

Despite the importance of sport and events, most countries are experiencing a decline in active sport participation (Van Sluijs, van Poppel, Twisk, Brug, & van Mechelen, 2005), while the demand for spectator sport fluctuates and fragments due to market forces (Andreff & Szymanski, 2006). These trends are occurring while obesity rates, life expectancy and feelings of isolation increase, which has implications for quality of life. Sport has the ability to directly and indirectly influence a number of aspects in a person's life. Sport and events can influence health and well-being, build social cohesion and communities, impact the economy and help shape national and cultural identities (Beaton & Funk, 2008). Why people play and watch sport requires a better understanding of sport consumer behaviour. Sport marketers are likely to find themselves at the forefront in the battle to improve quality of life as sport and leisure activities become central components of promoting healthy lifestyles, and building more integrated communities. In addition, the cost of replacing one customer is six times more expensive than retaining an existing customer (Rosenberg & Czepiel, 1983) and marketing budgets are always limited.

The study of sport consumer behaviour developed from the general field of consumer behaviour. Consumer behaviour emerged in the early 1980s from a variety of disciplines such as marketing, psychology, sociology, anthropology, communication, and education to examine consumption in many forms and contexts. A variety of topics are now investigated including attitudes toward entertainment and social services, purchase behaviour of durable and non-durable products, preference for services such as insurance, tourism, and hospitality, behaviour of household members, influence of culture on purchase intentions, decision-making, and information processing (Wells, 1993).

Within the last decade, a subset of consumer behaviour research has focused specifically on understanding sport consumption activities. This research primarily focuses on describing reasons for attendance and participation at sport events but also examines recreational sport and related consumption behaviours involving media usage, merchandise, services, and tourism (e.g., Funk, Toohey, & Bruun, 2007; Kwon & Armstrong, 2006; McDaniel, 2002; McDonald, Milne, & Hong, 2002; Pritchard & Funk, 2006; Trail & James, 2001; Wakefield & Sloan, 1995). This body of research has built a tradition of testing theories in natural populations to understand why individuals attach so much importance to a sport experience. This approach is useful and has application to business, community, and government sectors dedicated to the delivery of sport and related tourism, event, and recreation services and products.

Sport and Event Consumer Behaviour Defined

Sport and event consumer behaviour (SECB) is the process involved when individuals select, purchase, use, and dispose of sport and sport event related products and services to satisfy needs and receive benefits.

An established definition of sport and event consumer behaviour does not exist. Funk, Mahony, and Havitz (2003) suggest in their critique of prior sport consumer behaviour research that sport consumer behaviour represents consumer behaviour relative to the products and services offered in the sport and leisure industry. In terms of sport event behaviour, there are generally three main components from the tourism literature: (a) travel to participate in a sport event activity, (b) travel to watch a sport event activity, and (c) visiting a sporting attraction (Gibson, 2003). Building upon this information, SECB is defined as the process involved when individuals select, purchase, use, and dispose of sport and sport event related products and services. This process is created by a desire to seek sport consumption experiences that provide benefits and satisfy needs. This definition views SECB as a holistic process that describes how individuals make decisions to spend available resources of time and money on sport and event consumption activities.

- *Time* resources can represent the amount of time devoted to watching either a live sport event in person or via TV, radio, or Internet broadcast, participating in various sport competitions and events and involvement in fantasy leagues or tipping competitions, the use of sport in daily activities such as using the Internet to follow a sport, using sport as a topic of conversation at work and social gatherings, the use of sport language with such terms as "teamwork" and "off-sides" in business, and the amount of media coverage sport receives.

The time devoted to sport and event related consumption activities is not isolated and can include the interaction of multiple sport and non-sport consumption activities. For example, being a professional football fan can have an impact on consumption of football at other levels, or consumption of other spectator sports, or active recreational sport participation. Similarly, devoting time to train for a marathon will have consequences for other consumption activities. The level of attention devoted to sport impacts consumption behaviour not traditionally sport related. For example, individuals may decide on sport related home decorating, food and dining, movies, clothing, education, automobiles, and office supplies. Sport lifestyle purchases often occur among committed bikers, rock climbers, as well as die hard sport fans.

- *Money* resources reflect the financial commitment for the actual sport consumption activities. These activities can include the purchase of tickets to sporting events, memberships to clubs, travel to a sporting event, licensed merchandise, registration fees, sport equipment, subscriptions, media, etc.

Monetary decisions related to the individual budgeting process must be taken into consideration. An individual's financial position will impact the ability to engage in sport and related entertainment activities. An individual's ability to purchase a team membership, season tickets, or travel to compete in a marathon will be determined by the amount of disposable income.

This information provides an understanding of sport consumption thresholds to determine the supply and demand of various sport consumption settings. This places sport consumer decision-making for products and services in a larger marketplace.

Marketing Actions for Sport and Event Consumer Behaviour

Based upon the amount time and financial resources individuals devote to sport and related event consumption activities, sport consumer behaviour represents an important and central aspect of life. As a result, marketing actions should develop a better understanding of consumer decision-making before any strategies are developed. Such an approach involves asking general questions to develop marketing strategies designed to increase and sustain consumer demand for products and services. Some typical questions marketers need to ask sport consumers are listed in Box 1.1.

These questions are standard questions that any researcher or journalist would ask. A marketer wants to determine what type of individual purchases a specific running shoe for recreation, fitness, competition, or fashion. This information helps create market segments because not all consumers buy a pair of shoes for the same reason. These segments highlight desirable features and benefits; as well as the likelihood of replacing their old shoes with new features and benefits. This information becomes important to inform marketers on how to satisfy benefits and needs with new shoe models and match production frequency with which consumers buy replacements. With the emergence of environmental concerns and conservation, this is even more important for many sport products. A further discussion on how to use market research activities to produce information appears in Chapter 4.

The previous running shoe example provides a good example of how sport marketers can obtain information to serve their

---

Box 1.1: Marketing action questions

1. Who are our consumers?
2. What do they buy and how often do they use it?
3. Where do our consumers live?
4. Where, when, and how are our consumers exposed to our product/service?
5. How does our consumer use and dispose of the product/service?
6. How does the product/service make the consumer feel physically and feel about his/herself emotionally?

consumers. However, the unique nature of sport consumer behaviour requires additional understanding for how sport differs from other business products and services. Research that examines experiential consumption reveals that individuals perceive and weigh some consumptive experiences differently than others (Babin, Darden, & Griffin, 1994; Holbrook & Hirschman, 1982). For example, products like detergent, mustard, movies and banking can be perceived as important, but sport experiences differ in terms of the value and meaning consumers ascribe to them (Pritchard & Funk, 2006). This is due in part to the unique nature of sport and events.

Unique Aspects of the Sport and Event Product

A discussion of the unique aspects of sport products, events, and services appears in the Sport Marketing text by Mullin, Hardy, and Sutton (2007). The authors describe how marketing sport and related event products and services differ from traditional marketing in terms of 10 aspects and are worth reviewing to understand the unique nature of sport consumer behaviour:

1. Sport organisations must compete and cooperate:
   - Sport franchises in the English Premier League such as Manchester United and Chelsea must cooperate with each other for the success of the league; while at the same time compete for resources and market share. Marketing activities by Coke and Pepsi do not follow this approach.
2. Sport consumers are experts:
   - Managerial decisions such as player acquisition and strategies in sport do not go unnoticed and the sport consumer often considers himself/herself an expert on running the company. Marketers for Dell computers rarely communicate detailed design and technological information and rarely have radio talk shows devoted to company operations.
3. Supply and demand fluctuates:
   - Sport participation opportunities can be determined by the environmental factors such as climate. Marketers offer outdoor sports such as football and baseball in warmer months, while basketball is offered in colder months.
4. Sport is an intangible product:
   - While sport equipment is easy to understand, selling the benefits received and needs fulfilled from watching or participating in a sport event are hard to pinpoint. Marketing vicarious achievement, socialisation, and escape at a sport

event is more challenging than colour, size, and material for Addidas.

5. Simultaneous consumption:
   - Many sport products are produced and consumed at the same time. In recreational leagues, participants create the game product and if an opposing team does not show up the product is not produced or consumed. In spectator sport, spectators create the atmosphere found at games. Marketing such experiences is difficult when the game does not happen or is over.

6. Social facilitation via sport:
   - Sport is consumed in the presence of others. Less than 2% of spectators attend games by themselves and bikers and runners often ride in groups. Marketers for Frosted Flakes cereal or Cheer detergent rarely have to consider how their product created opportunities for socialisation.

7. Inconsistent nature of the product:
   - A major attraction to sport is its inconsistent nature and the outcome is uncertain. Often, a sport team or individual athlete has a chance to beat an opponent in competition and the action that occurs during competition will be different. Marketers for Toyota do not desire inconsistency in performance of its vehicles as consumers find no joy in wondering whether their car may breakdown.

8. Lack of control over the core product:
   - Sport marketers have little control over the core product. Managers make trades, the league controls rules and regulations, and athletes get hurt. Marketers for Sony rarely have to worry about whether materials in the plant will be available to make their cameras.

9. Reliance on product extensions:
   - Much of the sport experience involves elements not related to the core product. Consumers are entertained through halftime and pre-game promotions, music, and various activities. Marketers often attempt to sell the spectacle that surrounds the event more than the actual competition.

10. Consumer vs. industrial nature of sport:
    - Sport is both a consumer product and an industrial product. A Liverpool football game is consumed by spectators and the London Marathon by participants, while at the same time businesses are using the event to promote various products via sponsorship opportunities.

The 10 unique aspects of the sport event product highlight the need for sport marketing actions that build upon traditional marketing understanding. Sport events provide a number of benefits and opportunities to fulfil individual needs not found in the larger general marketplace. Successful marketing activities should incorporate these elements into strategies that turn the unique challenges into opportunities. A concise four-step sport marketing process will be introduced in Chapter 4 to help guide these activities.

Marketing actions related to sport events can be quite diverse. Marketing activities by the host destination attempt to shape the image of city and stimulate the economy. Tourism marketers also use sport events to reach specific target markets and position the destination to non-residents. Governments can use sport events to build community identification and create jobs. Sponsors of sport events can increase brand awareness, launch new products and services, and open new markets. Finally, sport and recreation organisations can use sport events to promote sport products and services. Regardless of the agenda behind events, marketing actions attempt to achieve fundamental objectives related to: revenue generation (e.g., admission, entry fees, concessions), marketing communications (e.g., mass media, sponsorship, product promotions), community building (e.g., bring fans and participants together), and relationship building (e.g., alliances between participants/spectators, host communities, sponsors, event organisers).

Summary

The introductory chapter provides a broad understanding of sport and event consumer behaviour and considers marketing actions. A comprehensive definition of sport and event consumer behaviour (SCB) was provided which incorporates the notion of mega, hallmark, major and local events. The amount of time and money sport and events receives illustrates the importance of consumer behaviour in our society. A brief discussion of marketing actions highlights how asking simple questions can increase knowledge of the types of benefits sought and needs fulfilled through sport events and illustrates how unique aspects of sport products required the development of sport marketing actions that differ from marketing many traditional products and services. Marketing actions related to the agenda and objectives for events were discussed. The rest of this book will examine these issues in more detail.

References

Andreff, W., & Szymanski, S. (2006). *Handbook on the Economics of Sport*. Cheltenham, UK: Edward Elgar Publishing Limited.

Babin, B.J., Darden, W.R., & Griffin, M. (1994). Work and/or fun: Measuring hedonic and utilitarian shopping value. *Journal of Consumer Research, 20,* 644–656.

Beaton, A.A., & Funk, D.C. (2008). An evaluation of theoretical frameworks for studying physically active leisure. *Leisure Sciences, 30,* 1–18.

Eitzen, D.S., & Sage, G.H. (2003). *Sociology of North American Sport* (7th Ed.). New York: McGraw-Hill.

Funk, D.C., Mahony, D.F., & Havitz, M. (2003). Sport consumer behavior: Assessment and direction. *Sport Marketing Quarterly, 12,* 200–205.

Funk, D.C., Toohey, K., & Bruun, T. (2007). International sport event participation: Prior sport involvement; destination image; and travel motives. *European Sport Management Quarterly, 7,* 227–248.

Gibson, H. (2003). Small-scale event sport tourism: Fans as tourists. *Tourism Management, 24,* 181–190.

Higham, J.E., & Hinch, T.D. (2003). Sport, space and time: Effects of the Otago Highlanders franchise on tourism. *Journal of Sport Management, 17,* 235–257.

Holbrook, M.B., & Hirschman, E.C. (1982). The experiential aspects of consumption: Consumer fantasies, feelings, and fun. *Journal of Consumer Research, 9,* 14–132.

Institute for Environmental Studies (1995). Guidelines and principles for social impact assessment. *Environmental Impact Assessment Review, 15,* 11–43.

Johnson, P.K., & Whitehead, J.C. (2000). Value of public goods from sports stadiums: The CVM approach. *Contemporary Economic Policy, 18*(1), 48–58.

Kwon, H., & Armstrong, K. (2006). Impulse purchases of team licensed merchandise: What matters. *Journal of Sport Management, 20,* 101–119.

McDaniel, S.R. (2002). An exploration of audience demographics, personal values, and lifestyles: Influence on viewing network coverage of the 1996 Summer Olympic Games. *Journal of Sport Management, 2,* 117–131.

McDonald, M.A., Milne, G.R., & Hong, J. (2002). Motivational factors for evaluating sport spectator and participant markets. *Sport Marketing Quarterly, 11,* 100–113.

Mullin, B.J., Hardy, S., & Sutton, W.A. (2007). *Sport Marketing* (3rd Ed.). Champaign, IL: Human Kinetics.

Pritchard, M.P., & Funk, D.C. (2006). Symbiosis and substitution in spectator sport. *Journal of Sport Management, 20,* 297–320.

Rosenberg, L., & Czepiel, J. (1983). A marketing approach for consumer retention. *Journal of Consumer Marketing, 1,* 45–51.

Trail, G.T., & James, J.D. (2001). The motivation scale for sport consumption: Assessment of the scale's psychometric properties. *Journal of Sport Behavior*, 24(1), 108–127.

Van Sluijs, E.M.F., Van Poppel, M.N.M., Twisk, J.W.R., Brug, J., & Van Mechelen, W. (2005). The positive effect on determinants of physical activity of a tailored, general practice-based physical activity intervention. *Health Education Research*, 20, 345–356.

Wakefield, K.L., & Sloan, H.J. (1995). The effects of team loyalty and selected stadium factors on spectator attendance. *Journal of Sport Management*, 9, 153–172.

Wells, W.D. (1993). Discovery oriented consumer research. *Journal of Consumer Research*, 19, 489–504.

CHAPTER 2

Sport and Event Consumer Motivation

Mark is a college student and an avid cyclist. He rides every week-end with his mates and organises a Tour de France watch party every year in July. Mark knows that his favourite athlete Lance Armstrong used a Trek bicycle during the tour. Mark graduates next month and wants to buy himself a special gift for his upcoming grad-uation. He then sees a bike store advertisement announcing a bike sale at a local shop in 2 weeks. Mark decides that a new Trek bicy-cle is exactly what he wants.

The previous story is a typical account of how decision-making occurs in sport consumer behaviour. Mark's involvement in cycling appears to be a critical element in his decision-making process to purchase a new Trek bike. This creates two questions. First, why does Mark's involvement in cycling motivate him to a purchase a Trek bike? Second, and equally importantly, how did Mark become such an avid cyclist? Mark's decision to purchase a Trek bike stems from a number of personal, psychological, and environmental factors. In other words, Mark's involvement moti-vates his decision-making process.

Chapters 2 and 3 are devoted to decision-making. This chapter will address the first question, providing an understanding for how individuals are motivated to make purchase decisions of sport and sport event related products or services. Chapter 3 provides a discussion of a decision-making sequence and intro-duces a framework developed within sport consumer behaviour to understand how an individual's level of sport or sport event involvement influences decision-making.

Involvement represents a state of motivation with regard to a product, an activity, or an object (Rothschild, 1984). This state of motivation reflects the level of arousal, interest, or, drive evoked by a particular sport stimuli or situation that influences consumer behaviour (Mitchell, 1979). In Mark's case, his involvement in cycling represents a strong and continued interest in the sport as a recreational hobby. The motivation to purchase a particular bike brand stems from Mark's graduation, Lance Armstrong, and the sales advertisement. To better understand this process, a simpli-fied model of sport consumer motivation is provided.

Sport Consumer Motivation Process

The sport consumer motivation process refers to the process that causes people to behave the way they do as consumers. Simply put, people are motivated to watch or participate in a sport or sport

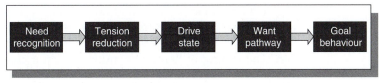

Figure 2.1
Sport and event consumer motivation process.

event activity because the behaviour has certain attractive outcomes. Motivation is an internal factor that arouses and prompts goal-directed behaviour (MacInnis, Moorman, & Jaworski, 1991). At the basic level, sport consumer motivation reflects desires to satisfy an internal need or receive a benefit through acquisition. This motivation process contains five basic stages: needs, tension, drive, want and goal; that occur in a sequence as illustrated in Figure 2.1 (e.g., Schiffman & Kanuk, 2001).

Need Recognition

The motivation process begins with a need recognition stage where an individual recognizes he or she has a need. This need is created when a discrepancy exists between the individual's present state and some ideal state. For example, Mark determines that he needs a new bike because his current bike is 5 years old (present state) and desires a new Trek model bike (some ideal state). There are a number of biological and psychological needs (e.g., internal and external) whcih individuals recognize that initiate the recognition stage. The psychologist Abraham Maslow (1954) proposes a hierarchy of needs that motivate people to action. These include physiological needs (water, air, sleep, food), safety needs (security, shelter, protection), belongingness needs (friendship, acceptance by others), ego needs (prestige, assert one's individual identity, personal accomplishment and achievement), and self-actualization needs (self-fulfilment, skill mastery, enriching experience). There are other needs but these provide a general guide to human behaviour relevant to consumers. The lack of any one need creates the discrepancy and creates tension.

Tension Reduction

The discrepancy between the present state and the ideal state creates a feeling of tension. Tension is an unpleasant state or feeling when a need remains unfulfilled. For example, when you get ready to give a presentation in front of an audience you may feel stress and this is similar to tension. Likewise, the anticipation of hitting a golf ball on the first tee with a group watching can create tension. The feeling of being uncomfortable on a crowded elevator that stops at every floor can also create tension. Individuals try to reduce or even eliminate tension in their lives through the consumption of products and services. For example, Mark may feel a sense of urgency to get a new bike if he wants to participate in a 60 K cycling event in a few weeks after graduation. Tension can develop from many types of needs and the magnitude or level of tension determines the urgency that engages the drive state.

Drive State

The drive state occurs when a person is aroused to reduce or eliminate an unpleasant state and restore balance. Think of the phrase: How motivated are you? The drive state can develop from either biological needs (i.e., I'm hungry), cognitive needs (i.e., I'm bored) or a combination of both. Although fulfilling biological needs is important, this book will focus more on cognitive needs because of the unique nature of sport and the expectation of achieving desirable outcomes. Within the drive state, the degree of pressure exerted on the individual to restore balance creates a "push" and reflects the strength of motivation. For example, Mark's strength of motivation reflects how unpleasant having an old bike makes him feel and whether he perceives a number of positive outcomes from a new bike can reduce this tension. The strength of motivation within the drive state pushes the individual toward considering various pathways capable of restoring balance.

Want Pathway

The want stage represents the pathway toward a specific form of consumption an individual chooses to reduce tension. A need can be satisfied or a benefit received in numerous ways and the specific path a person chooses comes from a unique set of experiences, socio-cultural upbringing, benefits desired, personality, etc. This list of choices is quite long. As a result, the want stage represents a "pull" that draws the person toward a product or service that provides opportunities to receive a desirable outcome and restore balance. In simple terms, reducing tension "pushes" a person forward and the pathway providing the most positive benefits to restore balance "pulls" that individual toward a specific consumption activity. In Mark's case, he believes that purchasing a new bike versus a new computer can reduce his unpleasant feeling of having an old bike.

Push–Pull Motivation

Push: The internal desire to eliminate an unpleasant state and reduce tension initiates motivation.
Pull: The pathway providing the most benefits to restore balance directs motivation.

The push–pull concept illustrates a two-dimensional approach to motivation. Crompton (1979) proposes push motivation represents the recognition of internal social–psychological needs unfilled and pull motivation reflects the seeking of external experiences that can satisfy these needs. Hence, people watch and play sport because an internal desire prompted by need recognition pushes them to seek sport consumption activities because they provide desirable outcomes (Iso-Ahola, 1982). Seeking represents the pathway that pulls or directs the individual toward goal-directed behaviour or acquisition of these desirable outcomes. This stage of the motivation process receives considerable attention from researchers in sport consumer behaviour. The reason for this attention is sport and event marketing professionals understand providing pathways (i.e., avenues to seek benefits and satisfy needs) is easier than creating the need in the first place. For example, making people hungry is harder than providing them the opportunity to eat pies and chips at a football match. As a result, marketing communication can focus on informing individuals how a sport product or service can provide positive outcomes that restore balance. To clarify this stage, we can use a non-sport and sport example.

The first example involves tension created from a basic need. We have two individuals, Bill and Mary, who are equally hungry and have the same drive to reduce the tension of being hungry. However, Bill likes to eat healthy (e.g., salads and yogurt) while Mary does not (e.g., pies and chips). This creates different wants or pathways that can reduce their hunger. The desire to eat creates the push, while the pull directs each down a different "food" pathway to fulfil the need.

The second example involves tension created from psychological needs. Lisa and Tom both feel an unpleasant state or tension created by a desire to escape their weekend routine of working on

Saturday afternoon. For the last 6 months, work has been hectic due to a new product launch at their company. Both like to watch professional football matches, but choose to follow different pathways to reduce tension. Lisa wants to purchase a ticket to attend next Saturday's home match, while Tom wants to go to a local sports pub to watch the match on TV. Hence, the same sport event offers the means to restore balance by reducing boredom, but can accomplish this via different pathways. The desire to escape the normal routine provides the push while the pull directs each down a different "football" experience (e.g., stadium vs. pub vs. TV).

Goal Behaviour

Goal behaviour represents the final point in the motivation process – the acquisition. Goal attainment occurs through a consumption activity that fulfils the need and reduces the tension. In Mark's case, when he purchases a new bike the action or behaviour reduces tension and restores balance. The unpleasant feeling of having an old bike drops or recedes. Mark's purchase represents his expectation that the bike and the specific brand Trek help him achieve desirable outcomes. The motivation process describes how a need pushes and pulls Mark toward buying a bike with certain positive benefits. This process is important for sport marketing, in which the objective is to communicate to consumers that the pathway or experience offered (i.e., product, event, service, brand) provides the best pathway to attain the goal and restore balance. Hence, sport marketers concern themselves with communicating the positive attributes and benefits of their products and services that can direct or pull the consumer along a specific pathway.

Revisiting the previous examples can help clarify this process. It is very difficult for a marketer to make Bill and Mary hungry. However, a sport marketer can communicate that the stadium restaurant has a full service menu with traditional fare (pies and chips) and a new heart smart selection (salads and sushi). For Mary, who likes pies and chips, a marketer will have more success motivating her to order a healthy salad than to make her hungry in the first place. Similarly, for Tom and Lisa, who are bored from working every Saturday, attracting them to watch a professional sport event is easier than making them want to escape their weekly Saturday routine. These examples illustrate how marketing creates a want in the form of specific pathways capable of pulling an individual towards a goal behaviour that can provide desirable outcomes through sport products and services. In summary, sport marketers have limited ability to create

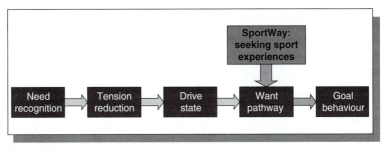

Figure 2.2
SportWay.

the push force operating within the motivation process, but can have considerable success providing and communicating pathways that pull and direct behaviour. Sport marketers can leverage pathways to attract and sustain consumer interest in their products and services.

With a better understanding of the motivation process, an examination of potential pathways that help achieve desirable outcomes follows. This examination will concentrate on the creation of the want pathway stage of the sport motivation process through the introduction of SportWay (see Figure 2.2).

SportWay: Seeking Sport and Event Experiences

The box SportWay illustrates a collection of potential pathways available for individuals to achieve desirable outcomes through sport and event-related goal-directed behaviour. SportWay represents how individuals seek out sport and event experiences that provide opportunities to receive benefits and satisfy needs. In other words, how the push force created from need recognition, tension reduction, and drive state is pulled toward a desire or "wanting" to seek out sport and event consumption activities because of expected positive outcomes. Within SportWay, numerous pathways exist. For example, a person can play or watch baseball, football, running, or golf. These SportWay paths allow individuals to seek out benefits and needs that ultimately lead to sport consumption activities.

> SportWay represents want pathways through which individuals seek out sport and event experiences that provide opportunities to achieve desirable outcomes.

An example using Rachel may be helpful to begin the discussion. Rachel recognises a need to spend more time with her family and wants to take her two children to a women's professional basketball game. Need recognition pushes Rachel to search potential pathways. The professional basketball game represents a specific pathway that Rachel desires to take toward goal behaviour. This desire develops because Rachel expects certain outcomes will occur as a result of attending the game, namely the opportunity to interact and bond with her children. However, there are added benefits of this pathway such as the wholesome environment found at women's professional basketball games, the performance of athletes, the excitement of the game, and reasonable admission prices. Taken together, the opportunity to satisfy a need and additional benefits received help motivate Rachel to take a sport pathway rather than another pathway such as taking her children to a movie.

The above example illustrates how the expectation of positive outcomes creates motivation for sport consumption activities. Motivation simply refers to an activated state that creates a desire to take a specific pathway to achieve a goal-directed behaviour (Mowen & Minor, 1998). Motivation represents a cognitive expression of a motive and a sport motive is an internal factor that arouses a person to engage in behaviour (Iso-Ahola, 1982). In other words, a motive initiates a sequence of cognitive events leading to behaviour (Weiss & Chaumeton, 1992). To clarify this sequence, the need recognised pushes an individual forward and the sport pathway that can satisfy the need or provide benefits pulls the individual toward a specific sport consumption activity (Funk, Toohey, & Bruun, 2007).

Research has identified a number of paths within SportWay that direct sport consumer behaviour. These pathways generally fall into two categories called hedonic and utilitarian motives. Hedonic motives are experiential in nature involving emotional responses that are subjective such as excitement, self-confidence, and fantasy (Holbrook & Hirschman, 1982). For example, Mary is bored from working, thus she desires to watch a professional football game with her friends for 2 hours. In Mark's case, buying a new bike allows him a chance to complete a 60 Km road race. Hedonic needs are found within the top three levels of the Maslow's hierarchy because sport provides opportunities for belongingness (friendship, acceptance by others), ego (prestige, assert one's individual identity, personal accomplishment and achievement), and self-actualization (self-fulfilment, skill mastery, enriching experience).

Utilitarian motives are more functional and represent the objective tangible attributes of a product or service that an individual desires. These typically represent the type of sport context, admission or purchase cost, marquee players and athletes, stadium and produce/service amenities (Gladden & Funk, 2002;

Wakefield & Sloan, 1995). For example, Bob likes to watch football and support his favourite player, but has a limited budget to attend professional football games. In addition, Bob does not like crowds. In Mark's case, utilitarian motives relate to the type of bike desired such as an aluminium bike, painted yellow, made by Trek, with Shimano components and within a certain price range. Sport products and services can provide opportunities for both hedonic and utilitarian motives to be satisfied. For example, Rachel can spend time with her children at a women's basketball game that provides an exciting wholesome atmosphere at a reasonable price with easy access to parking.

The next section will discuss prominent hedonic motives that direct individuals along SportWays. There are numerous hedonic and utilitarian motives in sport consumer behaviour, but this discussion will focus on a core set of hedonic motives identified through research. The reason for this approach is that the subjective nature of hedonic motives and the unique aspects of various sport experiences make these motives more difficult to understand than utilitarian motives. Utilitarian motives are important and examples throughout this book illustrate their role. The following section provides a core set of SportWay motives applicable to both physical engagement of active sport as participants and passive participation of sport spectators.

SportWay toward Consumption

Sport participation both active and passive creates numerous pathways for individuals to seek opportunities to receive benefits and satisfy needs through goal-directed behaviour. These pathways motivate an internal desire to seek out and experience sport or sport events to fulfil physical, social, and personal needs. Researchers have identified a number of sport consumer motives that push and pull individuals toward specific sport experiences. This information is used to develop tools in the form of research scales (i.e., questionnaires) to better aid marketers (cf., Beard, & Ragheb, 1983; Crompton, & McKay, 1997; Funk, & Bruun, 2007; Funk, Mahony, & Ridinger, 2002; Gladden, & Funk, 2002; Madrigal, 2006; Trail & James, 2001; Wann, 1995, Zhang & Lam, 1999). A detailed discussion of the scales and their content appears in Chapter 6. However, a common set of core motives to evaluate why individuals seek out sport experiences to receive benefits and satisfy needs does not exist.

Prior research has been instructive but a comprehensive list of motives capable of explaining the wide variety of push and pull motives in sport contexts led to a proliferation of scales. As a result, the number of motives and the length of the questionnaire grew considerably, making it difficult for sport marketing professionals to determine the best tool to use. Sport marketers require a more parsimonious measurement tool capable of measuring basic motives for attending and participating in sport events. In response to this scale proliferation, researchers are working to develop a core set of motives to bring parsimony to the study of sport consumer behaviour and create a manageable tool useful for practitioners and researchers.

James, Trial, Zhang, Wann, and Funk (2006) attempted to bring parsimony to this line of inquiry by proposing the SportWay Motives. The SportWay Motives represents a core set of needs and benefits (push and pull) provided by sport. These motives include socialisation, performance, excitement, esteem, and diversion. Subsequent research indicates the Big 5 is a valuable measure of sport consumers' motivation for professional team sports and successfully distinguishes between those that attend events

Table 2.1 SportWay Motives in Consumer Behaviour

SportWay	Description
Socialisation	Socialisation represents a desire for social interaction. Individuals are motivated to seek a sport event experience due to opportunities for the enhancement of human relationships through external interaction with other spectators, participants, friends, and family.
Performance	Performance represents a desire for aesthetic and physical pleasure. Individuals are motivated to seek a sport experience due to opportunities to enjoy the grace, skill, and artistry of athletic movement and physiological movement.
Excitement	Excitement represents a desire for intellectual stimulation. Individuals are motivated to seek a sport event experience due to opportunities for mental action and exploration from the atmospheric conditions created by the uncertainty of participation and competition and the spectacle of associated activities.
Esteem	Esteem represents a desire for competency. Individuals are motivated to seek a sport event experience due to opportunities for achievement and challenge that produce a sense of mastery and heighten a sense of personal and collective self-esteem.
Diversion	Diversion represents a desire for mental well-being. Individuals are motivated to seek a sport event experience due to opportunities to escape and remove themselves from daily work and life routines the create stress.

and those that do not (Beaton, Filo, & Funk, 2007). Table 2.1 provides a list of the Big 5 Sport Motives with an explanation of each motive. The core SportWay pathways are socialisation, performance, esteem, excitement, and diversion.

This list represents a common set of motives found among prior scales in the sport literature. As a result, these motives are both theoretically supported and practically useful to understand why people engage in sport consumer activities across various sport experiences. In addition, the motive labels create the acronym SPEED providing a useful means to remember the Big 5. This acronym further illustrates attempts to facilitate sport consumer research by reducing the number of motives to a manageable number of factors and improve knowledge sharing among academics and practitioners. In other words, get everyone on the same page or reading the same playbook. These five SportWay motives provide a common sense interpretation to guide day-to-day activities of marketers and researchers.

SPEED Motives

Socialisation
Performance
Excitement
Esteem
Diversion

The SportWay motives can facilitate future work in sport and event consumer behaviour by providing the ability to examine and compare "core" motives across a variety of sport contexts. These motives also represent a platform from which to build and identify additional contextual motives (e.g., utilitarian motives) for specific sporting events. For example, the desire to participate in an international sport event must consider core SPEED pathways (i.e., motives), but also probe deeper to understand the sport tourism context related to seeking an opportunity to experience, explore and learn about a foreign destination's culture (Funk, Toohey & Bruun, 2007).

Summary

This chapter provides a basic understanding of the motivation process that directs sport and event consumer behaviour. The desire to watch or participate in a sport event occurs within five stages involving need recognition, tension reduction, drive state, want pathway, and goal behaviour. This sequence illustrates how a need recognised creates internal tension that pushes an individual toward seeking pathways that provide opportunities to satisfy the need and receive benefits through behaviour. Within the want pathway stage, the idea of SportWay was introduced to illustrate how this push force can be directed along five core sport pathway motives of socialisation, performance, excitement, esteem, and diversion (SPEED). The SportWay can pull an individual toward engaging in sport consumption activities of watching and participating in sport.

References

Beard, J.G., & Ragheb, M.G. (1983). Measuring leisure motivation. *Journal of Leisure Research, 15,* 219–228.

Beaton, A.A., Filo, K., & Funk, D.C. (2007). Achieving parsimony in sport consumption motivations: A convenient truth. *Proceedings from the Sport Management Association of Australia and New Zealand,* Auckland, NZ.

Crompton, J.L. (1979). Motivations for pleasure vacation. *Annals of Tourism Research, October/December,* 408–424.

Crompton, J.L., & McKay, S.L. (1997). Motives of visitors attending festival events. *Annals of Tourism Research, 24,* 425–439.

Funk, D.C., & Bruun, T. (2007). The role of socio-psychological and culture-education motives in marketing international sport tourism: A cross-cultural perspective. *Tourism Management, 28,* 806–819.

Funk, D.C., Mahony, D.F., & Ridinger, L. (2002). Characterizing consumer motivation as individual difference factors: Augmenting the Sport Interest Inventory (SII) to explain level of spectator support. *Sport Marketing Quarterly, 11,* 33–43.

Funk, D.C., Toohey, K., & Bruun, T. (2007). International sport event participation: Prior sport involvement; destination image; and travel motives. *European Sport Management Quarterly, 7,* 227–248.

Gladden, J.M., & Funk, D.C. (2002). Developing and understanding of brand association in team sport: Empirical evidence from professional sport consumers. *Journal of Sport Management, 16,* 54–81.

Holbrook, M.B., & Hirschman, E.C. (1982). The experiential aspects of consumption: Consumer fantasies, feelings, and fun. *Journal of Consumer Research, 9,* 132–141.

Iso-Ahola, S.E. (1982). Toward a social psychological theory of tourism motivation: A rejoinder. *Annals of Tourism Research, 9,* 256–262.

James, J., Trail, G., Wann, D., Zhang, J., & Funk, D.C. (2006). Bringing parsimony to the study of sport consumer motivations: Development of The Big 5. *Symposium at the North American Society for Sport Management Conference,* Kansas City, MO, USA.

MacInnis, D.J., Moorman, C., & Jaworski, B.J. (1991). Enhancing and measuring consumers' motivation, opportunity, and ability to process brand information from ads. *Journal of Marketing, 55,* 32–53.

Madrigal, R. (2006). Measuring the multidimensional nature of sporting event consumption. *Journal of Leisure Research, 38,* 267–292.

Maslow, A. (1954). *Motivation and Personality.* New York: Harper and Row.

Mitchell, A.A. (1979). Involvement: A potentially important mediator of consumer behavior. *Advances in Consumer Research, 6,* 191–196.

Mowen, J.C., & Minor, M. (1998). *Consumer Behavior* (5th Ed.) NJ: Prentice-Hill.

Rothschild, M.L. (1984). Perspectives on involvement: Current problems and future directions. *Advances in Consumer Research, 11,* 216–217.

Schiffman, L.G., & Kanuk, L.L. (2001). *Consumer Behavior* (7th Ed). Englewood Cliffs, NJ: Prentice Hall.

Trail, G.T., & James, J.D. (2001). The motivation scale for sport consumption: Assessment of the scale's psychometric properties. *Journal of Sport Behavior, 24*(1), 108–127.

Wakefield, K.L., & Sloan, H.J. (1995). The effects of team loyalty and selected stadium factors on spectator attendance. *Journal of Sport Management, 9,* 153–172.

Wann, D.L. (1995). Preliminary validation of the sport fan motivation scale. *Journal of Sport and Social Issues, 19*(4), 377–396.

Weiss, M.R., & Chaumeton, N. (1992). Motivational orientations in sport. In S. Thelma (Ed.), *Horn Advances in Sport Psychology* (pp. 61–99). Champaign, IL: Human Kinetics Publishers.

Zhang, Q.H., & Lam, T. (1999). An analysis of mainland Chinese visitors' motivations to visit Hong Kong. *Tourism Management, 20,* 587–594.

CHAPTER 3

Consumer Decision-Making in Sport and Events

> What then is time?
> If no one asks me, I know what it is.
> If I wish to explain it to him who asks, I do not know.
>
> > Saint Augustine (354–430 AD)

Similar to Saint Augustine's view of "time" some 1600 years ago, the meaning of sport consumer behaviour remains difficult to describe. Individuals can describe what sport or sport event is important to them and when the activity takes on greater significance in their lives. However, like Augustine they struggle to describe "why" something is so important and "how" did it become so meaningful.

The challenge for sport marketing professionals and researchers is to identify key elements of the decision-making process that influence behaviours (Crompton & McKay, 1997). From Chapter 2, one element is the motivation process that pushes and pulls an individual toward specific pathways to satisfy needs and receive benefits. Five core SportWay pathways of socialisation, performance, escape, esteem, and diversion (SPEED) are prominent reasons individuals seek to engage in sport consumption activities. This chapter explores other key elements through a simplified decision-making sequence to illustrate how external and internal forces shape sport consumer behaviour.

The sport consumer decision-making sequence accounts for the selection of SportWay paths to acquire needs and benefits. As Figure 3.1 illustrates, the sport decision-making sequence

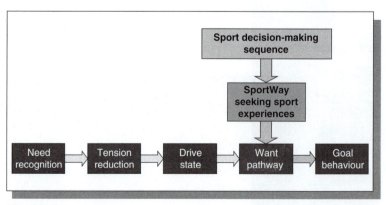

Figure 3.1
Motivation, SportWay and Sport Decision-Making.

influences the selection of potential SportWay paths that allow individuals to engage in sport consumption activities and acquire desirable outcomes. However, selection is a multifaceted process and does not necessarily follow such a simplistic process. In addition, consumer decision-making often involves an individual using a choice or combination of heuristics to determine decisions from memory. As a result, choice largely draws upon prior knowledge to evaluate new, consistent, and conflicting information and has particular importance in consumer decision-making (Bettman, Johnson, & Payne, 1991). The application of prior knowledge shapes many forms of sport consumer activity and work by Funk and James (2006) suggests the level of prior knowledge plays a central role in the developmental progression of sport consumer involvement. The next section discusses each phase of the sport decision-making sequence.

Sport Decision-Making Sequence

Figure 3.2 illustrates a simplistic view of how the sport and event decision-making sequence occurs within three major phases: inputs, internal processing, and outputs. The inputs phase represents a number of external forces that influence the evaluation of the sport object in the second phase. Inputs generally include sociological influences and marketing activities. The second phase represents internal processing of inputs via internal forces. These internal forces are unobservable cognitive processes such as motivation, personality, perception, and memory that shape the evaluation of the sport consumption experience and influence the output phase. The output phase represents psychological and behavioural outcomes. Psychological outcomes indicate the

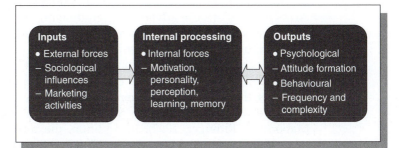

Figure 3.2
Sport decision-making sequence.

level of attitude formation. Behavioural outcomes represent the frequency and complexity of behaviour. The next section provides a detailed discussion of each phase.

Inputs Phase: External Forces

The input phase represents how external forces influence an individual's recognition of whether a product or service helps achieve a desirable outcome. These external forces consist of two categories and are major sources of environmental information that help individuals realise that SportWay paths can satisfy needs and provide benefits. The first information category occurs through a sport organisation's marketing actions. We can refer to the four P's of the marketing mix: product, place, price, and promotion with a special emphasis on promotion and product related customer service. For example, through advertising, Mary recognises how attending a basketball game provides an opportunity to spend time with her children at a reasonable price. Promotional communication can inform individuals how desirable outcomes can be acquired (e.g., SPEED motives) from engaging in sport and consumption activities and specific attributes (price, location, time) of the sport product and service. A more detailed discussion on marketing action occurs in Chapter 4.

The second environmental informational category is sociological influences that help individuals determine whether a sport consumption activity provides desirable outcomes. Sociological influences consist of information and recommendations we receive from family, friends, work colleague, neighbours, and non-commercial sources. These influences can also come from geography and climate, social class, gender, culture, values, and subculture membership. Remember the example of Mark in Chapter 2, inputs for his desire for a Trek bicycle were the environmental sources of him as a cycling enthusiast, Lance Armstrong, bike store advertising, graduation, his lifestyle, and parents whose custom is to buy a gift for graduation.

The inputs phase highlights the importance of understanding how environmental inputs shape the sport decision-making sequence. These inputs are critical in developing marketing activities that educate consumers regarding the acquisition of desirable outcomes through a sport product or service (Funk, Mahony, & Ridinger, 2002). In addition, the relative influence of each environmental input is significant. For example, promotional strategies such as the bike shop advertising generally have less impact than socialising agents and create the notion that positive word-of-mouth may be the most important asset a sport marketer possesses.

Internal Processing

The second phase of the decision-making sequence represents internal processing influenced by environmental inputs. The internal processing component encompasses a number of activities including need recognition, pre-purchase search, and evaluation of alternatives. The processes component contains many unobservable internal influences and attempts to understand the inner workings of an individual's mind otherwise known as the "mental box." Environmental inputs enter the mental box and then outputs emerge. Unfortunately, it is very difficult to see inside a person's head to understand how the mental box operates. Figure 3.3 provides an illustration to help understand the workings of the sport consumer mental box.

The processing of environmental inputs that occurs within the mental box is based on a person using internal psychological and personal forces. Psychological inputs represent intrinsic and extrinsic factors (e.g., hedonic and utilitarian needs, and benefits desired). Personal factors represent person-specific characteristics and dispositions (e.g., gender, body type, ethnicity, lifecycle, direct experience, personality). Hence, sport and event

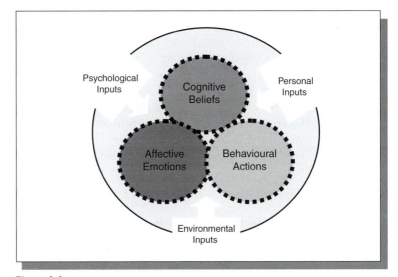

Figure 3.3
Internal processing.

consumer behaviour represent the product of processing internal (i.e., personal and psychological) and external (i.e., environmental) inputs. This processing occurs via three types of evaluations cognitive, affective and behavioural represented as gears in Figure 3.3. Think of gears in a machine or a clock that turn. The activation and movement of one gear creates movement in the other two gears. For example, information about a sport or event object activates the cognitive gear causing it to turn. This rotation causes the affective and behavioural gears to start rotating.

Internal processing represents the manner in which an individual evaluates external inputs and utilizes internal inputs conduct the evaluation. Processing activates the internal gears within the mental box to create the evaluation. The size and power of each gear (i.e., cognitive, affective or behavioural) determines how external and internal inputs are evaluated. For example, Alex may utilise the affective gear relying on feelings and emotions to evaluate inputs related to a sport or event object. In contrast, Pat may evaluate the same inputs utilizing a cognitive gear that reflects rational thinking and beliefs. Finally, Mackenzie may use the behavioural gear that draws upon physiological reactions to performing consumption actions. In other words, internal processing is the mechanism that activates the rotation and direction of attitudinal gears in Figure 3.3 and determines the evaluation of environmental, psychological and personal inputs.

The evaluation process represents a number of internal processes including motivation, perception, learning, memory, and personality. These processing mechanisms evaluate whether a person can obtain needs and benefits through a specific SportWay compared to alternatives (sport and non-sport). This evaluation process largely draws upon prior knowledge to evaluate new, consistent, and conflicting information to determine the degree to which engagement in a sport activity provides desirable outcomes. Hence, the existing level of knowledge, and particularly acquisition of knowledge, about a sport object are important to control the movement of the gears. The acquisition of knowledge occurs through a number of internal processes including motivation, perception, learning, memory, and personality.

Knowledge Acquisition through Motivation

Sport motivation as discussed in Chapter 2 reflects a process that directs sport goal directed behaviour to acquire attractive outcomes. Motivation is a sequence with five basic components, needs, tension, drive, want, and goal, that determine an individual desire and willingness to engage in cognitive or behavioural activities. This sequence illustrates how a need recognised creates internal tension that drives an individual toward seeking sport pathways (i.e., SportWay) that provide opportunities to satisfy the need and receive benefits. Reducing tension "pushes" a person forward and the pathway providing the most positive benefits "pulls" that individual to select a specific consumption activity to restore balance. For example, the introductory story of Mark in Chapter 2 illustrates how psychological and personal needs activate the motivation sequence to acquire knowledge to satisfy these needs. Subsequently, environmental inputs direct Mark toward a specific consumption activity (e.g., pre-purchase search and consideration of alternatives).

Push needs generally initiate motivation prior to pull forces in the decision-making process (Dann, 1996). Funk, Toohey, and Bruun (2007) suggest that the push–pull concept of motivation occurs through knowledge of psychological, personal, and environmental factors. The ability to evaluate the push–pull forces depends upon prior knowledge and environmental inputs. Environmental inputs help refine the recognition of a need and this recognition can direct an individual to engage in pre-purchase search for activity information, trial participation, and the evaluation of alternatives. The evaluation of this information stems from the activation of personal and psychological inputs. In other words, motivation to acquire knowledge can control the movement of the gears in Figure 3.3 to determine what different SportWay paths exist and which one is the best to achieve desirable outcomes.

Let us return to Mark's decision-making process to help clarify. Mark's friends who are cyclists, his graduation, respect for Lance Armstrong, and the store advertising are environmental inputs that influence Mark's motivation. This environmental input interacts with internal factors (personal and psychological inputs) within Mark and creates the recognition of a need for a new bike. Mark now seeks a specific Sportway goal behaviour in the form of a new Trek road bicycle because it satisfies various SPEED motives. He immediately visits five online bike websites to compare models and prices. He also spends considerable time on Ebay to gather information. On the weekend, he visits three local bike stores to compare various models and prices against his online research. Mark determines he can buy a bike cheaper online but is concerned with the risk and hassle of an online purchase. In addition, the traditional bike retailer has a good bike mechanic and provides a free annual tune-up. This example illustrates Mark's level of motivation to acquire knowledge but also depends upon perception.

Knowledge Acquisition through Perception

Perception influences the evaluation of a sport experience through acquiring, interpreting, selecting, and organising sensory information. Perception occurs when an individual interprets information through the sensory system (vision, smell, sound, touch, taste) and a cognitive filter that selects certain information from a vast array of stimuli. Perception depends upon the person, situation, and the object and sport consumers are constantly interpreting cues about sport products and services (e.g., attributes, benefits, risk of an activity or purchase). Sport consumers evaluate situational characteristics of the sport event environment through sensory arousal or pleasure (Donovan & Rossiter, 1982; Holbrook & Hirschman, 1982). Research in sport considers the role of situational or environmental effects in creating an "atmosphere" that augments the consumption experience (Madrigal, 2003). Sport offers an exciting atmosphere as a spectacle and the drama of uncertainty (Funk, Ridinger, & Moorman, 2003; Zuckerman, 1983). This environment influences the evaluation of a sport experience through processing sensory information and the cues inform evaluation leading to knowledge acquisition through learning.

Knowledge Acquisition through Learning

Learning is the acquisition of knowledge through education and experience. Knowledge develops from simple learning process such as observation to more complex associated learning process such as operant and classical conditioning. A sport consumer can learn through observing behaviours of others indirectly (e.g., watching on TV, reading about the event) or directly through engagement (attending or participating in a live sport event) (Funk & James, 2001). Hence, sport consumers may learn about sport objects through a learn-feel-do process or a do-feel-learn process. Learning also provides prior exposure and direct experience with a sport product or service. The basis of a future decision depends upon the level of knowledge learned from prior experiences. Sport consumers continue to engage in playing and watching sport activities because of past experiences, especially if an experience fulfils expectations.

Much of the learning in sport is complex with respect to goal directed behaviour and occurs through operant conditioning. For example, following a sport team to satisfy a need for affiliation or following a successful team to satisfy a need for self-esteem. Learning can also occur through formal and informal channels including school, church, community-based programs, parents, peers, coaches, and mass media (James, 2001). An individual has the ability to learn skills, understanding, values and wisdom by observing how to behave from others and learning to perform behaviours that produce positive outcomes. A person can also learn to avoid behaviours that lead to negative outcomes. Knowledge occurs as new information in the form of environmental inputs confirms or disconfirms preconceived notions. This acquisition of knowledge through learning influences how sport consumers store information in memory.

Knowledge Acquisition through Memory

The role of memory contributes to knowledge acquisition through an individual's ability to store, retain, and subsequently retrieve information. Memory involves the process of acquiring information through perception and learning and storing it over time until needed. The duration of memory and the ability to retain information depends upon sensory memory, short-term memory, and long-term memory. The perception of the atmosphere by a sport fan or participant during a sport event is an example of sensory memory. This information is then transferred to short-term memory allowing an individual to recall the atmosphere for as long as a minute. Unfortunately, short-term memory has limited capacity and duration which means that unless this process is repeated it will only be available for a certain period of time. If the process is repeated, then knowledge is transferred to long-term memory and can be available for an individual's entire life.

The evaluation of hedonic and situational experience depends upon the effects of memory. For example, an individual's knowledge of cricket contains both long-term and short-term memory. Short-term memory influences a spectator's evaluation of the cricket match experience while at the game, but also the ultimate selection of cricket as a sport activity to follow frequently depends upon long-term memory. Hence, the evaluation of a sport experience depends upon the prior knowledge structure and how new information is integrated and retrieved. The knowledge structure represents the complexity of memory from which a sport consumer evaluates external inputs. A sport consumer has a memory structure that consists of a network of inter-related nodes of knowledge on a specific sport object similar to a spider web. Figure 3.4 provides an illustration of an association network for a sport consumer. The figure represents associations linked to a professional sport team identified by Gladden and

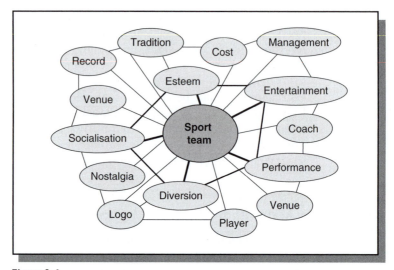

Figure 3.4
Example of an association network for sport fan.

Funk (2002). The association nodes contain unique knowledge about specific attributes and benefits of the sport team.

The associative network links the knowledge nodes together to form a memory schema. A schema is a mental structure that consumers use to organise current knowledge and provides a framework for future understanding. The schema represents the level of knowledge available to evaluate environmental inputs about the sport activity from perception and learning. This schema influences the storage and retrieval of information to evaluate the sport experience to determine whether need recognition, pre-purchase search and evaluation of alternatives.

Knowledge Acquisition through Personality

The previous discussion of motivation, learning, and knowledge illustrate how environmental inputs are internally evaluated using internal psychological and personal factors. An additional internal factor is the role of personality on knowledge acquisition. Personality represents a set of individual characteristics that uniquely influence internal processing (Ryckman, 2007). These characteristics shape internal processing by determining the level or degree of emotions and beliefs used in the evaluation (Kassin, 2003). Personality traits such as extraversion, openness, agreeableness, neuroticism, or conscientiousness (McCrae & John, 1992) influence the evaluation process. For example, specific traits such as self-monitoring inform the use of public association with athletic teams to enhance self-representation (Mahony, Madrigal, & Howard, 1999). In addition, some individuals have a stronger need for cognition that influences the evaluation processing of inputs.

The previous section provides an overview of how internal processing of environmental inputs creates knowledge about a sport object or experience. To clarify this process, Holt (1995) illustrates how knowledge is acquired through an evaluation of the consumption experience. Mary has a general level of awareness about baseball from various socialising agents (e.g., brother, mother, and TV). Her first experiential encounter occurs through search and trail behaviour while attending a game. While in the stands, Mary attempts to make sense of the baseball experience and to do this, must engage in an evaluative process. This process involves perception, learning, memory, and personality. Mary attempts to determine the type of actions and objects surrounding the baseball game, assign specific value and meaning to each action and object, and make connections to prior knowledge she has about baseball. The evaluation process contributes to Mary constructing value judgements regarding baseball and judgement made on situations, people, and actions. This evaluation leads to a short-term appreciation of her experience and her initial positive emotional response becomes part of long-term memory. Mary's association network or schema is developing. Mary has moved from knowing about baseball games to feeling that she likes attending baseball games.

The internal processing phase is a complex aspect of the sport consumer decision-making sequence. The evaluation of environmental, personal and psychological inputs is shaped by motivation, learning, perception, memory and personality. Hence, sport and event consumer decision-making is the product of evaluating external and internal inputs using three interlocking gears (see Figure 3.3).

This evaluation largely draws upon prior knowledge to determine the relative importance of each gear in the overall processing sequence and subsequently leads to the output phase.

Output Phase: Behavioural and Psychological Outcomes

The final stage of the decision-making sequence represents psychological and behavioural outcomes. Psychological outcomes indicate the formation of an attitude toward a sport object or experience. Research suggests an attitude possesses three main components or classes of evaluative responses: cognitive, affective, and behavioural intent that occur in a linear structure (Bagozzi, Tybout, Craig, & Sternthal, 1979; Fishbein & Ajzen, 1975). Cognitive outcomes represent a category of evaluative responses containing thoughts a person has about a sport object (Funk, Haugtvedt, & Howard, 2000). Cognitive outcomes are generally non-emotive and consist of knowledge-based beliefs about whether a sport experience provides needs and benefits. These beliefs describe knowledge-based association linked to a sport object (Gladden & Funk, 2002) (see Figure 3.4). Affective outcomes consist of feelings, emotions, or moods that people experience in relation to the sport object. Affective outcomes are emotive and consist of positive affect due to the desirability and the degree to which potential needs and benefits result. Behavioural intent consists of an individual's readiness to engage in a specific activity (Ajzen, 2001).

Psychological outcomes describe how attitude formation and change occur as cognitive thoughts influence feelings. These feelings in turn influence behavioural intent and actual behaviour. Sport consumer behaviour research often focuses on the affective component, but recent efforts seek to understand the cognitive component's relationship to feelings (e.g., Funk & Pritchard, 2006; Kang, 2002). The reason for the new approach is that the type of internal processing determines normative and subjective beliefs that can influence an individual's positive or negative feelings toward a sport object (Funk, Haugtvedt, & Howard, 2000). In other words, the acquisition of knowledge creates beliefs that influence feelings through the affective evaluation of the sport object or experience. The affective evaluation of a sport object influences a person's behavioural intent and ultimately the actual engagement of the consumptive behaviour.

Behavioural outcomes represent an individual's observable response with respect to a given sport object. These responses can include purchase behaviour, post-decision activities of purchase behaviour and post-experience behaviour. Sport purchase behaviour outcomes can take many forms as illustrated in Chapter 1 in terms of how individuals spend available resources of time and money on sport consumption activities. It may be easier to think of sport purchase behaviour as consisting of both experiential activities and traditional transactional activities. For example, the unique experiential aspects of sport products and services create simultaneous consumption. Simultaneous consumption occurs as sport fans and participants actually create and consume the product and service at the same time.

For example, the consumption of a football match has i related activities. Pat can watch a football match live, on TV, on radio, via the internet and use the newspaper and internet to read about the same match. Pat's love of football may also create participation in a recreational league and the purchase of team related merchandise. Purchase behaviour can be activities directly related to the experience of attending a live sporting event, watching and listening to the event broadcast on TV, Radio, Internet, attending a sports bar or live site to watch the event. Purchase behaviour can also include transactional activities like acquiring tickets or registering online or over the phone, purchase of sport equipment, and sport licensed merchandise.

Post-experience behaviour in sport is equally complex. This behaviour consists of consumption activities not related to the actual physical experience during a sport event. A major influence for post-experience behaviour is the evaluation of the experience. These activities can be reading about a recently competed event in the newspaper, on the Internet, listening to radio talk show, watching ESPN's highlight coverage, sharing thoughts and opinions among friends, family, and work colleagues. Such activities also stem from the evaluation of the experience in terms of service quality and satisfaction. For example, service quality considerations relate to were there enough bathrooms and were they clean, was parking accessible, what type of food was provided, and was the price reasonable. The post-experience evaluation also considers whether the event fulfilled the need or provided expected benefits. For example, were Pat's SPEED motives satisfied by the experience? Did Pat like the experience?

The double-headed arrow in Figure 3.2 illustrates how outputs can feed directly back into the internal processing phase. This feedback occurs because the evaluation of the experience influences future internal processing. Psychological and behavioural outcomes provide knowledge acquisition related to the sport object and experience. Such knowledge plays an important role in subsequent evaluations of environmental inputs. In other words, outputs serve to guide future decisions regarding sport consumption activities.

The proceeding discussion illustrates how a decision to engage in sport consumption activities occurs through a sequence of inputs, processes, and outputs. The decision-making sequence describes how external forces derived from a person's environment serve as inputs that interact with internal personal and psychological inputs to create attitudinal and behaviour outcomes. Hence, sport consumer decision-making is a product of evaluating personal, psychological, and environmental inputs.

This evaluation shapes a desire to seek SportWay paths that provide opportunities to satisfy needs and receive benefits. The specific SportWay chosen also represents an evaluation based upon knowledge and direct experience.

The sport decision-making sequence of inputs, processes, and outputs is important because it provides the necessary foundation to understand why individuals initially choose and continually engage in sport consumption activities. This understanding helps answer the second question posed in Chapter 2 in how did Mark become such an avid cyclist in the first place? This sequence provides the basic tools required to use a much larger framework to address why some individuals' engage more frequently in sport activities and form stronger psychological connections with sport and events than other individuals do. This framework is the psychological continuum model (PCM) (Funk & James, 2001, 2006) and describes how individual and social situational factors work together in the development of sport consumer involvement. Sport consumer involvement draws upon the decision-making sequence to produce different levels of involvement with sport objects. The object can be any related object (e.g., sport, team, player, event, activity). The PCM explains how inputs, processes, and outputs create a developmental progression. The rest of this chapter provides an overview of the PCM to lay the foundation for subsequent Chapters 5–8 in which a more detailed explanation of each stage occurs.

Psychological Continuum Model

PCM is a framework to organise prior literature from various academic disciplines applied to consumer behaviour to explain sport and event consumer behaviour (Funk & James, 2001). This framework suggests watching, playing, and engaging in continuous sport consumption activities progresses along four general hierarchical stages: awareness, attraction, attachment, or allegiance. A discussion of research and writing from various disciplines offers a means to understand and examine each stage. A revision to the PCM framework occurred in 2006 to include inputs, processes, and outputs to examine movement between the four stages (Funk & James, 2006). The PCM uses a vertical framework to characterise various psychological connections that individuals form with sport objects to explain the role of attitude formation that directs behaviours across a variety of sport consumption activities (see Figure 3.5) for a depiction of the PCM framework.

The PCM framework provides a systematic and detailed explanation accounting for the *how* and *why* in sport consumer

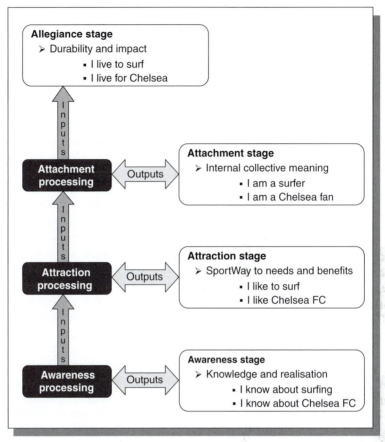

Figure 3.5
Psychological continuum model.

behaviour and has the ability to produce public theories. Public theories are based on data and empiricism. Public theories can be further classified in terms of their scope as either grand or middle-range theories (Henderson, Presley, & Bialeschki, 2004). Grand theories attempt to produce universal truths that operate irrespective of context. Middle-range theories are context specific. As a result, the PCM framework enables the creation of middle-range theories applicable for understanding conceptually distinct behaviours in sport, recreation, tourism, and leisure. These theories are important to guide researchers, practitioners, and policy makers to assist in theory development, facilitate collaboration, enhance the research–practice relationship and allow rigorous testing and evaluation of interventions, policies, and programs (Beaton & Funk, 2008).

The PCM offers a comprehensive framework to explain how personal, psychological, and environmental factors influence sport and event consumption activities in both active and passive forms (Beaton & Funk, 2008). The PCM framework in Figure 3.5 integrates the decision-making process previously discussed in this chapter. For example, the inputs and processing gears illustrated in Figure 3.3 operate within the PCM framework to determine how a person evaluates a sport or event object and produces different psychological and behavioural outcomes.

At first glance, Figure 3.5, appears quite complex. However, the figure simply integrates the sport decision-making sequence in a horizontal manner. Inputs are "grey arrows" and influence internal processing located in the "black boxes" that create outputs signified by "light grey arrows." The main difference is that outcomes are divided into four different stages (i.e., white boxes). The PCM framework suggests there is a unique decision-making sequence based upon the level of involvement. In other words, there is a unique input–internal processing–output sequence at each stage.

The white boxes on previous page represent four psychological outcomes labelled awareness stage, attraction stage, attachment stage, and allegiance stage. These stages represent a developmental progression individuals go through as they increase their level of involvement with a sport object. The black boxes represent three categories of internal processing labelled awareness processing, attraction processing, and attachment processing. The hierarchy of the boxes indicate an evaluation of the sport object differs based upon the prior level of involvement and produces different outputs.

The grey arrows are inputs that influence internal processing. Inputs are environmental factors and outputs from a preceding stage that feedback into processes (i.e., light grey arrows). As indicated by the double-headed light grey arrows, outputs serve as inputs in the processing boxes for the next higher stage. This represents the feedback loop previously discussed in the decision-making sequence. Hence, both grey and light grey arrows are inputs that influence internal processing. The PCM framework suggests that an individual progresses upward along the four psychological stages through the processing of internal and external inputs. Hence, the evaluation of a sport object at a specific level is a product of processing personal, psychological, and environmental inputs.

It may be helpful to think of a four-story building with an elevator. The white boxes represent floors and the higher up you go in the elevator the more involved you become with a sport object or activity. For example, the awareness stage is the ground floor where you enter and exit the elevator. The top floor, allegiance, is where you are fully committed and continuously engage in a specific sport consumption activity. However, the PCM elevator is a bit different in that a person must visit each floor for a period prior to proceeding to the next floor. As a result, a person may not skip a floor, but the amount of time spent on a specific floor depends upon the decision-making sequence. In other words, the level of advancement and length of time on a particular floor depend upon the evaluation of personal, psychological, and environmental inputs. This proposition is based on the application of prior knowledge and experience that shapes attitude formation and change in sport consumer activity. Attitude formation and change highlight movement within the PCM framework in terms of the developmental progression of sport consumer involvement.

Movement with the PCM Framework

Movement with the PCM elevator results from internal processing of inputs. Internal processing represents a number of internal mechanisms that control direction and speed of movement. Revisit Figure 3.3 and think about the three gears turning inside the PCM elevator. Internal mechanisms move gears and the gears move the levers that push and pull the individual between floors. The speed and direction of movement depend upon the relative influence of each gear. As indicated by the black boxes in Figure 3.5, there are three different internal processes based upon the stage. In other words, the internal mechanisms of motivation, perception, learning, memory, and personality operate in the processes of awareness, attraction, and attachment, but these mechanisms operate differently depending upon stage.

The awareness processing creates outcomes of knowledge and realisation that a sport object exists. Since awareness is the initial stage, inputs are external sources. Awareness stage outcomes are noted by two sport examples of *I know about surfing* and *I know about Chelsea FC* within the awareness stage box. The awareness stage outputs subsequently feedback serving as internal inputs along with new external inputs for attraction processing. The attraction processing creates outcomes of seeking SportWay opportunities that satisfy needs and receive benefits, as well as engaging in consumption behaviour related to the sport object and events. These needs and benefits represent the SPEED motives listed in Table 2.1. The examples of *I like surfing* and *I like Chelsea FC* illustrate the attraction stage box. The attraction outputs subsequently feedback serving as inputs along with new external inputs in the attachment processing.

The attachment processing creates the internal collective meaning of the sport object or experience. Attachment stage outcomes occur when SportWay benefits and the sport object are internalised taking on a collective emotional, functional, and symbolic meaning. This is noted by the example of *I am a surfer* and *I am a Chelsea fan* within the attachment stage box. The attachment stage outputs subsequently feedback into the attachment process serving as internal inputs along with new external inputs. As the attachment processing continues, the internal collective meaning becomes more durable in terms of persistence and resistance and has greater impact on cognitive activities and behaviour. This is noted by the examples of *I live to surf* and *I live for Chelsea FC* within the allegiance stage.

The hierarchy of stages within the PCM framework portrays how the internal processing of external and internal inputs progressively changes as the individual becomes more involved with a sport object. As illustrated by the white boxes in Figure 3.5, the statements form a hierarchical progression of greater psychological connection. The relative influence of inputs on internal processing gradually moves from external in awareness processing to a combination of external and internal within the attraction process to primarily internal in the attachment processing. In other words, the relative importance of personal, psychological, and environmental inputs change as a person moves upward. Changes to internal processing also occur creating different outputs within each stage as the level of psychological outcomes progressively increases from minimal to heighten and the level of behavioural outcomes moves from simple to complex.

If we return to our example of Mark the cycling enthusiast in Chapter 2, we can begin to understand how his involvement in cycling is a critical element for his decision to purchase a new Trek bicycle. This level of involvement determines the impact of external and internal forces such as the bike shop advertisement, Lance Armstrong, selection of graduation present, etc. Equally important is now we can understand how Mark became such an avid cyclist as we trace his progression through the PCM framework.

Mark's Awareness

Mark's introduction to road cycling occurred at the age of 15 years through a key socialising agent, his uncle Stan. Stan was elite triathlete, bought Mark his first bike at age four, and taught him how to ride. Mark, like many children, spent his primary school years riding a bike in the neighbourhood along with participating in many other sports. However, at 15 Mark went to watch his uncle participate in a regional triathlon championship and was impressed with the road bike component of the event. Mark and his uncle had often talked about cycling, even watched the Tour de France together a few times. Mark had ridden his mountain bike occasionally but until that moment, had never shown a desire for road cycling. Mark knew about cycling, but did not prefer cycling to other sport activities. Mark's progression to the attraction stage began when his uncle gave Mark one of his old road bikes to use and took him riding on Saturday. Over the next year, Mark began cycling a few times a month and decided he liked the idea of cycling.

Mark's Attraction

Mark began to realise that cycling provided him a number of positive outcomes or SPEED opportunities. He was able to meet other cyclists, make new friends and spend time with his uncle (social interaction). Mark received pleasure from the experience of riding through the hills on a sunny morning (performance) and the thrill of riding down hills at 50 kilometres per hour (excitement). Mark enjoyed being the fastest up the hills, usually rode in the front of the Pele ton, and considered one of the best riders (esteem). Finally, riding gave Mark a chance to get away from studying and weekend house chores (diversion).

Mark's Attachment

Mark progressed into the attachment stage relatively quickly and within a year began riding every Saturday morning and Tuesday evening. Cycling now was an important part of Mark's life as he entered college and he attached functional, emotional, and symbolic meaning to the sport. He often wore cycling clothes to class, spent time visiting bike shops, used the Internet to follow international cycling events, and joined the University's cycling club. Mark even travelled to a few regional cycling competitions with his friends who were predominantly cyclists.

Mark's Allegiance

Mark progressed into the allegiance stage during his last year of college as the strength of his connection to cycling became durable. Mark thought of cycling and related activities daily. He always found time to ride and follow the sport regardless of university and work requirements or other sport opportunities. Mark's connection to cycling impacts the amount of mental effort devoted to selecting and processing information, which primarily occurs through a cycling filter consistently guiding his behaviour. As a result, it is understandable how Mark's decision to ask his parents to buy him a new bike for his graduation was influenced by his involvement with cycling.

Please remember that few individuals beyond mechanical engineers know the intricate workings of elevators. Many know how to use an elevator and can observe inputs such as pushing a button and outcomes such as going from ground level to the third floor. However, the mechanical process involving simultaneous working of various parts such as pulleys, levers, cables, electric circuits, and timing belts operates unseen. This is similar to sport consumption where often we only observe the type and frequency of consumption behaviour without knowing the internal mechanisms that influence behavioural outcomes. The PCM provides an understanding of how both psychological and behavioural outcomes progressively increase as a person becomes more involved with a sport activity. This linear relationship serves to aid would be sport consumer behaviour engineers with means to understand how attitudes and behaviour work together. Figure 3.6 presents this relationship in a linear pattern.

Engagement

Figure 3.6 illustrates how psychological and behavioural outcomes increase as a person progresses through the stages of the PCM. Psychological engagement ranges from "minimal" to "enhanced" in the black box. It may be helpful to remember that psychological engagement represents attitudinal formation and change created through the decision-making sequence. Behavioural engagement progresses from "simple to complex" in the light grey boxes. The stage-based developmental engagement results from the activation of internal mechanisms within awareness, attraction, attachment processing located in the linear grey boxes.

Psychological engagement represents the level of attitude formation and change that occurs as a person becomes more involved with a sport object. The literature indicates an attitude forms from a psychological tendency expressed by evaluating a particular entity with some degree of favour or disfavour (Eagly & Chaiken, 2007). The authors suggest an attitude has three key elements: evaluation, entity, and tendency. *Evaluation* refers to

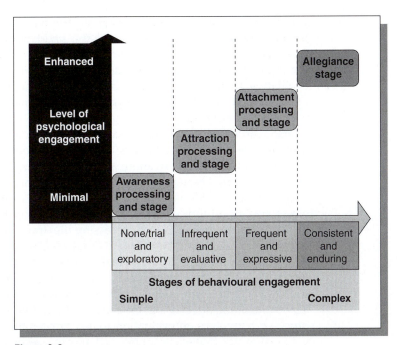

Figure 3.6
Psychological and Behavioural Engagement.

an evaluative response that creates cognitive beliefs, values and thoughts, affective feelings or emotions, and overt or intentional behaviours. *Entity* represents the focal object, tangible or intangible, capable of producing an evaluative response. *Tendency* refers to an enduring evaluative response or personal disposition. These key elements of an attitude suggest an individual who continually engages in sport consumption activities (i.e., allegiance stage in dark grey box) evaluates the focal sport experience with a high degree of enduring favour.

The integration of attitude formation and change to account for movement within the PCM framework suggest psychological engagement is the formation, function, and effect of attitude development. *Form* represents characteristics of the attitude that determine the quality of an attitude's internal nature (e.g., complex, consistent, rigid). *Function* represents the processes of determining an attitude's immediacy in retrieval from memory and its propinquity to self. *Effect* represents an attitude's capacity to resist change over time and its effect on information processing. As the person moves through the stages, his/her attitude evolves, becoming more highly formed (e.g., increases in complexity and strength). Behavioural engagement corresponds to psychological engagement, representing the type and frequency of consumption activities related to the sport object, and progressing from simple to complex. Figure 3.6 illustrates this progression with the boxes trial and exploratory, infrequent and evaluative, frequent and expressive and consistent and enduring.

Engagement results from the operation of internal mechanisms within awareness, attraction and attachment processing. As previously discussed, the acquisition of knowledge from which to evaluate the sport object occurs through a number of internal processes including motivation, perception, learning, memory, and personality. These processes represent general processes that shape evaluation. However, as a person engages a sport or event object, specific attitudinal processes emerge. These internal mechanisms represent three types of processing illustrated in Figure 3.3: cognitive, affective, and behavioural (Eagly & Chaiken, 1995).

Cognitive processing stipulates that a connection to a sport object forms from evaluating informational inputs derived from various sources including direct and indirect experience and socialising agents including advertising, media, friends, and family. Affective processing involves an evaluation that compares the sport object with a stimulus that elicits an internal affective response and after repeated activation the connection is formed (Bagozzi, Gopinath & Nyer, 1999). Behavioural processing creates a connection with a sport object based on an evaluation from past behaviour or consistent with behavioural intent (Funk & James, 2004). Behavioural processing outlines how physiological experiences can influence cognitive and affective elaboration ultimately leads to behavioural intent and is embodied in an individual's readiness to perform a specific behaviour (Ajzen, 2001). All the three types of processing occur within awareness, attraction and attachment, but the relative influence of these processing mechanisms change as the individual moves within the PCM framework.

Awareness Processing

Within the awareness processing, behavioural learning, and minimal cognitive evaluation prevail, creating a non-emotional connection with a sport object. This creates psychological engagement such as "I know about golf" and the awareness stage has been reached. A person devotes minimal cognitive effort toward a sport object and behaviour is simplistic. The level of psychological engagement occurs because minimal attitude formation has taken place based more upon preconceptions created from various socialising agents and information sources than direct experiences.

Behavioural engagement occurs through search and trail behaviour as the individual first becomes aware and explores a sport activity. Behaviour can range from non-existent to unplanned to random and correspond to limited knowledge and minimal prior experiences with related consumption activities. For example, a person may know about golf as a recreational and professional sport, have played in a work-related golf outing, went to the driving range with a friend, played putt-putt golf, watched a golf event on TV, and occasionally read golf stories in the newspaper.

Attraction Processing

Within attraction processing, a cognitive–affective form of processing emerges that evaluates the object in terms of benefits and needs. This type of processing introduces an emotional element to the connection. This creates psychological engagement such as "I like golf" or "Golf is a bit ordinary." The attraction stage is achieved when psychological engagement becomes more active and behavioural engagement increases in complexity. Psychological engagement is enhanced as the previous weak attitude toward the sport object changes and continues to form and take shape. This enhancement is driven by the activation of positive perceptions and discounting misconceptions about whether the activity offers desirable outcomes. Behavioural engagement ranges from infrequent to necessary and increases in complexity through learning and evaluation. This complexity occurs as the individual begins to participate and watch sports, internalise experiences, interpret and assign value and meaning to actions, constructs value judgements regarding situations and people, integrates a variety of elements of the activity to learn roles and interacts with fellow participants and spectators via mutual experience. For example, Pat would like to play a bit more golf so she can learn the rules and etiquette, be able to play better and not embarrass herself, enjoy the outdoors, spend time with friends and family, and network with work colleagues and potential clients.

Attachment Processing

Within attachment processing, the cognitive–affective evaluation becomes more complex creating a meaningful connection. This creates psychological engagement such as "I am a golfer." The attachment stage is achieved when the amount and intensity of cognitive activity considers the internal and external meaning of the sport object, enhancing psychological engagement. The formation of a person's attitude begins to strengthen, producing consistency between feeling and beliefs. The attitude evaluation functions in a manner that aligns the sport object with important, personally relevant and centrally aligned values and self-concept. Behavioural engagement increases in complexity as the type of actions performed and their frequency are linked to functional, emotional, and symbolic meaning. Behaviour becomes standard and repetitive creating opportunities for self-expression that can form the basis of behaviour related to self-developmental tasks, and integration with others within the subculture. Behaviours may still fluctuate due to traits and values that a person already possesses as part of their self-concept, but generally conform to expectancies, while uncertainty is resolved in norm referenced behaviour to produce authenticity of the perceived outcomes. For example, playing golf once a month, buying golf clubs, wearing golf related clothing to work and non-work related activities, subscribing to Golf Digest, following the PGA and European tour on the Internet, watching the British Open, and joining a golf club represent examples of expressive and frequent behaviour.

The final stage of allegiance represents attachment processing through affective–cognitive consistency. The attitude is highly formed, possessing the capacity to resist change over time, while also influencing information processing and guiding behaviour. This creates the most enhanced level of psychological engagement where the evaluative response is characterised by a high degree of prior experience and knowledge. For example, the statement "I live to golf" embodies this level of engagement. The enhanced level of cognitive complexity contributes to the strength of resistance allowing the individual to refute or block against persuasive communication that conveys negative information about a preferred object or attractive information about competing alternatives. Behavioural engagement increases in complexity as the behavioural actions that occur in attachment continue but increase in terms of breadth, depth, and frequency. Behavioural engagement forms the basis of continuance that represents behavioural consistency in terms of complex actions that are enduring and consistent. Specifically, the level of media use, merchandise purchased/used, expenditure on golf products, active participation, and length of time participating. This level of behaviour demonstrates engagement that is consistent and enduring.

The preceding section provides a basic understanding for how a person's involvement with a sport object progressively develops. This progression is depicted as occurring in a linear fashion corresponding to levels of psychological engagement (minimal to enhanced) and stages of behavioural engagements (simple to complex). Unfortunately, human behaviour is quite complex and rarely follows such a simplified linear pattern. In addition, some behaviour is more difficult to perform or has different meaning such as watching an event live vs. watching on television. Figure 3.6 includes dotted lines that separate each stage into boundaries to illustrate how psychological and behavioural engagement may not follow such a simplified linear progression. For example, Bob is a die-hard Manchester United fan, but does not attend matches for an entire season and only watches a few on TV. Hence, Bob would be located in the upper left hand area of Figure 3.6. This may occur because of work and family commitments, or financial constraints.

Bob represents a latently engaged individual (Backman & Crompton, 1991) because his attendance behaviour appears to be simple and less frequent often found in the awareness stage but he actually has a strong psychological connection often found in the allegiance stage. In contrast, you can have a spuriously engaged individual. For example, Sarah goes to every Manchester United match during a season and watches away games on TV. However, Sarah admits that she does not really care about ManU and only attends and watches matches to spend time with her friends. Hence, Sarah's behaviour appears to be enduring and routine, but her psychological connection to the team is similar to that found in the attraction stage. Sarah would be found in the lower right hand area of Figure 3.6.

Participant sport also has latent and spurious engagement. Mary may not run for a year but still refers to herself as a runner. Frank may not play golf for 6 months, but watches, reads, and talks about golf constantly. A number of constraints such as family, injury, work, money, lack of playing partner could prevent behaviour. In contrast, Carla may play golf once a month, but does so only to network within the local business community. Bill may run every third day after work but finds no joy in "pounding the pavement." If he could figure out how to run past the Pie and Chip shop at lunch, he would bin the Nike running shoes and settle for a movie.

These examples illustrate how a person's behavioural engagement level sometimes does not match his/her psychological engagement level. Most often, an enhanced psychological engagement does not correspond with greater behavioural complexity making the engagement relationship appear vertical. For example, indirect behaviour such as media use is a substitute for actual direct attendance behaviour (Pritchard & Funk, 2006). As a result, it is important to identify the breadth and depth of behaviour, as well as those behavioural acts that are more restrictive to perform. Chapter 9 provides a further discussion of this topic.

Summary

This chapter reveals how a decision to engage in sport consumption activities occurs through a sequence of inputs, processes, and outputs. The decision-making sequence is a product of evaluating personal, psychological, and environmental inputs that form attitudinal and behavioural formation and change outcomes. The PCM integrates this evaluative sequence into a hierarchical framework to describe how and why an individual progresses upward along four stages: awareness, attraction, attachment, and allegiance. The PCM framework suggests there are three unique decision-making processes: awareness, attraction, and attachment that contribute to the developmental progression. These processes are based on level of involvement and govern the evaluation of personal, psychological, and environmental inputs. As the level of involvement progresses, the type of processing increases the level of psychological engagement from minimal to enhanced and behavioural engagement from simple to complex.

References

Ajzen, I. (2001). Nature and operation of attitudes. *Annual Review of Psychology, 52*, 27–58.

Backman, S.J., & Crompton, J.L. (1991). Using loyalty matrix to differentiate between high, spurious, latent and loyal participants in two leisure services. *Journal of Park and Recreation Administration, 9(1)*, 1–17.

Bagozzi, R.P., Tybout, A.M., Craig, C.S., & Sternthal, B. (1979). The construct validity of the tripartite classification of attitudes. *Journal of Marketing Research, 16*, 88–95.

Bagozzi, R.P, Gopinath, M., & Nyer, P.U. (1999). The Role of Emotions in Marketing. *Journal of the Academy of Marketing Science, 27*, 184-206.

Beaton, A.A., & Funk, D.C. (2008). An evaluation of theoretical frameworks for studying physically active leisure. *Leisure Sciences, 30*, 1–18.

Bettman, J.R., Johnson, E.J., & Payne, J.W. (1991). Consumer decision making. In T.S. Robertson, & H.H. Kassarjian (Eds.), *Handbook of Consumer Behavior* (pp. 281–315). Upper Saddle River, NJ: Prentice-Hall.

Crompton, J.L., & McKay, S.L. (1997). Motives of visitors attending festival events. *Annals of Tourism Research, 24*, 425–439.

Dann, G.M.S. (1996). Tourists' images of a destination – an alternative analysis. *Journal of Travel and Tourism Marketing, 5*, 41–45.

Donovan, R.J., & Rossiter, J.R. (1982). Store atmosphere: An environmental psychology approach. *Journal of Retailing, 58,* 34–57.

Eagly, A.H., & Chaiken, S. (1995). Attitude strength, attitude structure, and resistance to change. In R.E. Petty, & J.A. Krosnick (Eds.), *Attitude Strength: Antecedents and Consequences* (pp. 413–432). Mahwah, NJ: Lawrence Erlbaum Associates.

Eagly, A.H., & Chaiken, S. (October 2007). The advantages of an inclusive definition of attitude. *Social Cognition, 25*(5), 582–602.

Fishbein, M., & Ajzen, I. (1975). *Belief, Attitude, Intention, and Behavior: An Introduction to Theory and Research.* Reading, MA: Addison-Wesley.

Funk, D.C., & James, J. (2001). The psychological continuum model: A conceptual framework for understanding an individual's psychological connection to sport. *Sport Management Review, 2,* 119–150.

Funk, D.C., & James, J.D. (2004). The Fan Attitude Network (FAN) Model: Propositions for exploring identity and attitude formation among sport consumers. *Sport Management Review, 7,* 1–26.

Funk, D.C., & James, J. (2006). Consumer loyalty: The meaning of attachment in the development of sport team allegiance. *Journal of Sport Management, 20,* 189–217.

Funk, D.C., & Pritchard, M. (2006). Responses to publicity in sports: Commitment's moderation of message effects. *Journal of Business Research, 59,* 613–621.

Funk, D.C., Haugtvedt, C.P., & Howard, D.R. (2000). Contemporary attitude theory in sport: Theoretical considerations and implications. *Sport Management Review, 3,* 124–144.

Funk, D.C., Mahony, D.F., & Ridinger, L. (2002). Characterizing consumer motivation as individual difference factors: Augmenting the Sport Interest Inventory (SII) to explain level of spectator support. *Sport Marketing Quarterly, 11,* 33–43.

Funk, D.C., Ridinger, L., & Moorman, A.J. (2003). Understanding consumer support: Extending the Sport Interest Inventory (SII) to examine individual differences among women's professional sport consumers. *Sport Management Review, 6,* 1–32.

Funk, D.C., Toohey, K., & Bruun, T. (2007). International sport event participation: Prior sport involvement; destination image; and travel motives. *European Sport Management Quarterly, 7,* 227–248.

Gladden, J.M., & Funk, D.C. (2002). Developing and understanding of brand association in team sport: Empirical evidence from professional sport consumers. *Journal of Sport Management, 16,* 54–81.

Henderson, K.A., Presley, J., & Bialeschki, M.D. (2004). Theory in recreation and leisure research: Reflections from the editors. *Leisure Sciences, 26*, 411–425.

Holbrook, M.B., & Hirschman, E.C. (1982). The experiential aspects of consumption: Consumer fantasies, feelings, and fun. *Journal of Consumer Research, 9*, 114–132.

Holt, D.B. (1995). How consumers consume: A typology of consumption practices. *Journal of Consumer Research, 22*, 1–16.

James, J.D. (2001). The role of cognitive development and socialization in the initial development of team loyalty. *Leisure Sciences, 23*, 233–262.

Kang, J. (2002). A structural model of image-based and utilitarian decision-making processes for participant sport consumption. *Journal of Sport Management, 16*, 173–189.

Kassin, S. (2003). *Psychology*. USA: Prentice-Hall, Inc.

Madrigal, R. (2003). Investigating an evolving leisure experience: Antecedents and consequences of spectator affect during a live sporting event. *Journal of Leisure Research, 35*, 23–48.

Mahony, D.F., Madrigal, R., & Howard, D.R. (1999). The effect of individual levels of self-monitoring on loyalty to professional football teams. *International Journal of Sports Marketing & Sponsorship, 1*, 146–167.

McCrae, R.R., & John, O.P. (1992). An introduction to the five-factor model and its applications. *Journal of Personality, 60*, 175–215.

Ryckman, R.M. (2007). *Theories of Personality* (9th Ed.). Belmont, CA: Wadsworth Publishing.

Zuckerman, M. (1983). Sensation seeking and sports. *Personality and Individual Differences, 4*, 285–293.

CHAPTER 4

Marketing Action for Sport and Events

At 26 years, Pat graduated with a Masters from Brighten University. Pat loves sports and frequently attends football and cricket matches with her friends and family. However, her first love has always been running so when she was offered a sport marketing job with Triple F Management she was over the moon. Triple F produces a number of sport events for participants and spectators and recently acquired the rights to produce the 4th annual Pig & Whistle Marathon event. The 3rd annual Pig & Whistle had 2,000 runners participating in a full marathon and 10 Km distances. Within the first month at Triple F, Pat took charge of marketing the Pig & Whistle scheduled to take place in seven months. Pat's supervisor at Triple F informed her that a 20% revenue increase was the marketing target for this year's event and her performance evaluation directly related to achieving this target.

Sport marketing action creates opportunities for individuals to satisfy needs and receive benefits through an exchange process. Sport marketing consists of activities designed to match needs and wants of consumers with sport products and services (Shilbury, Westerbeek, Quick, & Funk, 2009). For Pat, developing a marketing approach that positions the Pig & Whistle to attract new runners and entice previous event participants to return requires an understanding of sport consumer behaviour. Chapter 4 presents an overview of sport marketing and introduces a four-step sport marketing action procedure to position sport products and services within the total sport exchange process. A detailed discussion of each marketing action illustrates the role sport consumer behaviour has in developing sport marketing activities.

Sport marketing action within the sport industry has traditionally approached marketing activities by focusing on selling products and services (Mullin, Hardy, & Sutton, 2007). There are two general reasons for this approach. The first stems from the lack of trained staff working in the marketing capacity. Sport and recreation organisation often use part-time employees and other personnel as marketing staff who do not understand the marketing process. The second reason is the lack of market research being conducted that allows a sport organisation to understand consumer needs and wants. Together, these practices create a "selling" orientation for products and services rather than developing a "service" orientation approach that focuses on providing opportunities for individuals to achieve desirable outcomes.

The ultimate goal of sport marketing action is to build and sustain volume for an organisation. Three methods are used to achieve this goal. The first is to attract new customers through a traditional selling approach. The second method is to do more business with existing customers. The third method is to reduce the loss of existing customers. The latter two methods represent a consumer retention approach that incorporates a service orientation. The study of sport consumer behaviour provides the necessary information and knowledge to inform all the three approaches.

The sport exchange process occurs from the interaction between customer and sport service provider. As a result, sport marketing represents a series of activities that communicate positive outcomes achievable through the sport experience. As discussed in Chapters 1 and 2, sport products and services have unique aspects that allow individuals to seek opportunities to fulfil needs and receive benefits not found in the larger general marketplace. Utilitarian motives represent the objective tangible benefits of a product or service, such as the type of sport context, admission or purchase cost, marquee players and athletes, stadium and produce/service amenities (Gladden & Funk, 2002). Hedonic motives represent the intangible benefits of the experience and involve emotional responses (Robinson & Trail, 2005), such as SPEED motives. This requires sport marketing activities that augment traditional marketing activities by incorporating these unique aspects into strategies that communicate how utilitarian and hedonic benefits can be realised through sport consumption.

Sport marketers must understand what tangible and intangible benefits their product or service provides. This information helps the marketing professional meet the desires of potential and existing customers within the total sport exchange process. As a result, sport marketing action depends upon understanding the reasons for sport consumer behaviour as discussed previously in Chapters 2 and 3. The following section outlines how this knowledge informs the development of sport marketing activities. A sport marketing action (SMA) procedure employs four actions that serve as a simple guide to apply sport consumer behaviour to market sport products and services (see Figure 4.1 for a depiction of SMA). The SMA procedure has four interrelated actions labelled: strategic use of the marketing mix, select key target markets, study and evaluate the market, and selection information system. These actions generally occur in a circular sequence as outlined by the arrows in Figure 4.1 with the information systems supporting the other three actions.

The story of Pat at the beginning of the chapter is useful to understand the SMA procedure. Pat is responsible for marketing the Pig & Whistle. The sport and event management company

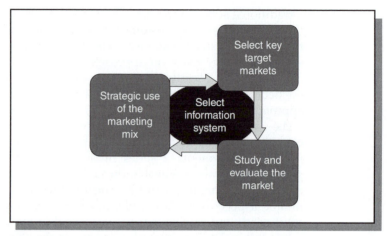

Figure 4.1
Sport marketing action.

Pat works for wants to increase participation by 20%. Pat decides she can reach this participation target by increasing first-time runners by 10% and repeat runners by 10%. She now begins to think about the type of marketing actions required to achieve this target.

The first action Pat takes is the strategic use of the marketing mix. This occurs through positioning the Pig & Whistle's marketing approach and incorporating the marketing mix elements. In other words, how to position the Pig & Whistle as a SportWay that allows an individual the opportunity to satisfy needs and receive benefits. For example, should Pat add a Half-marathon and a 5 Km Fun Run to the current event? Pat knows that most runners are participating in the event because of SPEED motives and positioning the event to provide these opportunities is a good marketing approach. However, Pat realises positioning the Pig & Whistle requires more information because to increase participation by 20%, she needs to market the event to attract both new runners and repeat runners. These two segments may have different needs and wants.

At this point, Pat moves to the second action in the SMA procedure and selects key target markets. She believes a decision to participate in the Pig & Whistle by new runners and repeat runners may result from different inputs, processes, and outputs based on the level of involvement. For example, new runners in the awareness or attraction stage of the PCM are probably influenced more by environmental inputs. In contrast, repeat runners in the attachment or allegiance stages rely more on internal forces to make participation decisions. Pat also realises that identifying additional segments within these two key target markets such as gender, age, location, and income could help in the marketing approach. In fact, Pat could position the event differently depending upon the target market selected. Unfortunately, Pat's company has limited information on previous races and in the past has not conducted sport marketing research. In fact, Pat was only able to find an alphabetised registration list of last year's participants and results in a word file on the office computer. Pat realises she needs more information and detailed information to better understand the key target markets selected.

Pat moves to the third action in the SMA procedure to study and evaluate the market with a specific focus on key target markets. The action requires an evaluation of last year's runners, potential runners, competitor events and the environment in which the Pig & Whistle operates. Pat begins to draw upon available published information regarding general trends of the running industry from newspapers, magazines, Internet sites, and academic and industry journals. She contacts a local running club and distributes a short survey to its members. Pat also visits a local sport store and interviews individuals buying running shoes as they leave for the parking lot. This information provides knowledge to develop a marketing report for her supervisor to strategically position marketing mix elements of the Pig & Whistle. Hence, Pat is now in a better position to develop a marketing approach that will achieve the target of 20% increase.

The fourth action of the SMA procedure is the selection of information systems to create knowledge. This action represented by a black circle in Figure 4.1 illustrates how information collected, stored, and retrieved informs the other three actions. In Pat's case, current information practices used by Triple F limited her ability to access information about key target markets to develop a marketing approach. Pat overcame this restriction by collecting information on target markets from published reports, surveys, and interviews. However, this action of studying and evaluating the market also dictates the software program required in terms of functionality to store and retrieve collected information for the SWOT analysis. The phrase "Knowledge is Power," is certainly appropriate for how an information system is the engine that drives the other three sport marketing actions. Hence, it is important for Pat to understand the types of engines that exist, which engine is best for the Pig & Whistle, and equally important is how this engine is stored, maintained, and used.

The previous example using Pat provides a brief overview of the SMA procedure. This procedure involves employing four actions, or 4-S's, that link sport consumer behaviour to sport marketing activities. The next section builds upon this understanding and offers a detailed discussion of each "S" action.

Action: Strategic Use of the Marketing Mix

Sport marketing action

Strategic use of marketing mix
Select key target markets
Study and evaluate market
Select information systems

The strategic use of the marketing mix involves the action of developing a marketing approach for a sport product or service to meet the needs and wants of current and potential consumers. The most common method is to position the marketing approach by incorporating the 4 P's of the marketing mix: product, price, place, and promotion. As illustrated in Figure 4.1, this approach requires understanding sport consumer behaviour (i.e., through study and evaluating the market) and linking this knowledge to marketing action.

The marketer has the ability to modify products and services to respond to changes in interest and demand. A modified version of football in Greece has become a popular recreational sport using 5-players a side competing on a smaller field. In England and India, modification to Cricket in the form of Twenty20 matches reduced the length of the contest to encourage larger crowds. The AFL in Australia continually introduces and evaluates new rules and regulations such as a 9-point goal to add excitement to the game. The emergence of X-Games and "Echo Adventure Challenges" provide new and interesting challenges. Equipment has also become specialised to meet various demands such as water-filled bats for softball, titanium bikes and oversized golf clubs. Technology can often be a larger driver of these modifications.

The sport consumption experience depends heavily upon the atmospheric conditions surrounding the event (e.g., music, cleanliness, number of participants and spectators) as well as personnel that deliver the product and service. The Internet also represents a relatively new element of this experience. Price is one of the most easily controlled aspects of the marketing mix, but increasing ticket or registration prices must be informed by understanding price tolerance among consumers. Promotion as communication strategy is the vehicle by which the marketer conveys information about the other marketing mix elements of product, price, and place. Although promotion receives the most attention from marketers, it only reflects decisions regarding positioning the other mix elements.

Sport marketing action should draw upon the study of consumer behaviour to help shape the positioning of products and services (Funk, Mahony, & Havitz, 2003). Positioning is an ongoing process requiring continual attention and knowledge to guide decisions. Knowledge of the sport consumer enhances the ability to maintain or modify various products and services to meet interests and demand. As in Pat's case, she must determine if the marketing approach of this year position the Pig & Whistle to attract previous runners to return and new runners to sign up. Asking a series of questions may help guide this marketing action. Figure 4.2 provides a list of such questions.

The strategic use of the marketing mix represents various activities that utilise product, place, price, and promotion to position the marketing approach. Not all mix elements require changing and modification decisions rely upon understanding

---

- What attributes and benefits of that event are most important for target markets?
- Can modifying aspects of the sport event better satisfy needs and provide benefits for the target markets?
- Will altering the delivery of event aspects increase demand?
- Can utilising training programs for volunteers and employees increase satisfaction?
- Are there alternative times that would increase demand?
- Are there alternative locations that would result in increased demand?
- Can the experience at the event be enhanced?
- How much are runners "willing to pay" for the event?
- What impact would lowering or raising prices have on demand or satisfaction?
- What are competitors charging?
- Are current advertising channels reaching intended target markets?
- Does the promotional or advertising message appeal to intended target markets?
- How can direct marketing and licensing activities increase demand?
- How can sponsorship activities increase demand?

Figure 4.2
Questions for positioning the marketing approach.

the sport consumer. Such consideration should also concentrate on differences that exist within a market.

Action: Select Key Target Markets

Sport marketing action

Strategic use of marketing mix
Select key target markets
Study and evaluate market
Select information systems

The second action of the SMA procedure involves selecting key segments on which to concentrate the marketing approach. For Pat, the purpose of segmentation is to create smaller clusters of current, past, and potential runners that share some meaningful characteristic. The action of segmentation provides the opportunity for specialisation and customisation to help position the marketing approach for specific segments. A common rule in marketing is the 80/20 rule where 80% of products and services are consumed by 20% of the market (Shilbury et al., 2009). In other words, a small number of consumers purchase all the products and services. Hence, the 20% are generally considered a segment of loyal consumers. Selection of a key market segment represents a target market and the selection of a target market depends upon

- *Size*: Are there enough customers in the segment to meet your profit objectives?
- *Location*: Is the segment in the right location?
- *Demand*: Can you meet the demands of the segment, provide the product, service, prices, and other elements?
- *Reach*: Can you reach the segment?
- *Benefits*: What are the attractive tangible and intangible features of product or service?

Figure 4.3
Segmentation requirements.

answering number of questions including: size, location, demand, reach, and benefits. The segmentation requirements are illustrated in Figure 4.3.

Traditionally target markets occur from five basic segmentation strategies: demographic, psychographic, product usage, benefits, and combination. A description of each strategy is listed in Figure 4.4.

The selection of key target markets can aid sport marketers in identifying current profitable segments as well as new potential segments to develop marketing approaches. In Pat's case, repeat participants and first time runners are two key target markets for the Pig & Whistle event. However, within these two segments she feels additional information would help clarify potential differences that may exist. This requires marketing action to better understand selected target markets.

The action selecting key target markets illustrates the benefits of understanding sport consumer behaviour as a means to direct the marketing approach. The selection of key target markets often requires information to better understand each target segment. In Pat's case, she feels repeat participants and first-time runners seek different needs and benefits based upon their level of involvement in running as a recreational activity and interest in participating in organised sport events. Hence, a means to differentiate individuals by prior sport involvement is required.

The psychological continuum model (PCM) framework discussed in Chapter 3 offers a means to segment individuals by level of sport involvement. The PCM provides a method to allocate individuals into appropriate stages to study and evaluate different needs and benefits useful in developing marketing

- *Demographic segmentation*: age, gender, income, education, ethnicity, profession, geographic location.
- *Psychographic segmentation*: attitudes, interest, opinions, involvement level.
- *Product usage segmentation*: frequency, type of participation.
- *Benefits segmentation*: desired attributes, benefits, SPEED.
- *Combination segmentation*: create a more defined target markets or new segments (e.g., gender X involvement level; gender X frequency, involvement level X income, age X socialisation). Whether this is advisable depends upon size, location, demand, and reach.

Figure 4.4
Segmentation strategies.

activities. A staging algorithm or "staging tool" allows a quick and simple procedure to segment participants into one of the four involvement stages: awareness, attraction, attachment, and allegiance. The staging tool is useful across any number of sport contexts so it is useful for both active sport (running, golf) and passive sport (spectators) participation. Instructions to assist in the staging process appears in Appendix A of this chapter. SPSS syntax is also available for large data sets by contacting the author. The next section provides a discussion of the staging tool with examples.

PCM Staging Tool

The PCM staging tool utilises information to allocate participants into one of the four PCM levels (Beaton, 2006; Beaton, Funk & Alexandris, in press). The staging tool is based on the concept of involvement (Rothschild, 1984). Involvement is a psychological construct and represents a person's level of interest, desire and motivation to engage in a sport and related consumption activities (Funk, Ridinger, & Moorman, 2004). The involvement construct has received widespread attention in the fields of marketing and consumer behaviour (Burton & Netemeyer, 1992; Laurent & Kapferer, 1985; Rothschild, 1984) as well as recreation and leisure (Funk, et al., 2004; Havitz & Mannell, 2005). A three-dimensional view of involvement dominates research today (Kyle & Mowen, 2005). These three dimensions are labelled pleasure, centrality, and sign, and each is explained in Box 4.1.

Box 4.1 Involvement facets

- *Pleasure* – the enjoyment derived from the activity.
- *Centrality* – how central the activity is to the individual's lifestyle.
- *Sign* – the self-expression, value, or level of symbolism of the activity.

A person's involvement level with a sport object (e.g., Chelsea FC, Surfing) is determined by measuring each of the three involvement facets to create an involvement profile. Figure 4.5 illustrates how involvement facets are then used to place

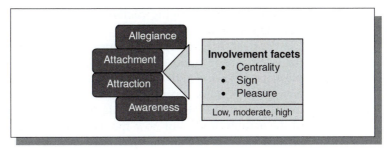

Figure 4.5
Involvement facets within the PCM framework.

Table 4.1 Involvement facets

	Pleasure facet	Centrality facet	Sign facet	Total score
Barto	7	4	4	15
Alecia	6	3	6	15

individuals into awareness, attraction, attachment, and allegiance stages of the PCM. A questionnaire collects this information from participants and spectators. The reason a three-facet profile is used instead of a total score is that each aspect of involvement contains important and different information.

As an example, Table 4.1 offers a hypothetical result for two individuals with the three involvement facets measured on seven-point Likert scales. A sport marketer obtains this information from a questionnaire distributed to participants or spectators. This can be done by asking an individual to rate their agreement with a series of involvement statements on a seven-point scale where 1 = strongly disagree and 7 = strongly agree. Barto and Alecia attended a Real Madrid match and completed a questionnaire with the involvement facets during the game. The involvement scores for Barto and Alecia are listed in Table 4.1.

Barto recorded values of seven for the Pleasure facet (7), and four on each of the Centrality (4) and Sign facets (4). Barto could be described as someone who participates for the inherent pleasure of the behaviour itself, and does not consider the activity as a central part of his life, or as a tool for expressing himself to others. Barto watches just for the fun of the activity itself, and is susceptible to changing preference for other SportWays (e.g., other teams or activities).

In contrast, Alecia recorded values of six for Pleasure (6), three for Centrality (3), and six for the Sign facet (6). Alecia derives pleasure from the activity and sees the activity as self-expressive, yet it is not a central part of her lifestyle. Alecia may have initially started watching Real Madrid for the enjoyment value of the activity itself, but now the team is beginning to take on a significant level of personal meaning in terms of self-expression (e.g., wearing a Real Madrid jersey to work). Alecia is unlikely to change her preference from Real Madrid to another team.

This example illustrates how each involvement facet creates a profile more beneficial than using a summated total score. In Table 4.1, using a summated or aggregated scale approach, Barto and Alecia have identical scores of fifteen (15). However, it would be a mistake to assume both Barto and Alecia have similar levels of involvement with Real Madrid. The level of involvement would be the same but different profiles would produce different behavioural and psychological outcomes. For example, Alecia may be in the attachment stage and less likely to change her preference from Real Madrid than Barto, who is in the attraction stage.

Funk and James (2001) discussed how involvement profiles are likely to vary across stages of the PCM. The Awareness profile will have low scores on all facets. The Attraction profile will have high scores on the Pleasure facet and low scores on the Sign and Centrality facets. The Attachment profile will have higher scores for Sign and Centrality and have the most diverse involvement profiles. The Allegiance profile will have high values across all facets of involvement. As a result, each stage of the PCM has a unique set of profiles based upon the level and combination of the three involvement facets. Appendix B illustrates these profiles.

Drawing upon this approach, Beaton, Funk and Alexandris (in press) created a method to split an involvement facet score into high, moderate and low. As depicted in Table 4.2, information from a questionnaire is used to combine the facets to create unique profiles and place individuals into awareness, attraction, attachment, and allegiance.

Each involvement facet is measured using three questions to ensure reliability. See Appendix A for questions. Table 4.2 illustrates an involvement facet of an individual. The scores from each of the nine questions are tabled. Looking at the Pleasure facet first, there are two questions P1 and P3 with a score of five, and one score of six for P2, resulting in a mean construct score of 5.33 (16 ÷ 3 = 5.33) for Pleasure. This procedure provides a Centrality mean score of 3.67 and Sign mean score of 6.33.

Table 4.2 Calculating involvement facets

	Pleasure	**Centrality**	**Sign**
Item 1	P1 = 5	C1 = 4	S1 = 7
Item 2	P2 = 6	C2 = 3	S2 = 6
Item 3	P3 = 5	C3 = 4	S3 = 6
Total Score	16	11	19
Average	**= 5.33**	**= 3.67**	**= 6.33**

Table 4.3 Classification of involvement facets

Low (L)	**Medium (M)**	**High (H)**
Mean score ∪4.49	Mean score 4.50 – 5.74	Mean score ∩5.75
Involvement profile		
Centrality 3.67 L	Pleasure 5.33 M	Sign 6.33 H

Once the mean construct score is created for each facet, a tripartite split is used to classify individuals into high, medium and low on respective facets. The tripartite split utilizes intervals to create a profile. Low classification is a mean score on a facet from 1.0 to 4.49. Medium is a mean facet score from 4.5 to 5.74. High classification is a mean score on a facet above 5.75 (see Table 4.3 for an illustration).

These classifications of low, medium, and high create an individuals unique involvement profile. For example, a profile from the three facet mean scores shown in Table 4.3 would be as follows. The Pleasure facet mean score of 5.33 would be considered "Medium." The Centrality facet mean score of 3.67 is considered "Low." The Sign facet mean of 6.33 considered "High." So the individual has a unique involvement profile of Centrality = L, Pleasure = M, and Sign = H as illustrated in the bottom of Table 4.3. The intervals are created in such a manner to be applicable across various sport settings.

For a given population, there are 27 possible profiles distributed across the stages of the PCM. These profiles are shown in Appendix B of this chapter and illustrate the potential profiles that can occur within the PCM stages. These profiles are based upon high, medium, and low facet scores on each of the three involvement dimensions. For example, a person in the attraction stage would have a profile consisting of (Pleasure = M, Centrality = L, and Sign = L). For allegiance, the profile would be (Pleasure = H, Centrality = H, and Sign = H). It should be observed that the attachment stage has the most diverse profiles supporting Funk and James (2001) theory of involvement staging. The appendix illustrates this diversity.

The profile is then used in the staging algorithm tool to classify individuals into PCM stages of awareness, attraction, attachment, and allegiance. The staging tool is a relatively simple algorithm (e.g., decision tree) developed to allocate subjects in line with the theoretical framework provided by the PCM. The algorithm is presented in Table 4.4.

The staging tool can seem quite complex at first glance. However, it is relatively simple once the process is completed a few times. Three examples follow to help clarify the application of the PCM staging tool. The first example represents the use

Table 4.4   Staging algorithm for PCM framework

Using the involvement profile ratings, complete the following six actions below *in order* until stage is determined

Action 1: If *All* three facets rated low (L), Stage = awareness

      If condition not satisfied then;

Action 2: If *Pleasure* facet is rated low (L), Stage = attachment

      If condition not satisfied then;

Action 3: If *Both* Centrality and Sign facets are rated low (L), Stage = attraction

      If condition not satisfied then;

Action 4: If *Either* Centrality and Sign facets are rated low (L), Stage = Attachment;

      If condition not satisfied then;

Action 5: If *Any Two facets are rated as high* (H), Stage = allegiance;

      If condition not satisfied then;

Action 6: All *Remaining*, Stage = attachment

of information collected by Pat from a survey of runners and spectators at a marathon to study and evaluate the market. To begin, look at Box 4.2. Dan has an involvement mean score of 6.25 for Pleasure. Based on Table 4.3 Dan's pleasure score is categorized as "high." His mean score of 5.25 for Centrality is categorised as "medium." Finally, Dan's mean score of 4.25 for Sign is categorised as "low."

Box 4.2

Example 1   Dan's involvement profile

Facets	Pleasure	Centrality	Sign
Scores	6.25	5.25	4.25
Ratings	H	M	L

Now look at Box 4.3. This illustrates the application of the staging algorithm provided in Table 4.4. Actions 1 through 4 are recorded until the classification is complete. Based upon this procedure, Dan is classified into the attachment stage regarding running (i.e., *I am a runner*).

Box 4.3 Application of algorithm

- **Consider Action 1**: Dan's involvement scores are not all low (L). As a result, this condition is not satisfied so proceed to next action.
- **Consider Action 2**: Dan's Pleasure facet is not low (L), so second action is not satisfied so proceed to next action.
- **Consider Action 3**: Both of Dan's Centrality and Sign facets are not low (L), so third action is not satisfied so proceed to next action.
- **Consider Action 4**: Dan has a Sign facet rated as low (L). Hence, fourth action is affirmative and Dan's classification is Attachment.

The next example is taken from a spectator attending an Italian Serie A football match. This example illustrates Carry's involvement with the Italian football team Juventas. Box 4.4 reveals that Carry has a Pleasure score of 6.5 (high), a Centrality score of 6.5 (high), and a Sign score of 6.5 (high). Now look at Box 4.5. This

Box 4.4

Example 2   Carry's involvement profile

Facets	Pleasure	Centrality	Sign
Scores	6.5	6.5	6.5
Ratings	H	H	H

Box 4.5 Application of algorithm

- Action 1: Carry's involvement scores are not all low (L). First action is negative so consider next action.
- Action 2: Pleasure facet is not low (L), second action is negative so consider next action.
- Action 3: Both Centrality and Sign facets are not low (L), third action is negative so consider next action.
- Action 4: Neither Centrality or Sign facets rated as low (L), fourth action is negative so consider next action.
- Action 5: Two facets are rated as high (H). Hence, fifth action is affirmative and Carry's classification is Allegiance.

illustrates the application of the staging algorithm from Table 4.4. Follow Actions 1 through 5 until the classification is complete. Based upon this procedure, Carry is classified into the allegiance stage regarding his psychological connection to Juventas (i.e., I *Live for Juventas*).

The last example illustrates Carl's level of involvement with a Motor Sport race event. Carl completed a online Internet survey regarding his level of interest in the Lexmark Indy 300. Box 4.6 reveals that Carl is "low" on all the three facets of Pleasure, Centrality, and Sign. Based upon Action 1 from Table 4.4, Carl is considered to be in the awareness stage (i.e., I *know about the Indy 300*).

The above examples illustrate how the PCM staging tool provides a sport marketer with the ability to allocate individuals into meaningful segments of awareness, attraction, attachment, and allegiance. As discussed in Chapters 2 and 3, motivation and the decision-making sequence (i.e., inputs, processes, and outputs)

Box 4.6

Example 3 Carl's involvement profile

Facets	Pleasure	Centrality	Sign
Scores	3.25	2.25	1.25
Ratings	L	L	L

differ for individuals based upon the level of sport involvement. This highlights the need for sport marketing action based on an understanding of sport consumer behaviour. Returning to Pat's situation, she can use the PCM staging tool in conjunction with other segmentation strategies of demographics, product usage, and benefits to compare individuals from the awareness stage to allegiance stage. For example, Pat can explore differences among individuals within the attraction stage using age, gender, income, frequency of running and benefits desired. This information can help position the Pig & Whistle to attract new runners. In addition, comparisons between attraction and attachment stage runners using segmentation strategies can help position the event for repeat participants. Taken together, this information will help Pat understand important differences between the two key target markets and develop an appropriate response to whether changes to the marketing mix elements are advisable.

The preceding section demonstrates the relative ease within which a person's involvement with a sport object can be determined. The PCM staging tool is useful across any number of sport participation contexts. This book provides instructions and a scoring sheet to assist in the staging process. The staging tool procedure allocates individuals into different segments to allow further study of existing as well as potential consumers. The PCM framework provides the ability to examine these target markets by exploring how personal, psychological, and environmental factors influence identified segments. In other words, discover how one segment differs on SPEED motives. This is advantageous and leads to the third action of the SMA procedure of studying and evaluating key segments identified by a sport marketer. The third SMA focuses on determining needs and benefits of these key target markets and necessitates gathering information.

Action: Study and Evaluate the Market

Sport marketing action

Strategic use of marketing mix
Select key target markets
Study and evaluate market
Select information systems

The third action of the SMA procedure is the evaluation of existing consumers, potential consumers, competitors and the environment in which the sport organisation operates. The sport marketer must read and conduct research both in general terms and the immediate environment. This information is important to understand general trends and typically consists of primary and secondary research activities that aid in future decisions regarding marketing strategies. Simply put, this action attempts to answer many of the questions listed in Figure 4.2.

Primary research activities can include a quantitative approach to collect information from spectators and participants such as (a) distributing surveys at games or online; (b) creating a database of existing customer names, phone and email addresses from credit card receipts; (c) developing a prospect list of potential new clients through sweepstakes and drawings; and (d) recording frequency and type of behaviour. Primary research can also include a qualitative approach that uses (a) structured and semi-structured interviews; (b) focus groups; and (c) observations to collect information. Primary research represents activities undertaken by the sport organisation to collect information directly from its clients to answer a specific question(s). For example, for a professional sport franchise these activities can range from an online survey seeking information on ticket prices, customer service, ticket packages, transportation, food service, licensed merchandise offerings, group characteristics, and benefits sought. A paper survey mailed to clients or an information collection box also is useful. Interviews and focus groups with current clients, perspective clients, and clients who have discontinued can also be helpful. Sport marketers utilise primary research activities when information related to a specific question is not available through secondary sources.

Secondary research activities draw upon available published information regarding general trends of the industry and primary research to answer questions. This information exists in secondary data sources such as government agencies, libraries and chambers of commerce, newspapers, magazines, Internet sites and academic and industry journals, as well as publications designed for a specific purpose (e.g., Sweeney Sports Report, Sport Business, Advertising Age, Sport Marketing Quarterly, Amusement Business) and can be used to keep abreast of current trends. The sport marketer should read and evaluate prior research and trends related to the industry both in general terms and the immediate environment. This type of information can inform type and frequency of marketing strategies as well as development of new products and services. For example, a SWOT evaluation and analysis is a secondary research activity that uses existing information to determine strengths, weaknesses, opportunities, and threats of a sport organisation's products and services.

The action of studying and evaluating the market highlights how the study of sport consumer behaviour provides information to develop the marketing approach. This action produces knowledge to inform the marketing approach to build and sustain volume. As Figure 4.1 illustrates, studying that action and evaluating the market leads to knowledge on how to strategically manipulate the marketing mix. Knowledge occurs from the packaging of information into recommendations and disseminating this knowledge to others within the organisation. Often this requires sport marketing professionals to prepare and write reports to summaries findings and make recommendations.

A simple process can guide the writing of a marketing report. This process consists of a series of actions recommended by Funk, Mahony, and Havitz (2003) in their assessment of sport consumer behaviour research. These actions are listed in Box 4.7. The purpose of the sequence is to help a sport marketer determine what activities are required to study and evaluate to market to produce the report. Sport marketing professionals have limited

---

Box 4.7 Actions for writing marketing reports

Action 1: Determine implementation of report.
Action 2: Test market final report contents.
Action 3: Specify information requirements.
Action 4: Determine data requirements.
Action 5: Search for existing secondary data.
Action 6: Design plan for primary research data.
Action 7: Conduct research.

time and budgets so decisions on where to invest resources are important. The purpose of this process is not to provide an in-depth discussion of a marketing report and the specific elements a report contains. The 7-Actions process helps a sport marketing professional determine actions to generate necessary information include in the report.

The 7-Actions process for writing a marketing report follows Wells' (1993) recommendation to reverse the normal research process. This procedure advocates starting at the end of the process (e.g., the report) and proceeding to the beginning (e.g., conducting the actual research). Pat's marketing actions for the Pig & Whistle help illustrate this process. The first action is to determine implementation of the report. This action considers how the sport organisation or researchers utilise the report. For Pat, submission of the report to her supervisor serves as the basis for developing the marketing approach for next year's event. What are the expectations of Pat's supervisor? The second action involves test marketing the final report contents. This action seeks to discover what the final report should contain (i.e., content) and how it should look (i.e., presentation). For Pat, this involves gathering examples of previous marketing reports and using a template from a graduate sport marketing class to develop the report. She then meets with her supervisor and other key event stakeholders to get feedback on the report contents.

The third action specifies the type of information required to produce the contents of the report. Pat determines the report should provide a SWOT comparison of two key target markets; first-time runners and repeat participants. Action 4 involves determining the kind of information needed to carry out the analysis. For Pat, comparing the two segments requires detailed information on running demographics and benefits desired. The fifth action is to search for secondary data already collected by commercial and non-commercial services. Pat can access academic journals, marketing reports, and governmental statistics to gather data on runner demographics and benefits desired.

Action 6 occurs only after secondary avenues are exhausted and involves designing primary research activities that will yield relevant data. Since previous secondary sources failed to compare first time runners and repeat runners on demographics and benefits desired, Pat needs to conduct some primary research. Pat conducts some interviews and focus groups to develop a questionnaire. The last action is actually carrying out fieldwork research. Hence, Pat distributes an Internet survey to local running club members. At this point, Pat would conduct the analysis, write the report, and determine if it had its intended effect from Action 1.

As illustrated by the 7-Actions, the initial action of determining the final product in the form of the marketing report directs subsequent actions. This approach provides an efficient and effective means to study and evaluate the market to develop the marketing approach. In addition, action seven suggests sport marketers should utilise primary research activities only when answers to specific questions are not available. Often, a combination of secondary and primary research actions provide information to improve understanding of how to position the marketing mix. However, how this information is obtained, stored, and accessed is equally important and leads to a fourth action.

Action: Select Information Systems

Sport marketing action

Strategic use of marketing mix
Select key target markets
Study and evaluate market
Select information systems

The selection of information systems represented by the black circle in Figure 4.1 illustrates how information informs the other three actions. Sport marketers require ongoing market information to make decisions due to the dynamic nature of the sport environment and as a result, need to establish an appropriate information system. Mullin et al. (2007) suggest a key to sport marketing success is the ability to collect information about consumers to position a marketing plan specifically designed to meet the needs of a specific segment. An information system is an, "ongoing," organised set of procedures and methods designed to generate, analyse, disseminate, store and later retrieve information for use in decision making (Stanton, Miller, & Layton, 1995).

An information system determines the ability to make informed marketing decisions regarding modifying or promoting a sport product or service. Hence, the quality and accessibility of this knowledge influences a sport marketer's ability to study and evaluate the market, select key target markets, and strategically position the sport event. The aforementioned phrase "Knowledge is Power," represents how information powers the circular motion, the other three marketing actions follow in

Figure 4.1. For example, once a specific change is made to one of the marketing mix elements, information is needed to determine if the change had the desired effect on a specified target market. As a result, sport marketing action should be considered a continuous circular procedure that requires a responsive environment. General management practices within a sport organisation and available technology often determine this SMA procedure. It is advisable to seek outside advice for this step after the required marketing informational needs have been determined. Often a SWOT analysis of technology will provide some direction for the type of system in terms of functionality.

Participation tracking software can allow a sport organisation to monitor various sport consumption activities. Computer software programs can collect information such as names, addresses, frequency and type of products and services used by current customers, and register first-time guests at a facility or event. EXCEL provides a good program widely accessible and has a number of functionalities to enter and retrieve demographic information from ticket sales and registrations. This software provides the opportunity to access specific information for the purpose of direct marketing activities via email and post. If primary research data is collected, then software programs such as SPSS store and easily retrieve information.

The use of the Internet and website design is also an important information consideration. The Internet has become a primary source of information for many consumers across a number of contexts (Oorni, 2004; Peterson & Merino, 2003). In sport marketing, the Internet provides a low cost widely accessed resource to support the other three sport marketing actions (Filo & Funk, 2005). In general, sport marketers can utilise the Internet in three different ways: (a) to provide information concerning both the sport organisation and its products, (b) to purchase or reserve products with delivery through mail, and (c) for transactions including the physical delivery of products (Van den Poel & Leunis, 1999). The provision of detailed information via the Internet can also induce movement from awareness to attraction by communicating how a sport event provides opportunities to satisfy needs and receive benefits (Filo, Funk, & Hornby, 2008).

Summary

Sport Marketing action represents activities designed to build and sustain volume through the sport exchange process. An overview of sport marketing reveals a service orientation approach drawing upon an understanding of sport consumer behaviour is advantageous. A Sport Marketing Action (SMA) procedure introduces four actions to apply sport consumer behaviour to market sport products and services.

The first action involves strategic management of the marketing mix to position the marketing approach. Answering a series of questions about each marketing mix element determines whether changes are advisable. The second action involves selecting key target markets to explore positioning. A number of segmentation strategies provide a means to identify attractive and profitable target markets. A staging tool introduces a mechanism to allocate individuals into stages of the PCM framework based upon the level of sport involvement. The third action involves studying and evaluating the market to understand differences within identified segments. A 7-Action process allows an easy way to develop marketing reports to communicate this information. The final action involves the selection of information systems to collect, store, and use information that informs the other three sport marketing actions.

Appendix A: PCM staging score procedure

STEP 1: Distribute to participant/spectator

Rank your level of agreement with the following statements using the guide below:

1	2	3	4	5	6	7
Strongly disagree	Disagree	Slightly disagree	Neither agree nor disagree	Slightly agree	Agree	Strongly agree

		1	2	3	4	5	6	7
P1	Playing/attending X offers me relaxation when pressures build up	1	2	3	4	5	6	7
C1	I find a lot of my life organised around playing/attending X	1	2	3	4	5	6	7
S1	Participating/attending X says a lot about who I am	1	2	3	4	5	6	7
C2	Playing/attending X has a central role in my life	1	2	3	4	5	6	7
S2	You can tell a lot about a person by seeing them play/watch X	1	2	3	4	5	6	7
P2	I really enjoy playing/attending X	1	2	3	4	5	6	7
S3	When I play/attend X I can really be myself	1	2	3	4	5	6	7
P3	Compared to other sports, playing/watching X is very interesting	1	2	3	4	5	6	7
C3	A lot of my time is organised around playing/watching X	1	2	3	4	5	6	7

STEP 2: Involvement facet calculation

Place the score from each statement above in the appropriate box (P1, etc.) below and calculate the total score for each column. Then divide each column total by three to obtain an average score for the three factors of Pleasure, Centrality, and Sign.

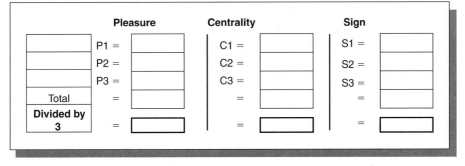

STEP 3: Profile facets

Use the scale below to rate the average score calculated in step 2 for Pleasure, Centrality, and Sign as low (L), medium (M), or high (H).

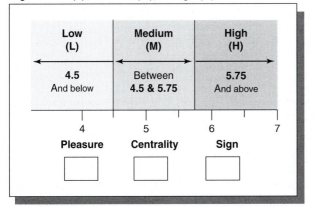

STEP 4: Determine stage

Using the ratings from step 3 above, complete the actions below IN ORDER until stage is determined

1. If **Pleasure** rank is (L) = Attachment, if not then

2. If **Both** Centrality and Sign are (L) = Attraction, if not then

3. If **any two** are (H) = Allegiance, if not then

4. All **else** = Attachment

Stage

Appendix B

Distribution of involvement profiles across PCM stages

Awareness			Attraction			Attachment			Allegiance		
P	C	S	P	C	S	P	C	S	P	C	S
L	L	L	M	L	L	L	L	M	M	H	H
			H	L	L	L	L	H	H	H	M
						L	M	L	H	M	H
						L	M	M	H	H	H
						L	M	H			
						L	H	L			
						L	H	M			
						L	H	H			
						M	L	M			
						M	L	H			
						M	M	L			
						M	H	L			
						M	M	M			
						M	M	H			
						M	H	M			
						H	L	M			
						H	M	L			
						H	M	M			
						H	L	H			
						H	H	L			

References

Beaton, A.A. (2006). *A study of sport participation: Operationalising a theoretical framework. Unpublished Honours Dissertation.* Gold Coast, AUS: Griffith University.

Beaton , A.A., Funk, D.C., & Alexandris, K. (in press). Operationalizing a theory of participation in physically active leisure. *Journal of Leisure Research.*

Burton, S., & Netemeyer, R.G. (1992). The effect of enduring, situational, and response involvement on preference stability in the context of voting behavior. *Psychology & Marketing, 9,* 143–156.

Filo, K., & Funk, D.C. (2005). Congruence between attractive product features and virtual content delivery for Internet marketing communication. *Sport Marketing Quarterly, 14,* 112–122.

Filo, K., Funk, D.C., & Hornby, G. (2008). The role of website content on motive and attitude change for sport events. *Journal of Sport Management.*

Funk, D.C., & James, J.D. (2001). The Psychological Continuum Model (PCM): A conceptual framework for understanding an individual's psychological connection to sport. *Sport Management Review, 4*, 119–150.

Funk, D.C., Mahony, D.F., & Havitz, M. (2003). Sport consumer behavior: Assessment and direction. *Sport Marketing Quarterly, 12*, 200–205.

Funk, D.C., Ridinger, L.L., & Moorman, A.M. (2004). Exploring the origins of involvement: Understanding the relationship between consumer motives and involvement with professional sport teams. *Leisure Sciences, 26*, 35–61.

Gladden, J.M., & Funk, D.C. (2002). Developing and understanding of brand association in team sport: Empirical evidence from professional sport consumers. *Journal of Sport Management, 16*, 54–81.

Havitz, M.E., & Mannell, R.C. (2005). Enduring involvement, situational involvement, and flow in leisure and non-leisure activities. *Journal Leisure Research, 37*, 152–177.

Kyle, G.T., & Mowen, A.J. (2005). An examination of the leisure involvement-agency commitment relationship. *Journal of Leisure Research, 37*, 342–361.

Laurent, G., & Kapferer, J.N. (1985). Measuring consumer involvement profiles. *Journal of Marketing Research, 22*(1), 41–53.

Mullin, B.J., Hardy, S., & Sutton, W.A. (2007). *Sport Marketing* (3rd Ed). Champaign, IL: Human Kinetics.

Oorni, A. (2004). Consumer objectives and the amount of search in electronic travel and tourism markets. *Journal of Travel and Tourism Marketing, 17*(2/3), 3–14.

Peterson, R.A., & Merino, M.C. (2003). Consumer information search behaviour and the Internet. *Psychology & Marketing, 20*, 99–121.

Robinson, M.J., & Trail, G.T. (2005). Relationship among spectator gender, motives, points of attachment, and sport preference. *Journal of Sport Management, 19*, 58–80.

Rothschild, M.L. (1984). Perspectives on involvement: Current problems and future directions. *Advances in Consumer Research, 11*, 216–217.

Shilbury, D., Westerbeek, H., Quick, S., & Funk, D.C. (2009). *Strategic Sport Marketing* (3rd Ed). Crows Nest, NSW: Allen & Unwin.

Stanton, W.J., Miller, K.E., & Layton, R. (1995). *Fundamentals of Marketing* (3rd Ed). Sydney: McGraw-Hill.

Van den Poel, D., & Leunis, J. (1999). Consumer Acceptance of the Internet as a Channel of Distribution. *Journal of Business Research, 45*, 249–256.

Wells, W.D. (1993). Discovery oriented consumer research. *Journal of Consumer Research, 19*, 489–504.

PART 2

Provides the reader with a comprehensive understanding of Awareness, Attraction, Attachment, and Allegiance with marketing strategies to promote sport consumption within each stage and concludes with a discussion of perceived constraints that modify or inhibit behaviour.

Consumer Awareness of Sport and Events

In August, Mike travelled to Darmstadt Germany from his home in Toronto, Canada, to celebrate the 95th birthday of his partner's grandfather. During his visit, Mike's cousin Helko invited him to attend a football match on Saturday. The match held in Stadion Bieberer Berg outside of Darmstadt is where the Offenbach Kickers play in the second division of the Bundesliga. Mike has watched many FIFA World Cup matches on television, but has no prior knowledge of the Bundesliga, the Offenbach Kickers nor has ever attended a football match. While travelling to the match, Mike asked Helko many questions about the Kickers, the Bundesliga, and football in general. Upon entering the stadium, Mike along with other spectators received an official Offenbach Kicker flag provided by the team's telecommunication sponsor Evo. Helko also purchased a match day program for Mike and translated the information. During the match, Mike watched and learned how and when to participate in the rituals at the match and was amazed at exciting atmosphere created by 15,000 plus fans. Mike also enjoyed cheering the Kickers to a 3–2 win in the 87th minute.

Awareness marks the initial introduction of an individual to a sport object. This introduction can happen at different points throughout a person's life and depends upon a number of personal, psychological, and environmental determinants. As the above example of Mike illustrates, his introduction to the Offenbach Kickers occurred from attending a soccer match with his relative Helco while visiting Germany. Hence, awareness represents an outcome indicating that a person forms an understanding that a sport object exists.

Discussion of the PCM (psychological continuum model) framework in Chapter 3 indicates that the awareness stage represents the initial point at which a person forms a psychological connection with a sport object. The acknowledgment of a sport, team, event, or any recreational activity suggests a general level of understanding. Awareness stage outcomes describe basic levels of introduction, and mark the low end of the vertical continuum within the PCM framework. As depicted in Figure 5.1, the awareness stage represents the entry point through which a person enters the PCM elevator (e.g., ground floor or Level 1).

The PCM framework views the awareness stage as a psychological outcome derived from awareness processing that consists of inputs, processes, and outputs (see Figure 3.5). The framework offers a review of relevant literature to help understand awareness processing. This chapter presents a detailed

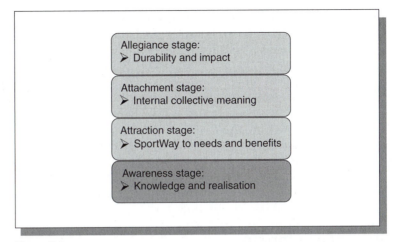

Figure 5.1
PCM framework.

understanding of the inputs, processes, and outputs that contribute to awareness.

Awareness Processing

The awareness processing represents a number of inputs, processes, and outputs that can shape decision-making and sport consumption behaviour. Most notable is the focus on the consumer socialisation process as an important means to describe how a sport object is introduced to an individual (James, 2001). Prior research generally attempts to examine socialisation within two fundamental areas: (a) "when" do people become aware of a sport object and (b) "how" do people become aware of a sport object. See Figure 5.2 for an illustration of awareness processing.

The PCM framework proposes that awareness processing accounts for when and how individuals learn skills, knowledge, and attitudes related to functioning as sport consumers in the

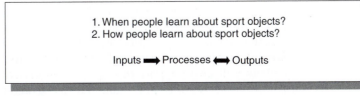

Figure 5.2
Awareness processing.

society. The awareness process has inputs, processes, and outputs that shape psychological and behavioural outcomes. Socialising agents represent environmental inputs and serve as important catalysts to influence social learning. Social learning creates outputs representing various levels of awareness for sport objects and behaviour that subsequently feedback into future learning processes through knowledge acquisition. As a result, the awareness process is a developmental process through which prior learning continues to shape ensuing learning contributing to various levels of awareness. For example, prior awareness levels as a child influences social learning as a teenager and this level of awareness subsequently influences social learning as an adult.

Awareness Inputs

Environmental inputs for awareness processing are external to the individual. The social science literature indicates that individuals form impressions and opinions from information provided by a variety of external sources. These sources are labelled socialising agents and represent persons, institutions, and organisations that communicate norms, attitudes, and behaviour through social interaction (Bush, Smith, & Martin, 1999). Sport socialisation research often seeks to understand the impact of socialising from two different perspectives: socialisation into sport, and socialisation through sport (Eitzen & Sage, 2003). A number of socialising agents introduce or draw individuals to sports as participants and spectators (James, 2001). The most common socialising agents are parents, peer group, coaches, mass media, schools, church, community-based programs, and cultural beliefs. These socialising agents represent environmental catalysts that influence awareness through social learning.

Socialising Agents for Sport Consumers

Family is an influential socialising agent and in many cases family members develop similar preferences for sports, teams, and recreational activities. For example, if one family member plays golf, children or siblings will often adopt that activity. Parents are particularly important in the early years (James, 2001). If a parent is a fan of football or a team such as Manchester United, many family members will also support that sport code or team. As a child matures, peers become important socialising agents due to the pressure to conform to the group. A teenage girl that plays softball is likely to have a group of friends that play and watch the sport.

The environment plays an important role in awareness. Sport clubs, schools, and universities influence the introduction of sport through curriculum and programs. Geographic considerations determine the type of sport activities offered. An individual who grew up in Austria is more likely to ski while an Australian is more likely to surf. Environmental considerations such as pollution, overpopulation, urban sprawl, and drought have important implications for accessibility and offerings. For example, recreational running in cities such as Mexico City and Athens can be difficult restricting opportunities for individuals. Technology can shape sport awareness through innovation of equipment and services and the movement toward online experiences. Among socialising agents, the mass media and sport subculture play important roles.

Mass Media

Television, newspapers, and the Internet represent key mass media sources for adult sport consumers. These mass media sources can influence awareness directly or indirectly through word-of-mouth from other socialising agents (e.g., friends, family, and colleagues). In a meta-analysis on mass media influence, Emmers-Sommer and Allen (1999) suggest that mass media becomes increasingly important in shaping the attitudes and behaviour of children as they mature. Mass media also continues to be an important source in shaping adult consumption activities (Rose, Bush, & Kahle, 1998; Trevino, Webster, & Stein, 2000).

Mass media's role as a socialising agent for sport consumers is well known. Research has identified media's role for participants and spectators (Burnett, Menon, & Smart, 1993), the role of sport event coverage on television (Duncan & Brummett, 1989; McDaniel, 2002), use of informational recreational brochures (Manfredo & Bright, 1991), role of social behaviour while watching (Gantz, 1981), the style of commentary during games (Comisky, Bryant, & Zillman, 1977), sport editorials in newspapers (Funk & Pritchard, 2006), and the use of the Internet by professional sport teams (Beech, Chadwick, & Tapp, 2000). Mass media along with other socialising agents produce awareness through sport subcultures.

Sport Subculture

Prior to initial and infrequent participation, awareness of an activity occurs as information about a specific sport subculture comes from various socialising agents. An individual becomes aware of a specific sport activity and its subculture from various socialising agents such as family, search and trial, peers, and media prior to participation (Donnelly & Young, 1988; Funk & James, 2001). A subculture is a subgroup of society that self-selects based on shared beliefs, rituals, and commitment to a particular sport consumption activity (Schouten & McAlexander, 1995). Initial awareness forms from positive or negative preconceptions and misconceptions about the subculture. Reference groups play a large role in awareness as the individual has less information and direct experience with the sport object. Reference groups can be normative or comparative including family, work, friends, Internet, celebrity, and experts that provide both general and specific awareness of sport objects. This research indicates that reference groups and mass media are important socialising agents that influence awareness and sport consumption related activities through a social learning process.

Awareness Processes

Awareness processing represents the activation of internal mechanisms that shape the evaluation of environmental inputs regarding a sport object or consumption experience. Chapter 3 discusses a number of general processes including motivation, perception, learning, memory, and personality that contribute to this evaluation and knowledge acquisition. However, as the person begins to engage with the sport object, specific attitudinal processes emerge. These internal processes represent a type of attitudinal processing that employ cognitive, affective, and behavioural evaluations. Cognitive processing occurs from the evaluation of informational inputs derived from advertising, media, friends, and family (i.e., socialising agents). Behavioural processing evaluates the sport object based on direct or actual experience. Affective processing evaluates whether or not the sport object is liked. In other words, general processes lead to attitudinal processing of environmental inputs and this evaluation creates initial attitude formation within awareness. Processing of environmental inputs whether it is general or attitudinal depends upon personal and psychological forces.

Personal Forces

Personal forces represent person-specific characteristics and dispositions. These personal factors are intrinsic forces created by the recognition of a need. Funk and James (2004) suggest sport objects and experiences allow for the expression of individual characteristics and dispositions. Personal forces can include gender, body type, peers, life-stage, ethnicity, culture, personality, and prior experience. Ridinger and Funk (2006) observed a number of differences in the reasons for attendance in US college basketball games based on spectator- and team-gender. Funk, Toohey, and Bruun (2007) observed that an individual's cultural background and gender shapes perceived travel benefits for participating in an international marathon in Australia. Participation in sport and exercise tends to differ along gender lines for motives of socialisation, enjoyment, body-related concerns, competition, and ego-related concerns (Recours, Souville, & Griffet, 2004).

Physical characteristics influence consumption decisions based upon body type. An individual weighing 100 kg, standing 180 cm may find team and contact sports more enjoyable than running and biking that benefit a lighter frame and endurance. An individual's life-stage in terms of being young, middle aged, elderly, single, married, with or without children may determine the evaluation of sport opportunities. The life-stage is a series of stages that correspond to transitions and not only to age and situation but values, identities and attitudes. An individual may find sports that are embedded in his/her ethnic and cultural fabric more enjoyable such as football among African-American and Hispanics (Armstrong, 2001; McCarthy, 1998). A British immigrant to Japan is more likely to follow a sport that resonates with his/her nationality such as cricket before following sumo wrestling.

An individual's personality and learning can also influence processing of environmental inputs. Self-concept is the interaction of how we view ourselves (own view), images of how we think others view us (perceived self), images of how we would like to be viewed (desired or ideal self), how we interact with references groups, and how this group views us (public self). Personality traits can explain why a person prefers football, cricket, tennis, sky diving, bushwalking, skiing, or yoga. Hawkins, Best, and Coney (1992) suggest that individual consumers purchase products that most closely match their own personality. In most cases, personalities usually emerge in the early stages of an individual's development and often coincide with the Awareness stage. Prior experience and exposure to the sport product or service is important for awareness processing and can create positive or negatives experiences in the initial stages of awareness.

The person-specific characteristics and dispositions represent personal inputs that determine the type of attitudinal processing used to evaluate the sport object or experience. Personal inputs interact with environmental inputs and shape awareness processing. However, psychological forces also play an important role as personal inputs.

Psychological Forces

Psychological forces are internal to the consumer and represent intrinsic and extrinsic benefits. These forces are a set of beliefs and feelings regarding the benefits a particular sport product or service provides. These benefits can be hedonic and utilitarian. Hedonic benefits are experiential in nature involving emotional responses that are subjective and create a desire to satisfy internal needs or receive intangible benefits through acquisition (Holbrook & Hirschman, 1982). Hedonic benefits represent the SPEED motives discussed in Chapter 2. Utilitarian benefits represent the functional tangible attributes of a product or service that an individual desires. Utilitarian benefits can be a function of price, product features, and accessibility.

Psychological and personal forces create the internal push to seek out a sport object or experience that fulfils physical, social, and personal needs and provides benefits. This internal push influences the attitudinal processing of environmental inputs. Within awareness processing, limited knowledge and prior experience exist; so behavioural and cognitive processing generally prevail. As previously discussed, much of the processing occurs through social learning as the social aspect of sport is an important component of the consumer's decision-making process.

Social Learning Process

Social learning process accounts for the development of awareness toward leisure in general (Iso-Ahola, 1980), recreation activities (Burch, 1969), sport participation (McPherson, 1976), and competitive sport teams (James, 2001). Specific agents such as parents, peers, and mass media represent environmental factors that interact with the learner to convey and exchange information, social mores, and values (John, 1999). This perspective suggests that social learning influences the development of preferences for sport products and services from early childhood through maturity (Bandura, 1986; Crawford, Godbey, & Crouter, 1986; Hoff & Ellis, 1992). Awareness of sport objects can stem from observational learning both active and passive, modelling behaviour of others based on context, reinforcement of appropriate behaviour in a given situation, and social interaction. Socialising agents that influence prior social learning as a child can also shape adult awareness of various sport objects. Hence, the impact of various socialising agents on cognitive learning processes change as a person matures and transitions through different life-stages.

Research indicates that mass media has a direct and indirect impact on cognitive learning (Drew & Weaver, 1990). Media's influence on learning occurs from two primary avenues: (a) the cognitive effects of how information is framed and processed (e.g., how sport events are perceived) and (b) the potential persuasiveness of media content (e.g., sport news coverage, editorials). Mass media can shape awareness by influencing the way individuals think and feel about their social, political, and economic environment. Entman (1989) states, "The media do not control what people prefer … they influence public opinion by providing much of the information people think about and shape how they think about it" (p. 361). For example, media coverage of a sport event influences the level of awareness by controlling what individuals know about a sport event in the absence of actual observation or first-hand knowledge.

Awareness processing influences the amount of cognitive, affective, and behavioural processing devoted toward a sport object during social learning. In general, behavioural learning and minimal cognitive evaluation prevail creating a non-emotional connection with a sport object. As the individual increases awareness of a sport object, the emotional connection begins to form and affective processing begins to emerge. Mike's attendance at the Offenbach game fits within this type of processing toward football. Mike knows about football as a recreational and competitive professional sport, but never watches or plays, rarely watches the sport on television and only occasionally reads a story in the newspaper. However, he is now aware of a second division Bundesliga football team in Germany and the type of experience that results from attending a live soccer match. This awareness level represents an output.

Awareness Stage Outcomes

Awareness processing illustrates how environmental inputs and internal forces influence outcomes such as knowledge, attitudes, values, and behaviours of sport consumers through the process of social learning. Awareness stage as an output indicates that an individual has formed an initial psychological connection with a sport object. Mike can now state, "I know about the Offenbach Kickers." Mike's awareness reflects a connection based upon the knowledge and realisation that the team exists. Awareness outcomes for the most part reflect a psychological connection with a sport object that lacks an emotional component. Level of awareness can range from simply acknowledging a sport, team, or activity exist, to understanding basic rules and etiquette of a specific sport, to distinguishing between different leagues, events, and athletes, to being able to associate sport objects with geographic locations and sponsors. For Mike, he may now know about the Offenbach Kickers, but emotionally he is neutral and does not like the team over other sport objects.

Within the awareness stage outcomes, minimal attitude formation has occurred and behaviour ranges from non-existent to sporadic and exploratory (see Figure 3.6). The various socialising agents create preconceptions of the sport object and the minimal direct and indirect experience occurs through search and trial behaviour. Search and trial behaviour reflects behavioural learning processes through modelling, reinforcement, and social interaction. The limited psychological and behavioural engagement occur because processing stems from preconceptions created from environmental inputs rather than direct experiences and knowledge. However, for Mike, the positive experience of attending a football event may have subsequent influence on affective processing in future entertainment decisions.

Awareness processing may take place multiple times. This occurrence creates different outcomes that can incrementally feedback into social learning and build various levels of knowledge and realisation. Only as a connection continues to develop and a person moves toward the attraction stage, do emotional characteristics emerge and a distinct preference for a specific sport object form. The level of awareness as an output interacts with subsequent social learning processes as well as new environmental inputs. If the connection continues to mature, various levels of knowledge, realisation and recognition occur and can create an understanding that different sport objects exist. For example, when Mary hears the word "basketball," she can distinguish the sport from football and cricket. However, Cheri can distinguish these sports and recall a specific team (e.g., the Toronto Raptors) that play in the National Basketball Association (NBA) league when cued by the word "basketball." This level of knowledge signals movement upward within the awareness stage for Cheri.

The previous discussion outlines the inputs, internal processing, and outputs within the awareness stage sequence of the PCM framework. Awareness outcomes reflect the processing of environmental inputs through internal psychological and personal forces that govern general and attitudinal processing. Inputs emerge from the general social learning process. This sequence accounts for how individuals learn that sport objects exist and begins to distinguish between various sport objects. The inputs, processing, output sequence occurs multiple times and represents a developmental process contributing to various levels of awareness. The awareness process represents the initial entry point within the PCM framework. Hence, awareness is an important concern for sport marketing professionals and academics attempting to develop a sport league or event. The rest of this chapter provides a discussion of sport marketing action applicable to the awareness stage.

Awareness and Sport Marketing Action

Sport marketing action

Strategic use of marketing mix
Select key target markets
Study and evaluate market
Select information systems

Marketing action in the awareness stage draws upon the sport marketing action procedure (SMA) discussed in Chapter 4. The SMA provides marketing levers that can foster initial entry into a sport (i.e., awareness stage of the PCM framework) and induce incremental movement upward. The primary focus is strategically positioning the marketing mix to meet the needs and wants of potential key target markets. This approach relies upon information on the sport consumer within various life-cycle positions as well as understanding the marketing environment. As a result, this approach allows for the integration of the awareness process and life-cycle positioning.

Sport marketing activities within the awareness stage should attempt to position the sport product or service to accomplish two outcomes: (a) entice an individual to enter the PCM elevator by acknowledging that a sport object exists and (b) increasing the level of awareness and incrementally building momentum en route to the attraction stage. Such activities incorporate designing a marketing approach for an individual, but also indirectly influence an individual through socialising agents. For example, creating opportunities to increase social learning opportunities is advisable. As a result, positioning the marketing approach should consider the awareness process and the differential influence of various socialising agents at different points in the life-cycle.

Awareness strategies
- Entice individual to trial and search creating realisation that a sport object exists.
- Increase level of awareness and incrementally build momentum en route to the attraction stage.

Awareness Process and Life-Cycle Positioning

General awareness of a sport object often begins during childhood, but continues to be relevant over time. For example, awareness can occur through the emergence of new sport activities, events, and teams, or an individual moving to a city with a particular team, or a parent supporting a child's interest in an unfamiliar sport. Regardless of one's life-cycle position, the degree to which socialising agents moderate the introduction to sport and the value placed on sports (i.e., the importance of sport from a societal perspective) continues to be important for sport marketing action. Marketing strategies should focus primarily on environmental factors such as the influence of family, peers, the mass media, and other socialising agents.

Traditional forms of marketing are useful in creating awareness since the stage involves search and trial behaviour. Advertising and selling techniques can communicate specific attributes and benefits of the sport product to influence socialising agents. As new teams and sport events enter the sport landscape, promotional efforts can entice socialising agents to engage search and trial behaviour as well as word-of-mouth. Marketers can utilise promotions such as discounts (e.g., two for one tickets or early registration), the record of the opposing team, T-shirt and coupons in race packets, entertainment such as live music, special events including championship or all-star events or signing of a marquee player (e.g., David Beckham at Real Madrid and LA Galaxy). Marketing to socialising agents should communicate opportunities to satisfy hedonic needs (e.g., excitement), the success of the team (achievement), or the financial considerations (e.g., entertainment value) are appropriate (Funk & James, 2001).

Marketers can strategically position the marketing mix to create and highlight unique attributes and benefits for a new consumer experience. However, since minimal cognitive effort takes place within awareness, the use of a simple and quick message that reduces time needed to read or think about the message is advisable. Marketing action can take a proactive role in fostering awareness by managing media relations within the local community (Nichols, Moynahan, Hall, & Taylor, 2002). For example, using a multi-feature coverage within the sport section (e.g., a three-part series over corresponding Sundays) creates exposure and repetition to enhance awareness (Pritchard & Funk, 2006). Such newspaper features should also use pictures, imagery and other key scenes to facilitate the encoding of the communication (Shimp, 1997).

Awareness processing can occur at different points in an individual's life and the relative influence of socialising agents that shape awareness change. The introduction of a sport object and the various levels of awareness stem from a number of personal, psychological, and environmental determinants that interact with socialising agents. Factors that influence awareness outcomes directly or indirectly depend upon the interaction of such determinants as age, gender, ethnicity, income, education, culture, and family structure with other socialising agents (Bush et al., 1999). Table 5.1 provides a general guide to different life-cycle positions related to age and the various socialising agents that may influence awareness. This guide links the fundamental areas of "when" and "how" individuals learn about sport objects within the awareness stage of the PCM.

The PCM staging tool allows marketers to segment consumers based upon the level of awareness. In other words, use involvement facets and the PCM staging algorithm to classify individuals. This creates the opportunity to explore the "when" and "how" awareness occurs. This helps understand the relative contribution of various socialising agents in the introduction of a sport object or experience. The awareness segmentation can be used in conjunction with other segmentation strategies. Table 5.1 highlights age and how it interacts with socialising agents to help position the marketing approach for awareness. Age ranges when people learn about sport objects, represent examples of general boundaries and are not intended to be absolute. In addition, the socialising agents that influence age ranges are not definitive. Table 5.1 illustrates how the sport marketing action of

Table 5.1   Awareness stage and life-cycle positioning

When people learn about sport objects	How people learn about sport objects

● Life-cycle positions
  1. Childhood
    – 0–5 years
    – 6–12 years
  2. Adolescence (13–19 years)
  3. Adulthood
    – 20–35 years
    – 36–54 years
    – 55+ years
	● Socialising agents
	  1. Parents
	  2. Siblings
	  3. Relatives
	  4. Friends
	  5. School
	    – Teacher(s)
	    – Coach(es)
	    – Peers/friends
	  6. Media
	    – News
	    – Programming
	  7. Promotions
	    – Advertising
	    – Special events
	  8. Community
	  9. Geographic proximity
	  10. Spouse/partner

studying and evaluating sport consumer behaviour can guide segmentation and positioning, but further research to clarify ages and agents in a specific market is advisable.

Marketing Awareness to Children

Marketing action to create awareness in children under 5 years of age should concentrate on positioning the marketing approach for important socialising agents such as parents, siblings, and relatives. Parents are often the primary socialising agent for introducing a sport object to a child in the early period of the life-cycle phase. Parents expose children to sport activities and events they participate in and watch. James (2001) reports children can demonstrate characteristics of sport and team awareness by the age of five. Prior research also reveals parents are the primary socialising agents for recreational sports during the preschool years (0–5 years of age) (Kenyon & McPherson, 1973).

Marketing activities can influence awareness by providing opportunities for parents to introduce a sport object. For example, parents can dress their children in clothes with a sport logo from a favourite sport team or event. Research also indicates fathers play an important role in introducing children to a sport object by talking about and/or watching specific sports and events on television (Kolbe & James, 2000). Hence, selecting fathers as a key market segment is advisable. Although fathers have a central role in introducing children, particularly boys to sports this may be changing as the notion of the nuclear family evolves.

A marketing approach can also utilises siblings and relatives to influence a child's early interest and help shape introduction to a particular sport object. Younger children become aware of an older sibling's sport consumption activities and often adopt such interest. Relatives can buy licensed sports equipment, merchandise, and other paraphernalia as presents exposing a child to their sport preferences. Even the social network of a parent or sibling can influence awareness through exposing various interests in sport activities.

Marketing activities designed for children represent a means to create awareness indirectly by influencing a socialising agent. For example, marketing a minor league baseball game so that a parent realises the opportunities to satisfy needs and receive benefits (e.g., SPEED) can be achieved. The goal is to create an experience that entices a parent to bring the child to the game or watch the game on television. The marketing approach should also consider how to attract parents based on their level of involvement with the team.

The decision-making sequence that results in taking a child to a football match differs depending upon the level of involvement. For example, external inputs such as advertising and promotions may influence fathers in the awareness stage of the PCM. In contrast, a parent in the attachment stage rely more on internal processes to make parental decisions. The PCM staging algorithm represents a useful tool to segment the potential influence of socialising agents based upon level of involvement.

Marketing action to create awareness for children 6–12 years of age should concentrate on positioning the marketing approach to use a greater number of socialising agents. The later childhood life cycle phase increases awareness through a widening influence of socialising agents. Once a child transitions to primary school, a wider social network introduces a greater variety of different sport objects and levels of awareness. An introduction to sport can come from playing and interacting socially with neighbourhood friends. The education system also plays a critical role in socialising a child into sport. During primary school years, teachers, coaches, physical education instructors, and peers become important socialising agents.

Marketing activities should position the approach to create awareness, but also build upon prior awareness levels. Children learn and become more aware of a number of sports and events. Participating in community sport leagues and youth groups contribute to awareness. In addition, the media also begins to have more influence. Interviews with children 5, 6, 8, and 9 years old indicate that television introduces non-traditional sports (e.g., gymnastics and swimming), particularly for girls (James, 2001). Children are now able to differentiate between specific sports, teams, and events (e.g., high school, club, professional, hallmark event). The use of marketing strategies can now utilises both indirect and direct approaches to foster a child learning the basic rules of play, start distinguishing between sports and teams, and understanding the different levels of play.

Marketing Awareness to Adolescents

Marketing activities for adolescents should begin to position the marketing approach directly to influence the individual. The adolescent life-cycle phase 13–19 years of age builds upon prior awareness levels as the relative influence of socialising agents begins to shift. Parents, relatives, and siblings can continue to have important roles, but this influence begins to fade. Hence, the opportunity to create targeted introductions emerges. For example, in Chapter 3 Mark's introduction to road cycling occurred at the age of 15 through a key socialising agent, his uncle Stan, who was an elite triathlete. During this adolescent phase, school, friends, and the mass media become more prominent in creating awareness. At this point, awareness of sport objects begins to lead to actual participation through search and trial behaviour. However, an individual may be aware of participation opportunities (both passive and active) but does not engage, or if participation does occur it may be coerced (Stebbins, 2005). The decision to initiate participation is also dependent upon perceived ability to perform the activity (Netz & Raviv, 2004) or perceived constraints (i.e., cost, location, and accessibility) to participation (Carroll & Alexandris, 1997). Marketing activities may need to help the adolescent overcome perceived constraints. The primary focus at this level is on mass media outlets of television and the Internet as well as word-of-mouth.

Marketing Awareness to Adults

The adult life-cycle phase marks a continued shift in the range of possible socialising agents to introduce a sport object. In this case, the potential socialising agents may narrow down. For adults, mass media, friends, spouse/partner, co-workers, and community become important (Funk & James, 2001). Awareness relative to adults and the socialisation process still includes family and relatives, but these agents become substantially less influential. The education system also becomes less prominent unless an adult has children. Adults have well-defined attitudes and preferences toward sport objects so the awareness process often corresponds to changes in living conditions and the sport environment. Adults are influenced by geographic proximity (moving to a new community), the influence of one's spouse/partner, co-workers' attitudes and behaviours, and even the emphasis a community places on sport or supporting the home team or community sport event.

Once an individual knows that sports and teams exist, he or she may return to the awareness level when new sports and teams emerge. Adults can experience an introduction and become aware through new sports and events (X-Games, Adventure Challenge), expansion teams are created (Baltimore Ravens of the National Football League), and leagues form (Arena Football League, Women's United Soccer Association) during their lifetime. The role of the media becomes an important element of introduction. With adults, awareness of sports and teams focuses more on the traditional role of media and promotion through the introduction of new sport products and services (a new sport, event, team, or league). Research illustrates the important socialising role that mass media plays in shaping the awareness of consumers toward a new sport object amongst adults within a community (Dalton, Beck, & Huckfeldt, 1998; Moy, Pfau, & Kahlor, 1999).

Conclusion

This chapter outlines the awareness stage of the PCM framework. Awareness represents a sequence of environmental inputs, internal processing, and outputs. Environmental inputs range from a wide variety of external sources including persons, institutions, and organizations that communicate norms, attitudes, and behaviour through socialisation. Prominent environmental inputs in sport consumer behaviour are socialising agents of family, peers, education institutions, mass media, and subculture. Internal processing is the evaluation of these inputs based on psychological and personal forces that govern general and attitudinal processing as well as the social learning process. Awareness outcomes such as knowledge and behaviour indicate that an individual has formed an initial psychological connection with a sport object.

The awareness stage represents the initial entry point within the PCM framework. A discussion of sport marketing action applicable to awareness was given to provide marketing levers that foster initial entry into the PCM framework and induce incremental movement upward. One approach that utilises life-cycle position was highlighted to allow for the integration of the awareness and life-cycle segmentation. This approach provides a general guide to different life-cycle positions related to age and the various socialising agents that may influence awareness. This guide links the fundamental areas of "when" and "how" individuals learn about sport objects within the awareness stage of the PCM. Marketing actions designed to foster awareness in children, adolescents, and adults were presented.

References

Armstrong, K. (2001). Black women's participation in sport and fitness: Implications for sport marketing. *Sport Marketing Quarterly, 10*, 9–18.

Bandura, A. (1986). *Social Foundations of Thoughts and Action*. Englewood Cliffs, NJ: Prentice-Hall.

Beech, J., Chadwick, S., & Tapp, L. (2000). Surfing in the Premier League: Key issues for football club marketers using the Internet. *Managing Leisure, 5*(2), 51–64.

Burch, W.R. (1969). The social circles of leisure: Competing explanations. *Journal of Leisure Research, 1*, 125–147.

Burnett, J., Menon, A., & Smart, D.T. (1993). Sports marketing: A new ball game with new rules. *Journal of Advertising Research, 33*, 21–35.

Bush, A.J., Smith, R., & Martin, C. (1999). The influence of consumer socialization variables on attitude toward advertising: A comparison of African-American and Caucasians. *Journal of Advertising, 28*, 13–24.

Carroll, B., & Alexandris, K. (1997). Perception of constraints and strength of motivation: Their relationship to recreational sport participation in Greece. *Journal of Leisure Research, 29*, 279–299.

Comisky, P., Bryant, J., & Zillman, D. (1977). Commentary as a substitute for action. *Journal of Communication, 27*, 150–153.

Crawford, D.W., Godbey, G., & Crouter, A.C. (1986). The stability of leisure preferences. *Journal of Leisure Research, 18*, 96–115.

Dalton, R.J., Beck, P.A., & Huckfeldt, R. (1998). Partisan cues and the media: Information flows in the 1992 presidential election. *American Political Science Review, 92*, 111–126.

Donnelly, P., & Young, K. (1988). The construction and confirmation of identity in sport subcultures. *Sociology of Sport Journal, 5*, 223–240.

Drew, D., & Weaver, D. (1990). Media attention, media exposure, and media effects. *Journalism and Mass Communication Quarterly, 67*, 740–748.

Duncan, M.C., & Brummett, B. (1989). Types and sources of spectating pleasures in televised sports. *Sociology of Sport Journal, 6*, 195–211.

Eitzen, D.S., & Sage, G.H. (2003). *Sociology of North American Sport* (7th Ed.). New York: McGraw-Hill.

Emmers-Sommer, T.M., & Allen, M. (1999). Surveying the effect of media effects: A meta-analytic summary of the media effects research in human communication research. *Human Communication Research, 4*, 478–497.

Entman, R.M. (1989). How the media affect what people think: An information processing approach. *Journal of Politics, 51*, 347–370.

Funk, D.C., & James, J.D. (2001). The Psychological Continuum Model (PCM): A conceptual framework for understanding an individual's psychological connection to sport. *Sport Management Review, 4*, 119–150.

Funk, D.C., & James, J.D. (2004). The Fan Attitude Network (FAN) Model: Propositions for exploring identity and attitude formation among sport consumers. *Sport Management Review, 7*, 1–26.

Funk, D.C., & Pritchard, M. (2006). Responses to publicity in sports: Commitment's moderation of message effects. *Journal of Business Research, 59*, 613–621.

Funk, D.C., Toohey, K., & Bruun, T. (2007). International sport event participation: Prior sport involvement; destination image; and travel motives. *European Sport Management Quarterly, 7*, 227–248.

Gantz, W. (1981). An exploration of view motives and behaviors associated with television sports. *Journal of Broadcasting, 25*, 263–275.

Hawkins, D.I., Best, R.J., & Coney, K.A. (1992). *Consumer Behavior: Implications for Marketing Strategy*. Boston, MA: Irwin.

Hoff, A.E., & Ellis, G.D. (1992). Influence of agents of leisure socialization on leisure self-efficacy of university students. *Journal of Leisure Research, 24*, 114–126.

Holbrook, M.B., & Hirschman, E.C. (1982). The experiential aspects of consumption: Consumer fantasies, feelings, and fun. *Journal of Consumer Research, 9*, 132–141.

Iso-Ahola, S.E. (1980). *The Social Psychology of Leisure and Recreation*. Dubuque, IA: William. C. Brown.

James, J.D. (2001). The role of cognitive development and socialization in the initial development of team loyalty. *Leisure Sciences, 23,* 233–262.

John, D.R. (1999). Consumer socialization of children: A retrospective look at twenty-five years of research. *Journal of Consumer Research, 26,* 183–213.

Kenyon, G.S., & McPherson, B.D. (1973). Becoming involved in physical activity and sport: A process of socialization. In G.L. Rarick (Ed.), *Physical Activity: Human Growth and Development* (pp. 303–332). New York: Academic Press.

Kolbe, R.H., & James, J.D. (2000). The internalization process among team followers: Implications for team loyalty. *International Journal of Sport Management, 4,* 25–43.

Manfredo, M.J., & Bright, A.D. (1991). A model for assessing the effects of communication on recreationist. *Journal of Leisure Research, 23,* 1–20.

McCarthy, L. (1998). Marketing sport to Hispanic consumers. *Sport Marketing Quarterly, 7,* 19–24.

McDaniel, S.R. (2002). An exploration of audience demographics, personal values, and lifestyles: Influence on viewing network coverage of the 1996 Summer Olympic Games. *Journal of Sport Management, 2,* 117–131.

McPherson, B.D. (1976). Socialization in toe the role of sport consumer: A theory and causal model. *Canadian Review of Sociology and Anthropology, 13,* 165–177.

Moy, P., Pfau, M., & Kahlor, L. (1999). Media use and public confidence in democratic institutions. *Journal of Broadcasting and Electronic Media, 43,* 137–158.

Netz, Y., & Raviv, S. (2004). Age differences in motivational orientation toward physical activity: An application of social-cognitive theory. *The Journal of Psychology, 138,* 35–48.

Nichols, W., Moynahan, P., Hall, A., & Taylor, J. (2002). *Media Relations in Sport*. Morgantown, WV: Fitness Information Technology, Inc.

Pritchard, M., & Funk, D.C. (2006). Dual routes to consumption: Examining the symbiotic and substitutionary nature of sport attendance and media use. *Journal of Sport Management, 20,* 299–321.

Recours, R.A., Souville, M., & Griffet, J. (2004). Expressed motives for informal and club/association-based sports participation. *Journal of Leisure Research, 36,* 1–22.

Ridinger, L., & Funk, D.C. (2006). Looking at gender differences through the lens of sport spectators. *Sport Marketing Quarterly*, *3*, 123–134.

Rose, G.M., Bush, V.D., & Kahle, L. (1998). The influence of family communication patterns on parental reactions toward advertising: A cross-national examination. *Journal of Advertising*, *27*, 71–85.

Schouten, J.W., & McAlexander, J.H. (1995). Subcultures of consumption: An ethnography of the new bikers. *Journal of Consumer Research*, *22*, 43–61.

Shimp, T.A. (1997). *Advertising, Promotion and Supplemental Aspects of Integrated Marketing Communications* (4th Ed). Forth Worth, TX: Dryden Press.

Stebbins, R.A. (2005). Choice and experiential definitions of leisure. *Leisure Sciences*, *27*, 349–352.

Trevino, L.K., Webster, J., & Stein, E.W. (2000). Making connections: Complementary influences of communication media choices, attitudes and use. *Organization Science*, *111*, 163–182.

Consumer Attraction to Sport and Events

> **Catch a wave and you're sitting on top of the world!**
>
> "Don't be afraid to try the greatest sport around
> Everybody tries it once
> Those who don't just have to put it down
> You paddle out turn around and raise
> And baby that's all there is to the coastline craze
> You gotta catch a wave and you're sittin' on top of the world"

The passage from The Beach Boys song "Catch a Wave" illustrates how Julie became attracted to surfing. Julie recently moved to San Diego, California from Austin, Texas and works in public relations for the San Diego Padres of Major League Baseball. Julie has been aware of surfing for as long as she can remember from movies, songs, magazines, and advertising. Now she lives in San Diego where the surfing culture is very strong she is keen to give it a go. A work colleague invites her to catch a wave one Saturday morning and she agrees. Julie stops by the local surf shop to buy some baggies. After more than a few attempts, Julie is able to stand up and rides her first wave. After one particular long ride, she begins to understand what it feels like to be "sittin' on top of the world."

Julie decides surfing is something she might like to do more often and enrols in four Saturday morning lessons at the local surf club. After the lessons, Julie decides to buy herself a used long-board and purchases a rash shirt. During one Saturday session, she gets a friend to video her surfing and posts the video on a video sharing website for her friends back in Texas. After an early Saturday morning session, a friend invites Julie to stick around and play beach volleyball. At first she declines, but then decides to play because she has always wanted to play beach volleyball. The next Saturday she plays volleyball after surfing. Saturday next, just 3 months after catching her first wave, Julie sleeps in so she can meet her new friends at midday to play beach volleyball.

The emergence of Julie's surfing activity illustrates the Attraction stage within the psychological continuum model (PCM) framework illustrated in Figure 6.1. Attraction represents an increased psychological connection with a sport or event object from the Awareness stage. Attraction is a connection that results from an interaction of processing personal, psychological, and environmental inputs. The product of this interaction creates interest and liking for a sport or event object because it provides opportunities to satisfy needs and receive benefits. Attraction results from the emergence of internal processing as

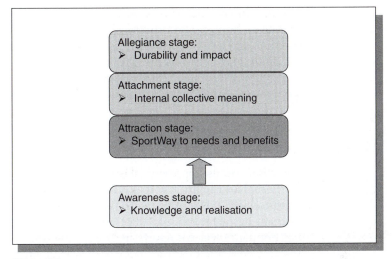

Figure 6.1
PCM framework.

an individual compares and evaluates different sport objects and opportunities to determine whether to engage in one specific sport activity. Selecting a favourite sport, event, or team because of the desirable outcomes suggests a person has moved from Awareness to the Attraction stage. This chapter offers a comprehensive understanding of the Attraction stage and provides marketing recommendations.

The Attraction stage represents a sequence of input, internal processes, and outputs. This sequence describes how an individual's psychological connection with a sport object progressively develops and continues to take shape from the Awareness stage. The developmental progression marks the transition from "I know about golf" to "I like golf." Figure 6.2 illustrates

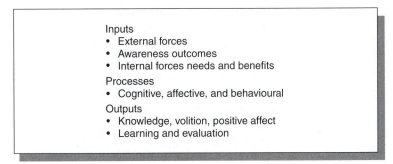

Figure 6.2
Attraction processing.

how previous awareness outcomes, external and internal forces, operate as inputs. The processes represent the role of cognitive, affective, and behavioural processing of inputs to create outputs. Attraction stage outputs are psychological outcomes that consist of liking and preference for a specific sport object and increase behavioural learning and evaluation.

Attraction Inputs

Attraction inputs represent existing awareness outputs as well as external and internal forces. Chapter 5 reveals acknowledging a sport object exists but having no emotional connection signals a person has achieved a level of awareness. A person may know that popular spectator sports in North America include football, baseball, basketball, and ice hockey. However, an individual may not like or dislike any of these sports and will not invest time, money, or emotions to engage in consumption-related activities.

The level of Awareness serves as the initial input within attraction processing. Within the Awareness stage, movement toward attraction occurs as an individual moves progressively from acknowledging a sport object exists to distinguishing between different sport objects, rules, and levels of sport experiences. Building upon this knowledge acquisition, increasing levels of awareness allow an individual to compare and contrast different sport activities, engage in simple search and trial behaviour, and make the conscious decision that one activity provides outcomes that are more desirable. For example, prior to moving to San Diego, Julie was aware of surfing but did not consider it a favourite sport activity. However, within a month, the introduction of external forces combined with internal forces help to shape her attitude and behaviour toward surfing.

The PCM framework suggests that within attraction processing, the Awareness stage outcomes combine with external and internal forces to facilitate movement toward attraction. Within the awareness processing sequence, inputs were primarily external and processing of those inputs utilised internal, personal, and psychological forces. Within the attraction processing sequence, the inputs also reflect Awareness stage outcomes derived from internal forces used in the awareness processing sequence. Environmental forces are still influential inputs, but personal and psychological forces begin to play a larger role as inputs.

As discussed in Chapter 5, external inputs represent environmental forces while internal inputs represent person-specific and psychological forces. Environmental forces stem from sociological influences including family, friends, work colleagues, neighbours, and other non-commercial sources (socialising agents) through information and recommendations. Environmental information also comes from a sport organisation's marketing actions. These forces provide information regarding the utilitarian attributes of a sport product or service that an individual desires. These inputs also focus on hedonic and intangible features including emotional needs and experiential benefits that a person desires from a sport product or service.

Attraction inputs also stem from characteristics of the individual and the sport consumption environment (i.e., person x situation). These characteristics can shape how individuals perceive and assess certain product features as well as the experience. Sport as a hedonic service depends upon technical and functional aspects of the experience (Hightower, Brady, & Baker, 2002). Technical elements of the sport product experience involve perceptions of athletic competition such as the skill of performance or act of performing (Deighton, 1992) and the climate evoked by the event (e.g., excitement, camaraderie, wholesome) (Funk, Ridinger, & Moorman, 2004). Situational characteristics encountered during consumption at the sport event can stimulate sensory arousal and pleasure (Holbrook & Hirschman, 1982).

Sport events have situational or environmental atmospheric conditions that evoke positive effect during the course of an event (Madrigal, 2003). These external inputs influence internal processing. This perspective also incorporates the notion that the sport and recreation settings (e.g., playing golf vs. watching a football match live vs. watching a football match at a pub), or the specific type of activity (running a 10 Km race vs. Marathon) provide attractive opportunities to experience the environmental surroundings (Williams, Patterson, Roggenbuck, & Watson, 1992). The entertainment and drama surrounding the sport event spectacle are integral parts of influencing how sport consumers think about the product experience (Swanson, Gwinner, & Larson, 2001). The exciting atmosphere and social interaction at events are other attractive components (Pons, Mourali, & Nyeck, 2006).

Functional attributes involve perceptions of services encountered at the venue that augment the consumption experience (Kelley & Turley, 2001). These services consist of tangible and intangible elements or hard and soft attributes (Driver & Johnston, 2001; Wakefield & Blodgett, 1999). Tangible service features include perceptions of "hard" physical aspects of events (stadium design, cleanliness, venue parking, food and beverages, etc.). Intangible service features represent "soft" customer service attributes performed by service personnel at events (crowd control, responsiveness, reliability, communication, etc.). Taken together, hard and soft aspects of the experience can bundle together to form inputs that influence internal processing (Janiszewski & Cunha, 2004). The blending of these forces represents a complex array of psychological, personal, and environmental inputs that shape attraction processing.

Attraction Processing

Attraction processing represents a collection of processes that describes how internal and external inputs are evaluated. Figure 6.3 illustrates how attraction processing occurs in a fashion similar to internal processing discussed in Chapter 3. See Figure 3.3 to review internal processing. Attraction processing is the internal mechanism of the interlocking gears. As discussed in Chapter 3, general processes including motivation, perception, learning, and memory continue to influence the evaluation process through knowledge acquisition. In Chapter 2, the motivation process describes how people are motivated to watch a sport or participate in a sport event, because the activity has certain attractive outcomes. A need-recognised creates internal tension that drives an individual toward seeking sport pathways that provide opportunities to satisfy the need and receive benefits. Reducing tension "pushes" a person forward and the pathway providing positive benefits "pulls" that individual to select a situation to restore balance. Needs push the individual forward as benefits (tangible and intangible) pull the individual towards specific sport experiences. Attraction processing represents the push–pull evaluation of the interaction of psychological, personal, and environmental inputs.

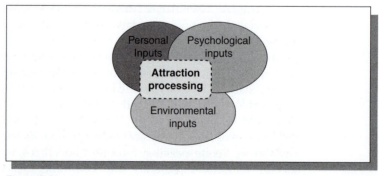

Figure 6.3
Attraction Processing.

Similar to awareness processing, attitudinal processing emerges that utilises cognitive, affective, and behavioural evaluations. Cognitive and behavioural processing evaluate the sport object or experience ability to provide attractive needs and benefits. Affective processing evaluates whether these benefits are desirable or not. In other words, the evaluation of inputs and the relative influence of each attitudinal process create continued attitude formation from the Awareness stage to the Attraction stage.

Within Attraction processing, cognitive-affective processing begins to prevail as the evaluation of the sport object compares needs and benefits with desires. This processing introduces an emotional element to the connection. This creates attitude formation such as "I like surfing" or "Surfing is a bit ordinary." Attraction processing reflects an increased psychological activity to evaluate the sport object and behavioural engagement increases in complexity. The previous weak attitude toward the sport object changes and continues to form and take shape. Attraction processing occurs through activation of positive perceptions and discounting misconceptions about whether the activity offers desirable outcomes. Behavioural engagement increases from infrequent to necessary and introduces complexity through learning and evaluation. The individual begins to participate and watch sports, internalise experiences, interprets and assigns value and meaning to actions, and constructs judgments regarding situations and people. The integration of environmental, personal, and psychological inputs reflects a variety of forces to help the individual learn roles and interact with fellow participants and spectators via mutual experience.

Processing of External Inputs

The processing of environmental inputs coincides with the acquisition of knowledge. External inputs continue to play an important role in attraction processing. Socialising agents operate as key external forces in the early development of an emotional psychological connection with a sport object. Mass media and particularly television, newspapers, Internet, and various forms of advertising continue to shape attraction by building upon awareness levels to process information and realise engaging in a sport activity provides desirable outcomes (e.g., Cobb-Wallgreen, Ruble, & Donthu, 1995). The influence of friends, family, work colleagues, whether directly or indirectly, through word of mouth contributes as well. Sport marketing activities also serve as inputs by communicating specific attributes and benefits of the sport product or service (Gladden & Funk, 2002). Environmental inputs help explain why people are drawn to a particular sport object because the mode of experience or situational attributes (Williams et al., 1992). For example, Julie's new geographical proximity and recruitment by a work colleague represent environmental sources that interact with her awareness of surfing and facilitate movement toward liking surfing.

The influence of subculture continues as a prominent input source in attraction processing. The surf subculture was an important reason for Julie's decision to surf. Surfing has many characteristics such as an underlying sentiment that informs beliefs, customs, rituals, and modes of symbolic expression popularised by the mass media (Schouten & McAlexander, 1995). This ethos represents a set of values subscribed to varying degrees by all surfers and one Julie learned in the Awareness stage. Within the first month, Julie underwent training in physical aspects of surfing via lessons, but also began learning characteristics of the subculture ethos (take on a new identity, learning values of group) and determining whether the preconceived notion of the subculture in the awareness stage was accurate (e.g., expectations were confirmed or disconfirmed) (Donnelly & Young, 1988).

Processing Using Internal Inputs

The evaluation of environmental inputs also draws upon person-specific characteristics and psychological inputs. Personal characteristics (e.g., gender, age, income, lifecycle) and physical characteristics (e.g., height, weight, and physical ability) remain important. Person-specific inputs help direct decisions toward a sport experience (Graeff, 1996). A decision to initiate, and later continue participation, is dependent upon perceived ability to perform the activity (Netz & Raviv, 2004) or perceived constraints such as alternative activities (Carroll & Alexandris, 1997). For example, given Julie's situation, she had to decide whether to continue surfing or to play beach volleyball.

Psychological inputs also play a role, while increasing in complexity. An important internal input of attraction is the psychological connection with the sport object originates from volition. Both children and adults may be aware of sport objects but do not engage in consumption-related activities unless coerced (Stebbins, 2005). Awareness often does not involve volitional choice. Volition is the act of free will and only when an individual consciously and willingly selects a favourite sport activity does attraction occur. A child may choose a specific football team as his/her favourite, because the sport team is the father's favourite. This level of connection is often weak and if the father changes teams, so would the child.

- Volition represents an important psychological characteristic to distinguish attraction from awareness.

Volition

Volition is also important for adults. Individuals who move to a new community may begin supporting a local sport team or event to gain in-group status. A desire for membership status within a group, either normative or comparative, has considerable influence on sport consumer decisions (Kahle, Kambara, & Rose, 1996). For example, when a sport team is successful some individuals will begin to follow that team for social benefits. The term "fair weather fan" describes this type of behaviour. However, once the individual makes new friends, supporting the team may no longer be important. In Julie's case, moving to a new community with a strong surf subculture influences her selection of surfing to "fit in" among work colleagues and make new friends.

Volition helps push the individual toward a specific sport object or sport experience that offers the opportunity to achieve desirable outcomes. Mannell and Iso-Ahola (1987) report recreation and leisure activities are sought, because they provide opportunities for self-determination, sense of competency or mastery, challenge, learning, exploration, relaxation, and social interaction. Funk and colleagues (2004) suggest spectator sport consumers are sought because they provide psychological benefits of drama, vicarious achievement, aesthetics, excitement, escape, socialisation, community pride, and wholesome environment for consumers. Regardless of the context, the desire to satisfy internal needs or receive intangible benefits through acquisition has received considerable attention in the literature.

Prior research has identified a number of discrete psychological needs and benefits that spectator sport provides. Wann (1995) examined eight psychological benefits for spectators: eustress, self-esteem, escape, entertainment, economic (gambling), aesthetic, group affiliation, and family. Trail and James (2001) extended the number of benefits with achievement, acquisition of knowledge, aesthetics, drama, escape, family, physical attraction, physical skills of players, and social interaction. Madrigal (2006) also measures similar benefits including a spectator's desire for fantasy, flow, aesthetics, camaraderie, vicarious achievement, performance evaluation, physical attraction, and celebrity attraction.

Other sport scholars have investigated more utilitarian benefits including marquee player, head coach, entertainment value, success, players as role models, service quality, use of technology, management practices, community pride, logo design, promotions and price (Beech, Chadwick, & Tapp, 2000; Gladden & Funk, 2002; Hansen & Gauthier, 1989; Hill & Green, 2000; Mahony, Nakazawa, Funk, James, & Gladden, 2002; Zhang, Pease, Hui, & Michaud, 1995). McDonald, Milne, and Hong (2002) integrated a number of benefits applicable to both spectator and participant motives related to: risk-taking, stress reduction, aggression, affiliation, social facilitation, self-esteem, competition, achievement, skill mastery, aesthetics, value development, and self-actualisation. Funk, Toohey, and Bruun (2007) examined benefits related to escaping everyday routines, social interaction, prestige of destination, relaxation, relaxation while on vacation, desire to experience culture of a foreign destination, and desire for knowledge exploration.

The previous discussion illustrates the wide variety of needs and benefits that shape attitudinal processing (cognitive, affective, and behavioural) and lead to attraction. Table 6.1 provides an amalgamation of internal and external inputs from sport, tourism, recreation, and event research that shape consumer behaviour. The list represents a general guide to various needs and benefits that direct individuals to engage in sport consumption activities. The psychological inputs include the core SPEED motives as basic needs and benefits discussed in Chapter 2. Personal inputs represent person-specific characteristics and disposition. Environmental inputs are notable forces that shape attraction to sport objects.

The complexity of sport consumer behaviour makes developing an exhaustive list of inputs particularly difficult. The various psychological, personal, and environmental forces that influence attraction are numerous. In addition, there are additional inputs that sport provides the opportunity to achieve such as motives for charitable giving within sport events. For example, research reveals a number of motives including reciprocity, self-esteem, need to help others, and the desire to improve the charity that determine charitable giving (Amos, 1982; Hibbert & Horne, 1996; Ritzenheim, 2000). These four benefits interact with psychological and personal needs to influence attraction to sport events aligned with charitable causes (Filo, Funk, & O'Brien, in press). For example, The American Cancer Society's Relay for

Table 6.1 Internal and external inputs

Internal inputs	Environmental inputs	
● Psychological		
Socialisation	Parking	Management practices
Performance	Food service	Special events
Entertainment	Venue cleanliness	Promotions
Esteem	Crowding effect	Price discounts
Diversion	Crowd control	Nostalgia/tradition
Volition	Access to technology	Marquee athletes
● Person-specific	Destination attributes	Community pride
Gender	Merchandise design	Customer service
Age	Charity/cause	Wholesome environment
Ethnicity/culture	Athlete role model	Sport knowledge
Direct experience	Price	Entertainment value
Knowledge	Heritage and culture	Geographic proximity
Learning ability	Safety and security	Event/team success
Body characteristics	Style of play	Media
Lifecycle	Subculture	Activity type
Personality		

An individual evaluates whether a sport object or experience provides opportunity to satisfy needs and receive benefits based on psychological, personal, and environmental inputs.

Life provides an opportunity to not only realise SPEED motives, but also additional charity benefits as well. Hence, the charity-based sport event provides an individual with the environment to receive psychological and personal needs and benefits not related to sport.

The PCM framework suggests inputs of prior awareness, external and internal forces collectively facilitate movement from awareness to attraction. The evaluation of these inputs occurs through cognitive, affective, and behavioural processing and produces outputs. Attraction processing occurs multiple times as the individual gains a better understanding of the sport experience and potential benefits and alternatives. Unfortunately, measuring attraction processing is difficult for researchers. Hence, measuring inputs and outputs is more advantageous for marketers. In other words, the inputs, which also serve as outputs listed in Table 6.1, are measurable. For example, attraction processing creates motivation, as well as the strength of desire for specific benefits that produce outputs in terms of level of attitude formation and behaviour.

Attraction Stage Outcomes

Attraction outputs result from cognitive, affective, and behavioural processing. Attraction stage represents a psychological connection based on various beliefs, feelings, and behavioural intentions toward a sport object. The level of knowledge acquired from the Awareness stage contributes to prior expectations to evaluate the sport experience based on potential outcomes. For example, the evaluation compares actual performance from behavioural processing with prior expectations. There are three possible outcomes of this evaluation. First, actual performance matches expectations leading to a neutral feeling. Second, if performance exceeds expectations, positive disconfirmation of expectations occurs and leads to satisfaction. Third, when performance is below expectations, negative disconfirmation of expectations occurs and leads to dissatisfaction. When the evaluation produces positive affect and the individual volitionally selects a sport object or experience, cognitive, affective, and behavioural outcomes occur (i.e., affection and enthusiasm for an activity begins to develop).

Psychological Outcomes

Cognitive Outcomes

Cognitive outcomes indicate the development of a set of beliefs associated with the sport object. The association network illustrated in Figure 3.4 provides an instructive means to understand cognitive outcomes. Gladden and Funk (2002) suggest sport team associations represent a set of knowledge-based thoughts, images, and ideas that come to mind when an individual thinks of a particular sport team. These associations represent hedonic benefits and utilitarian attributes such product delivery, logo, stadium, success, head coach, management, tradition, star player, escape, nostalgia, pride in place, identification, and peer group acceptance. These cognitive associations represent beliefs about whether a sport experience provides attractive needs and benefits. Cognitive formation provides direct experience and is reported to have greater clarity, held with more confidence and consistent with behaviour than attitudes not based upon direct experience (Ajzen, 2002). This creates knowledge that accompanies an individual's beliefs about the sport object.

Affective Outcomes

Affective outcomes consist of feelings, emotions, or moods that people experience in relation to the sport object (Funk & Pritchard, 2006). Affective outcomes represent how desirable a person evaluates potential needs and benefits associated with the sport experience. At this point, the individual begins to attach emotion to various cognitive associations. For example, an individual may attend a football game, because she believes the experience provides opportunities for socialisation, and this outcome is highly desirable. An individual may enter a 10K running event because he believes that it provides opportunities for personal accomplishment that he considers important. If the response is positive, the individual begins to like and develop a preference for a specific recreational activity (Beard & Ragheb, 1983; Crompton & Love, 1995; Henderson, 2003; Iso-Ahola, 1982).

However, if the response is negative, more evaluation takes place. For example, an individual may not enter a 10K, because she feels the opportunity for personal accomplishment is not great enough in comparison to a marathon. Consumers can often balance the number of positive and negative associations through a cognitive-affective evaluative process. The volitional decision to choose and like a sport object signifies attitudinal complexity that evaluates a number of psychological, personal, and environmental inputs. Within attraction, the previous weak attitude in the awareness stage continues to form and take shape. The resulting emotion subsequently influences behavioural outcomes.

Behavioural Outcomes

Behavioural outcomes within the Attraction stage represent both behavioural intention and actual behaviour. Behavioural intent is an individual's readiness to perform a given behaviour and serves as the antecedent of observed behaviour. Actual behaviour represents a wide range of activities. An individual attracted to a sport team may watch the team on television, attend games, and even wear team apparel. As the level of psychological engagement increases, the level of behavioural engagement becomes more complex through learning and evaluation. For example, Julie's initial attitude toward surfing was weak, but over a 3-month period, her attitude continued to take shape as she devoted more psychological and behavioural effort into surfing. This formation occurs through learning and evaluation as she began surfing, internalising the experiences, interpreting and assigning value and meaning to actions, constructing value judgments regarding situations and people, integrating elements of surfing to learn roles and interacting with fellow surfers via mutual experience.

However, if the evaluation is negative or conflicting positive and negative associations occur, the connection may not continue to develop and remain unstable. A key characteristic of attraction is that psychological connection with the sport object is still forming and preferences are not yet enduring. In other words, attraction outcomes are relatively unstable. A decision not to participate indicates a negative evaluation of the potential outcomes or the presence of constraints. For example, given Julie's situation, she had to decide whether to continue surfing or play beach volleyball. This suggests attraction still represents a relative low-level psychological connection with a sport object. For example, positive associations with a sport object are present, but the network is still forming and not complex (e.g., the spider web in Figure 3.4 is a work in progress). This low level of connect supports research indicating the greatest number of dropouts for a sport activity occurs within the first 3 months of initial participation (Guillot, Kilpatrick, Hebert, & Hollander, 2004). In fact, this timeframe corresponds to Julie's transition to beach volleyball. Her connection with surfing was not able to withstand attractive alternatives.

Research on sport spectators illustrates the instability of the psychological connection in the Attraction stage. A number of external forces can induce movement from awareness of a sport team to attraction however this connection may not endure. This phenomenon represents the notion of basking in reflected glory when a connection is successful (BIRGing; Cialdini, Thorne, Walker, Freeman, & Sloan, 1976). However, when a team begins to lose support the connection erodes as individuals attempt to cut off reflected failure (CORFing) (Snyder, Lassegard, & Ford, 1986). For example, the Florida Marlins of major league baseball won the World Series in 1997 and during the championship season, there was no shortage of Marlins fans. However, the next year they were one of the worst teams in baseball and ticket sales and television ratings dropped dramatically.

The Attraction stage provides a number of opportunities and challenges for sport marketers. External inputs such as marketing activities can influence the progression from Awareness stage to Attraction stage. An individual's knowledge structure and attitude formation are less stable and susceptible to change providing opportunities to influence the evaluation process through marketing activities. As discussed in Chapter 3, attitude formation and change occurs as cognitive thoughts influence feelings, and feelings in turn, influence behavioural intent and actual behaviour. Hence, external inputs provided through marketing actions can influence cognitive thoughts. However, this instability of attitude formation within the Attraction stage also creates a challenge since an individual is more likely to change behaviour to an alternate consumption activity. The example of Julie's switch from surfing to beach volleyball illustrates this challenge. The rest of this chapter deals with marketing attraction within the attraction stage.

Attraction and Sport Marketing Action

Sport marketing action

Strategic use of marketing mix
Select key target markets
Study and evaluate market
Select information systems

Marketing action to foster attraction receives considerable attention. This phase of marketing action involves moving a consumer from initial awareness of a sport product or service to attraction. Sport marketers can employ a number of strategies, since the individual is already aware of the sport object and has previously engaged in some form of search and trial behaviour. Marketing activities generally have more success in getting a consumer to try a sport product a second time vs. the initial time. In addition, the sport marketer generally has more information on the individual to use the sport marketing action (SMA) procedure.

Internal and external inputs are important for sport marketing in terms of positioning the marketing mix. Internal inputs are experiential in nature involving emotional responses that are subjective. In contrast, external inputs can represent the functional attributes of a product or service that an individual desires. Internal inputs are more enduring. Taken together, information regarding inputs can be used to guide sport marketing activities. For example, sport marketing activities for attraction can focus mainly on promoting desirable inputs (i.e., functional attributes and intangible benefits) to spectators and participants aware of the sport object.

Tools to Measure Inputs

The study of sport consumer behaviour has provided a number of tools to measure psychological, environmental, and personal inputs in order to guide marketing actions. James, Trail, Zhang, Wann, and Funk's (2006) development of the Big 5 Sport Motives can successfully distinguish between intangible outcomes desired by those that attend events and those that do not (Beaton, Filo, & Funk, 2007). A number of environmental measures also exist to assess contextual benefits and attributes of a sport event experience (Funk et al., 2004; Wakefield & Sloan, 1995). Person-specific measures can be derived from demographics. Taken together, this research provides sport marketers with diagnostic tools to understand sport consumer decision-making, as well as levers to manage movement.

The SMA provides marketing levers to foster movement upward from awareness to attraction. The individual has already entered the PCM elevator and now marketing actions should attempt to facilitate movement through traditional selling as well as a service orientation approach. Sport marketing activities within the Attraction process should attempt to position the sport product or service to accomplish three outcomes: (1) to increase the level of awareness and incrementally build momentum *en route* to the attraction stage, (2) to do more business with existing customers, and (3) to reduce the loss of existing customers. The study of sport consumer behaviour provides the necessary information and knowledge to inform this approach by communicating the opportunities to satisfy needs and received benefits.

Attraction strategies

- Increase level of awareness to facilitate movement toward attraction.
- Do more business with current customers.
- Increase level of attraction and incrementally build momentum *en route* to the attachment stage.

Tools to Measure Attraction

Marketing action within the attraction stage requires a more complex approach. The marketing approach should position the sport experience based on the specific needs and benefits desired of a specific target market. For example, increasing the level of awareness and doing more business with existing consumers require different strategies. The PCM staging tool provides a means to allocate individuals into meaningful segments to understand how the influence of external and internal forces differ based upon the level of sport involvement. The PCM framework provides the ability to manage target markets by exploring how personal, psychological, and environmental factors can be used to develop marketing actions to foster attitude formation and change.

Attitude formation that occurs within attraction represents a level of involvement with a unique profile. Involvement is an important attraction outcome and facets of involvement exert a differential influence on an individual's psychological connection with a sport object. Chapter 3 indicates sport involvement has three main facets: pleasure, centrality, and sign. Funk and James (2001) suggest a person in the Attraction stage will have a profile high in pleasure while low in sign and centrality. In contrast the Awareness profile will have low scores on all three facets. The PCM staging tool allows the development of marketing levers to build and sustain involvement. This stage has the most marketing levers for a sport marketer.

Financial Levers

Funk and James (2001) suggest the use of relationship marketing activities such as financial bonding (Zeithaml & Bitner, 2003) to facilitate movement from awareness to attraction. The relationship marketing activity of financial bonding illustrates how providing incentives serves to create attraction. Adults already have the awareness of the sport object and financial incentives such as lower prices or discount promotions could entice attendance at events and induce learning and evaluation. Cross-promotional efforts can also provide additional initiatives such as hosting a pre- or post-gathering at a local pub or restaurant. This approach also provides the opportunity for social bonding where participants can continue to share food, drink, and their event experiences.

Social Levers

The internal processing that occurs within the attraction process is important as it informs understanding of how consumers learn through evaluation. Marketing decisions often rely upon the assumption that consumers take in information about products and learn to prefer some alternatives. Marketing activities should continue to target socialising agents within various lifecycle positions discussed in Chapter 5 to aid this learning process. Mass media can influence introduction as well as positive affect by shaping subjective and normative beliefs of socialising agents. The learning and evaluation of a subculture also plays an important role in fostering attraction. Individuals strive for positive responses from social behaviour according to the norms of the subculture. The use of marketing collateral to introduce a sport, event, team, opposing team, or marquee athlete can shape evaluations of the sport experience (Mattila, 1999). This approach continues the use of awareness strategies to increase the likelihood of search and trial behaviour to develop associations.

Social leverage strategies can use festivals and supporting events to provide various entertainment offerings (bands, gala, and auctions) to create an inclusive, celebratory community component. In describing ancillary events, Chalip (2006) highlights how arts and music events can complement sporting events. Event parties have been found to be attractive to event participants as they allow individuals to celebrate with others of similar interest (Green & Chalip, 1998). European and Asian football marketers have relied upon activities tailored to membership clubs to create opportunities for individuation and integration (i.e., expression of a unique identity and membership as part of a group) to attract new members through social networking.

Experiential Levers

Managing the experience represents another lever to create attraction. Attraction builds upon knowledge gained through search and trial behaviour in the Awareness stage. This creates an opportunity to manage the learning and evaluation process and stimulate the initial experience. This approach requires management of product characteristics and situational effects through customer service and service quality. Product characteristics reflect tangible service aspects of the consumptive experience including variety of food choices at the venue, accessibility of parking, and cleanliness of the venue (Wakefield & Sloan, 1995). When service elements fail to perform at an event, negative experiences result, creating negative attitude outcomes (Kelley & Turley, 2001).

Situational effects also shape perceptions of the sport experience. The link between environmental inputs and consumer inferences about sport experiences is well established. Situational or environmental effects create the atmosphere that augments the consumptive experience and shapes the perceptions of the product. For sporting events, the social atmosphere and excitement of game day is an integral part of the experience (Madrigal, 2003; Mason, 1999). Marketers can highlight unique attributes and benefits of the experience for a consumer, differentiating the sport experience offered from competitors (Gladden & Funk, 2002). The notion of theming involves the use of symbols, colours, and decorations to enhance the event (Chalip, 2006). ING, a corporate sponsor of marathons, attempts to colour the racecourse orange with decorations to make the event more attractive to runners and spectators.

Cause-Related Levers

A sport event can provide the environment to satisfy psychological and personal needs and benefits related to charitable causes. Cause-related motives at sport events aligned with charitable causes include reciprocity, self-esteem, need to help others, and the desire to improve the charity (Filo, Funk, & O'Brien, in press). Marketing activities can highlight these features of the sport event that an individual may enjoy through participation and consumption. This approach can also adopt the notion of Corporate Social Responsibility (CSR). CSR can be an effective cause-related marketing tool to gain sustainable competitive advantage by enhancing the image of a sport event and attracting consumers (Amis, Pant, & Slack, 1997). Filo, Funk, and Neal (2007) suggest that corporations should strategically align with sport events to allow for CSR and the meaning elicited by the event among participants to work jointly. The role of public relations that implement community relation programs can also be beneficial to gain community understanding and increase support of a sport event.

Sponsorship Levers

Sport events can use corporate sponsorship as a vehicle to provide needs and benefits. Sport marketers can use sponsorship in the communications mix to increase the attractiveness of attending or participating in a sport event. Corporate sponsors can be used to add value without increasing cost through premium giveaways and lotteries. Sport sponsorship provides the opportunity to display CSR programs that align with charitable causes. Strategic alliances can be formed between the sport event, the sponsor, and the charitable cause to enhance the attractiveness of the experience. CSR is an additional benefit for some consumers to bolster the event's attractiveness.

Brand Levers

Marketing communication can highlight the opportunity to satisfy hedonic and pleasure-based needs associated with the sport object. The development of knowledge-based association occurs through information and repetition. Promotional efforts should introduce and reinforce positive associations linked to a sport object. SMAs should devise promotional material that communicates the positive psychological, personal, and environmental features. This entails first understanding what benefits a sport experience can provide depending upon the involvement profile. Overall, communicating SPEED opportunities is a good place to start, but contextual attributes and benefits should be included.

Gladden and Funk (2002) report unique attributes and benefits are associated with sport team brands and can be used to develop marketing communication to build brand image. In other words, these attributes and benefits help develop content for promotion and advertising. Attributes are the features of a particular brand including four product-related attributes; team success, star player, head coach, and management. There are also four non-product-related attributes including logo design, venue, product delivery, and tradition. Benefits represent the meaning and value consumers attach to the product and include escape, identification, peer group acceptance, pride in place, and nostalgia. Marketing communication should concentrate on building and reinforcing attractive attributes and benefits that sport consumers associate with a specific sport or team (Funk & James, 2001).

Communication strategies should also consider the variety of mediums (email, mail, and special "limited access" events) as well frequency and repetition to introduce, enhance and reinforce associations. SMA should provide repetitive advertising and information, encourage familiarity, offer a variety of inducements, create attention-grabbing point-of-purchase (POP) displays, and if possible, distribute in multiple outlets. Sport also receives substantial media exposure and building strong relationships with local media is critical and sport organisations should take a proactive stance towards media relations (Nichols, Moynahan, Hall, & Taylor, 2002).

Internet Levers

The emergence of the Internet to initiate sport marketing activities has become an effective and efficient means to create attraction. The Internet and new media have emerged as integral mechanisms in the planning, marketing and managing of local, regional, national and international sport events (Filo & Funk, 2005; Shilbury, Westerbeek, Quick, & Funk, 2009). Research indicates visiting a website is a self-selecting behaviour and only consumers with an existing interest or attraction toward a particular product or service will engage in information search behaviour (McQuitty & Peterson, 2000). The Internet is becoming the initial and primary source of information for consumers (Peterson & Merino, 2003) and providing quality and detailed content will aid information retrieval during a visit. The determination of what information content to provide on a website can be developed from understanding the psychological, personal, and environment forces that shape sport consumer decision-making (Filo & Funk, 2005).

A challenge for sport marketers is to learn consumer information requirements. This understanding can shape Internet marketing communication (Beech et al., 2000; Filo & Funk, 2008). Filo, Funk, and Hornby (in press) developed an event information template (EIT) with 15 distinct themes that a sport marketer should include on a website: event ticket procurement, venue site, shopping locations, accommodations, event schedule, local attractions, entertainment opportunities, travel costs, public transport, food and concessions, location of event, parking, safety and security measures, weather forecast and conditions, and traffic conditions. See Appendix for a depiction of the EIT. The EIT is beneficial for consumers evaluating the event during the information search process. The template can also be modified to reflect the nature of the event including details such as registration, merchandise purchase, fundraising, and sponsor product trial. These websites represent low cost marketing mechanism for potential spectators and participants to search for information during the pre-consumption search (Oorni, 2004).

The provision of information represents marketing communication capable of moving consumers from the Awareness stage to the Attraction stage. Filo and Funk (2008) report attractive psychological and environmental benefits can be used to shape website content. Once identified, the provision of attractive informational themes can increase satisfaction with an on-line experience when consumers are engaged in directed information retrieval (Filo, Funk, & Hornby, in press). The provision of targeted information themes can be utilised to enhance the experience, foster a more favourable attitude and behavioural intentions among consumers with minimal attitude formation toward a sport event. In other words, internal inputs push a desire for information and external information-based content pulls the consumer toward attraction to the event. Sport marketers should focus on providing information content complemented by images and multimedia to enhance information retrieval.

Summary

This chapter provides a comprehensive understanding of the Attraction stage. Attraction results from processing prior Awareness stage outcomes, new environmental forces and internal forces. Attraction processing occurs multiple times as the individual evaluates a number of personal, psychological, and environmental inputs. This processing generates attitudinal and behavioural learning and evaluation and allows a sport consumer to evaluate potential outcomes and alternative opportunities. The product of this evaluation and learning creates interest, enjoyment and favouritism for a sport object when it provides opportunities to satisfy needs and receive benefits. Attraction processing creates attitudinal complexity and when the evaluation produces positive affect, the individual chooses to like a sport object and engage in sport consumption-related activities.

Marketing action for attraction should rely upon utilising personal, psychological, and environmental inputs to position the marketing mix. The PCM staging tool allows for the development of marketing levers to build and sustain attraction. Notable marketing levers for a sport marketer within the Attraction stage include financial, social, experiential, cause-related, sponsorship, brand, and the Internet.

Appendix

Event Information Template (EIT) for Sport Event Website
Informational themes beneficial to include as content for a sport event website
Fifteen EIT themes can increase behavioural intention towards the sport event and create favourable attitudes among consumers low in motivation to attend the event.
1. Event schedule 2. Event ticket procurement 3. Location of event 4. Venue site 5. Public transport 6. Entertainment opportunities 7. Accommodations 8. Parking 9. Food and concessions 10. Traffic conditions 11. Local attractions 12. Safety and security measures 13. Shopping locations 14. Travel costs 15. Weather forecast and conditions

References

Ajzen, I. (2002). Residual effects of past on later behavior: Habituation and reasoned action perspectives. *Personality and Social Psychology Review, 6,* 107–122.

Amis, J., Pant, N., & Slack, T. (1997). Achieving a sustainable competitive advantage: A resource based view of the sport sponsorship. *Journal of Sport Management, 11,* 80–96.

Amos, O.M. (1982). Empirical analysis of motives underlying individual contributions to charity. *Atlantic Economic Journal, 7,* 45–52.

Beard, J.G., & Ragheb, M.G. (1983). Measuring leisure motivation. *Journal of Leisure Research, 15,* 219–228.

Beaton, A.A., Filo, K., & Funk, D.C. (2007). Achieving parsimony in sport consumption motivations: A convenient truth. *Proceedings from the Sport Management Association of Australia and New Zealand,* Auckland, NZ.

Beech, J., Chadwick, S., & Tapp, A. (2000). Towards a schema for football clubs seeking effective presence on the internet. *European Journal for Sport Management, 7*(Special Issue), 30–50.

Carroll, B., & Alexandris, K. (1997). Perception of constraints and strength of motivation: Their relationship to recreational sport participation in Greece. *Journal of Leisure Research, 29*, 279–299.

Chalip, L. (2006). Towards social leverage of sport events. *Journal of Sport & Tourism, 11*(2), 1–19.

Cialdini, R.B., Thorne, A., Walker, M.R., Freeman, S., & Sloan, L.R. (1976). Basking in reflected glory: Three (football) field studies. *Journal of Personality and Social Psychology, 34*(3), 366–375.

Cobb-Wallgreen, C.J., Ruble, C.A., & Donthu, N. (1995). Brand equity, brand preference, and purchase Intent. *Journal of Advertising, 24*, 25–40.

Crompton, J.L., & Love, L.L. (1995). The predictive validity of alternative approaches to evaluating quality of a festival. *Journal of Travel Research, 34*(1), 11–25.

Deighton, J. (1992). The consumption of performance. *Journal of Consumer Research, 19*, 362–372.

Donnelly, P., & Young, K. (1988). The construction and confirmation of identity in sport subcultures. *Sociology of Sport Journal, 5*, 223–240.

Driver, C., & Johnston, R. (2001). Understanding service customers: The value of hard and soft attributes. *Journal of Service Research, 4*, 130–139.

Filo, K., & Funk, D.C. (2005). Congruence between attractive product features and virtual content delivery for Internet marketing communication. *Sport Marketing Quarterly, 14*, 112–122.

Filo, K., Funk, D.C., & Hornby, G. (2008). The role of website content on motive and attitude change for sport events. *Journal of Sport Management.*

Filo, K., Funk, D.C., & O'Brien, D. (in press). It's really not about the bike: Exploring attraction and attachment to the events of the Lance Armstrong Foundation. *Journal of Sport Management.*

Filo, K, Funk, D.C., & Neale, L. (2007). Corporate social responsibility and sport event sponsorship. *Proceedings from the Australian and New Zealand Marketing Academy (ANZMAC) Conference,* Dunedin, NZ.

Funk, D.C., & James, J.D. (2001). The Psychological Continuum Model (PCM): A conceptual framework for understanding an individual's psychological connection to sport. *Sport Management Review, 4*, 119–150.

Funk, D.C., & Pritchard, M. (2006). Responses to publicity in sports: Commitment's moderation of message effects. *Journal of Business Research, 59*, 613–621.

Funk, D.C., Ridinger, L.L., & Moorman, A.M. (2004). Exploring the origins of involvement: Understanding the relationship between consumer motives and involvement with professional sport teams. *Leisure Sciences, 26,* 35–61.

Funk, D.C., Toohey, K., & Bruun, T. (2007). International sport event participation: Prior sport involvement; destination image; and travel motives. *European Sport Management Quarterly, 7,* 227–248.

Gladden, J.M., & Funk, D.C. (2002). Developing and understanding of brand association in team sport: Empirical evidence from professional sport consumers. *Journal of Sport Management, 16,* 54–81.

Graeff, T.R. (1996). Using promotional messages to manage the effects of brand and self-image on brand evaluations. *Journal of Consumer Marketing, 13,* 4–18.

Green, B.C., & Chalip, L. (1998). Sport tourism as the celebration of subculture. *Annals of Tourism Research, 25,* 275–291.

Guillot, J., Kilpatrick, M., Hebert, E., & Hollander, D. (2004). Applying the transtheoretical model to exercise adherence in clinical settings. *American Journal of Health Studies, 19,* 1–10.

Hansen, H., & Gauthier, R. (1989). Factors affecting attendance at professional sports events. *Journal of Sport Management, 3,* 15–32.

Henderson, K.A. (2003). Women, physical activity, and leisure: Jeopardy or wheel of fortune? *Women in Sport and Physical Activity, 12,* 113–125.

Hibbert, S., & Horne, S. (1996). Giving to charity: Questioning the donor process. *Journal of Consumer Marketing, 13*(2), 4–13.

Hightower, R., Brady, M.K., & Baker, T.L. (2002). Investigating the role of physical environment in hedonic service consumption: An exploratory study of sporting events. *Journal of Business Research, 55,* 697–707.

Hill, B., & Green, B.C. (2000). Repeat attendance as a function of involvement, loyalty, and the sportscape across three football contexts. *Sport Management Review, 3,* 145–162.

Holbrook, M.B., & Hirschman, E.C. (1982). The experiential aspects of consumption: Consumer fantasies, feelings, and fun. *Journal of Consumer Research, 9,* 132–140.

Iso-Ahola, S.E. (1982). Toward a social psychological theory of tourism motivation: A rejoinder. *Annals of Tourism Research, 9,* 256–262.

James, J., Trail, G., Wann, D., Zhang, J., & Funk, D.C. (2006). Bringing parsimony to the study of sport consumer motivations: Development of the big 5. *Symposium at the North*

American Society for Sport Management Conference, Kansas, MO, USA.

Janiszewski, C., & Cunha, M. Jr. (2004). The influence of price discount framing on the evaluation of a product bundle. *Journal of Consumer Research, 30*, 534–546.

Kahle, L.R., Kambara, K.M., & Rose, G. (1996). A functional model of fan attendance motivations for college football. *Sport Marketing Quarterly, 5*, 51–60.

Kelley, S.W., & Turley, L.W. (2001). Consumer perceptions of service quality attributes at sporting events. *Journal of Business Research, 54*, 161–166.

Madrigal, R. (2003). Investigating an evolving leisure experience: Antecedents and consequences of spectator affect during a live sporting event. *Journal of Leisure Research, 35*, 23–48.

Madrigal, R. (2006). Measuring the multidimensional nature of sporting event performance consumption. *Journal of Leisure Research, 38*, 267–292.

Mahony, D.F., Nakazawa, M., Funk, D.C., James, J.D., & Gladden, J.M. (2002). Motivational factors influencing the behavior of J. League spectators. *Sport Management Review, 5*, 1–24.

Mannell, R.C., & Iso-Ahola, S.E. (1987). Psychological nature of leisure and tourism experience. *Annals of Tourism Research, 14*, 314–331.

Mason, D.S. (1999). What is the sports product and who buys it? The marketing of professional sports leagues. *European Journal of Marketing, 33*, 402–418.

Mattila, A.S. (1999). The role of culture in the service evaluation process. *Journal of Service Research, 1*, 250–261.

McDonald, M.A., Milne, G.R., & Hong, J. (2002). Motivational factors for evaluating sport spectator and participant markets. *Sport Marketing Quarterly, 11*, 100–113.

McQuitty, S., & Peterson, R.T. (2000). Selling home entertainment on the Internet: An overview of a dynamic marketplace. *Journal of Consumer Marketing, 17*, 233–248.

Netz, Y., & Raviv, S. (2004). Age differences in motivational orientation toward physical activity: An application of social-cognitive theory. *The Journal of Psychology, 138*, 35–48.

Nichols, W., Moynahan, P., Hall, A., & Taylor, J. (2002). *Media Relations in Sport*. Morgantown, WV: Fitness Information Technology, Inc.

Oorni, A. (2004). Consumer objectives and the amount of search in electronic travel and tourism markets. *Journal of Travel and Tourism Marketing, 17*(2/3), 3–14.

Peterson, R.A., & Merino, M.C. (2003). Consumer information search behaviour and the internet. *Psychology & Marketing, 20*(2), 99–121.

Pons, F., Mourali, M., & Nyeck, S. (2006). Consumer orientation toward sporting events. *Journal of Service Research, 8,* 276–287.

Ritzenheim, D.N. (2000). One more time: How do you motivate donors? *New Directions for Philanthropic Fundraising, 29,* 51–68.

Schouten, J.W., & McAlexander, J.H. (1995). Subcultures of consumption: An ethnography of the new bikers. *Journal of Consumer Research, 22,* 43–61.

Shilbury, D., Westerbeek, H., Quick, S., & Funk, D.C. (2009). *Strategic Sport Marketing* (3rd Ed.). Crows Nest, NSW: Allen & Unwin.

Snyder, C.R., Lassegard, M.A., & Ford, C.E. (1986). Distancing after group success and failure: Basking in reflected glory and cutting off reflected failure. *Journal of Personality and Social Psychology, 51,* 382–388.

Stebbins, R.A. (2005). Choice and experiential definitions of leisure. *Leisure Sciences, 27,* 349–352.

Swanson, S.R., Gwinner, K., & Larson, B.V. (2007). Take me out to the ballgame: What motivates fan game attendance and word-of-mouth behavior. *American Marketing Association Conference Proceedings,* 12, Chicago, IL, pp. 176–177.

Trail, G.T., & James, J.D. (2001). The motivation scale for sport consumption: Assessment of the scale's psychometric properties. *Journal of Sport Behavior, 24*(1), 108–127.

Wakefield, K.L., & Blodgett, J.G. (1999). Customer responses to intangible and tangible service factors. *Psychology & Marketing, 16,* 51–68.

Wakefield, K.L., & Sloan, H.J. (1995). The effects of team loyalty and selected stadium factors on spectator attendance. *Journal of Sport Management, 9,* 153–172.

Wann, D.L. (1995). Preliminary motivation of the sport fan motivation scale. *Journal of Sport & Social Issues, 19,* 377–396.

Williams, D.R., Patterson, M.E., Roggenbuck, J.W., & Watson, A.E. (1992). Beyond the commodity metaphor: Examining emotional and symbolic attachment to place. *Leisure Sciences, 14,* 29–46.

Zeithaml, V.A., & Bitner, M.J. (2003). *Services marketing: Integrating customer focus across the firm.* New York: McGraw-Hill.

Zhang, J.J., Pease, D.G., Hui, S.C., & Michaud, T.J. (1995). Variables affecting the spectator decision to attend NBA games. *Sport Marketing Quarterly, 4,* 29–39.

CHAPTER 7

Consumer Attachment to Sport and Events

The Brisbane Lions are important to Alex. Alex likes to watch football and after moving from Sydney to Brisbane in 2004, began following the Lions in the Australian Football League. Alex's initial attraction came from the club's success of three premiership wins in 2001, 2002, and 2003. Over the last few years, Alex's friends and co-workers have noticed a change in his behaviour. Alex watches nearly every Lions' game on TV often becoming quite emotional during the game. Alex became a Cat club member to get access to tickets, visits the club's web site for news and the online chat forum, wears Lion merchandise to work on casual Friday, and is rarely seen at the pub, supermarket or a barbeque without some sort of Lions gear. In addition, during every season, Alex contemplates getting a team tattoo. Alex's decision to increase membership level to the Pride category came in 2007 despite the club's lack of success in making the playoffs for three straight years. Alex feels being a Lions' fan is about supporting the team regardless of success. The club runs the "Read to Succeed" after school clinic on Wednesdays and during the off-season offers a monthly clinic to teach football skills and get teenagers more physically active. Alex even enroled in the Lions' "Skills for Life" seminar in conjunction with the local university.

The above story illustrates Alex's attachment to the Brisbane Lions. The personal meaning of the Lions for Alex reveals a psychological connection that is emotional, functional, and symbolic. Alex has certainly moved beyond merely liking the team in the attraction stage. The question is how did Alex develop such a personal connection toward this sport team? How did Alex go from *"I like the Lions"* to *"I am a Lion."*

Alex is in the attachment stage of the Psychological Continuum Model (PCM) framework illustrated in Figure 7.1. Alex's position within the PCM suggests external and internal forces pushed and pulled him upward from attraction. Within the attraction stage, Alex's psychological connection formed based on the desirability of achieving hedonic and utilitarian benefits and fulfilling needs. Within the attachment stage, Alex places greater meaning on the Lions and this meaning is emotional, functional, and symbolic. For Alex, the Lions have become integrated into his self-concept and congruent with important values.

Attachment emerges when desirable outcomes from the attraction stage collectively join together producing a stronger more passionate connection to the sport object. Alex's psychological connection with the Lions is more meaningful because of an internal alignment between the team and Alex. The PCM framework

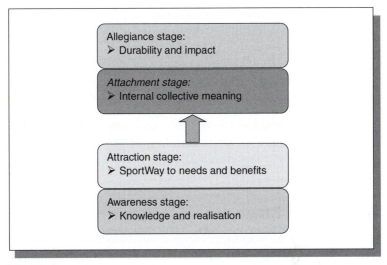

Figure 7.1
PCM framework.

proposes that as an individual internalises a sport object, the object becomes part of a larger, more complex network of associations that contribute to a person's self-identity (Funk & James, 2004).

The Lions still provide needs and benefits, but these outcomes have evolved. This can be readily observed when Alex chooses to enter social situations that promote the benefit of expressing a desired self-concept. Another benefit is when supporting and engaging in consumption activities related to the sport object allows expression of personal values such as warm relationships with others, sense of accomplishment, self-fulfilment, a sense of belonging, fun, and enjoyment in life. For Alex, being a fan of the Brisbane Lions provides a chance to enjoy the fun and excitement of a sport event in a safe environment. While at games or in other social contexts, Alex feels part of a group that shares a common purpose to support the team and gains a sense of achievement and self-respect. Supporting the team allows him to foster meaningful relationships with friends and family. In addition, the Lions' run a number of educational and social programs in the Brisbane community to promote mental and physical well being.

Attachment builds upon the attraction stage by creating a stronger, more subjective emotional connection. Discussion of attraction in Chapter 6 describes a process in which psychological, personal, and environmental inputs influence an individual to begin liking a sport experience and engaging in sport and event consumption activities. However, the psychological connection within attraction is relatively unstable because the level of psychological engagement is relatively low and behaviour is simple. Attachment introduces stability, complex behaviour and meaning to the connection through a collective strengthening of internal associations linked to a sport object. This chapter offers a comprehensive understanding of the attachment process and provides marketing recommendations to help activate this process.

Attachment Stage

Attachment represents a universal human experience that occurs throughout an individual's lifecycle (Schultz, Kleine, & Kernan, 1989). The attachment sequence describes a developmental progression from the attraction stage via social-structural and individual processes to create a stronger more subjective psychological connection with a sport object (Funk & James, 2006). The attachment process facilitates movement up the PCM elevator through the creation of a meaningful personal connection with a favourite object and enhances the liking of the object as it assumes a deeper significance. For example, Alex places more internal meaning on the Lions. Within attachment, psychological and personal inputs begin to play a more influential role than environmental inputs.

The PCM framework outlines attachment processing as a key internal mechanism for movement within the top two floors of the PCM elevator. Attachment processing consists of a sequence of inputs, internal processes, and outputs. This process describes how the psychological connection with a sport object progressively develops and takes shape from attraction. The developmental progression marks the transition from "I like golf" to "I am a golfer" based upon the influence of psychological, personal and to a lesser degree environmental factors. Within the attachment process, internal factors begin to play a more predominant role in moving an individual up the PCM framework. Box 7.1 lists attraction outcomes and internal forces related to values and self-concept as internal inputs for attachment processing. These processes include complex cognitive and affective evaluation of inputs Attachment stage outputs indicate a strengthening in the connection as the sport object takes on emotional, functional, and symbolic meaning and behaviour becomes more frequent and expressive.

Box 7.1 Attachment processing

Inputs

- External forces
- Attraction outcomes
- Internal forces

Processes

- Cognitive–affective evaluation
- Soldering

Outputs

- Attitudinal strengthening
- Personal meaning, trust
- Frequent and expressive behaviour

Stimulus–Response Perspective to Attachment

The PCM framework allows for the adoption and integration of complementary models and frameworks to understand various stages of the developmental progression. In terms of attachment stage, Bloch and Richins (1983) offer a model describing a sequence of three consecutive sectors: sources→importance→ responses. The source sector develops from characteristics of the consumer and the product. In other words, sources stem from the interaction between the person and the situation. Sources are equivalent to attraction inputs listed in Box 7.1 as well as Table 6.3 that shape how consumers process (perceive and evaluate) the significance and value of a sport object. Sources shape the importance sector and signify the attachment of meaning to interrelated qualities of a person's attitude about the sport object. Importance represents a strong attitude and is the personal concern or significance one attaches to an attitude toward a sport object (Funk, Haugtvedt, & Howard, 2000). To attach great importance is to care passionately and be deeply concerned about matters linked to that attitude. Importance governs or mediates the impact of related cognition on consumer response (Morgan & Hunt, 1994) as salient enduring or situation-specific goals are attached to the sport object. In other words, attachment as a process stimulates ongoing (enduring) and task-related (situational) responses. The stimulus–response perspective is instructive for understanding the attachment processing sequence that includes inputs, internal processes, and outputs.

Attachment Inputs

Attachment inputs represent external forces, existing attraction outcomes and new internal forces. Environmental forces come from the various socialising agents previously discussed and marketing actions by sport organisations. External forces are primarily informational and situational within attachment. Attraction outcomes represent the level of psychological and behavioural engagement previously achieved. Table 6.3 illustrates a number of psychological, personal, and environmental reasons why an individual is attracted to a sport object. Attraction outcomes represent prior experience about whether a sport experience provides various needs and benefits, feelings about how desirable these outcomes are to the individual, intentions to engage in consumption activities, and actual behaviour.

Service quality and customer service also operate as inputs. Both functional and technical elements discussed in Chapter 6 underscore the key role environment plays in the sport experience (Baker, Grewal, & Parasuraman, 1994; Kelley & Turley, 2001). Managing the experience surrounding sport events so individuals can achieve benefits such as socialisation, excitement, and diversion are positive ways to stage performances. The tension and uncertainty of the event's technical side is important and certain segments may value service expectations of the functional product (stadium cleanliness, parking, food and beverage, crowd control, etc.) as key to whether or not an individual will return (Hightower, Brady, & Baker, 2002; Wakefield & Sloan, 1995).

The level of psychological engagement from the attraction stage indicates attitude formation based upon three factors. The first is a set of cognitive beliefs regarding the sport object's ability to provide opportunities to satisfy needs and receive benefits. The second is volition, feelings, and liking of a sport object. Third, is the readiness to perform a given behaviour. Behavioural engagement represents learning and evaluation of a range of activities. Within attachment, these outcomes become internalised versions formed through interactions and serve to define the relationship between the self and object. Movement from attraction to attachment occurs when these outcomes are evaluated using additional internal forces related to personal values and self-concept (Funk & James, 2006).

Values

Values are concepts and beliefs related to desirable end states or behaviours regardless of specific situations. Values guide decision-making for behaviour and are ordered by relative importance (Schwartz & Bilsky, 1987). Prior research has uncovered a number of general values (e.g., Rokeach, 1973) and within consumer behaviour the list of values (LOV) (Kahle, Beatty, & Homer, 1986) represents a parsimonious list. The LOV includes nine values: self-respect, security, warm relationships with others, sense of accomplishment, self-fulfilment, sense of belonging, being well respected, fun and enjoyment in life, and excitement. The values can also be ordered in importance for the individual (Kahle & Kennedy, 1989).

Homer and Kahle (1988) further classified values into three dimensions external, internal, and fun/excitement. External values relate to interaction with others and consist of sense of belonging, warm relationships with others, security, and being well respected. Internal values involve less reliance on others and include self-fulfilment, sense of accomplishment, and self-respect. Goal-specific values relate to hedonism and comprise of fun, enjoyment and excitement. Values represent an important influence to assist in understanding meaning behind consumer activities (Kahle & Kennedy, 1989) by influencing the formation of attitudes towards objects (Perkins & Reynolds, 1988). The meaning consumers place on products and services depends upon internal, external and goal-specific values (Kahle, 1985) and are appropriate for sport event participation.

Recent work on sport events has examined the meaning that participants attach to a charity sport event (Filo, Funk, & O'Brien, in press). Participant attachment embodies three value-laden facets: Camaraderie, cause, and competency. Box 7.2 lists these three general themes that attachment embodies. Camaraderie represents the solidarity and friendship developed by participants.

Box 7.2 Sport participant attachment

- *Camaraderie*: Embodies the sense of solidarity and belonging that a sport event provides.
- *Competency*: Embodies physical, health, fitness, and entertainment aspects of the sport event.
- *Cause*: Embodies the inspiration and instrumental goals of participation.

Sport events provide strong social component that facilitates social interaction, allows individuals to express a connection with others and integrate the self with others. Competency represents the physical challenge a sport event provides along with the excitement and enjoyment of participating. Competency reflects a person's belief in what he/she can achieve through challenging themselves physically and provides a means to differentiate themselves from others through the training and successful completion of the event. Cause represents the inspiration and instrumental goal of participation including raising awareness and supporting the cause. Cause portrays a self-definitional aspect as participants use sport as a means to express themselves and support a cause in which they believe. The three values illustrate how individuals can be oriented to different parts of the sport event experience (Robinson & Trail, 2005).

Self-Concept

Funk and James (2004) propose the formation of a sport self-concept occurs from internalisation. In other words, a sport object becomes an integral part of one's self-image. Writings on identity indicate sport identity is broken down into group and personal identities (Heere & James, 2007). Group identity refers to an existing group membership (e.g., I'm a Lions fan) that through categorisation of the self with members of the group (e.g., Tajfel & Turner, 1986). Group identity reflects a social categorisation of the self into in-group and out-group status based upon social similarities and differences such as race, class, gender, and nationality (Turner & Oakes, 1989). Group identity moves the self-concept into more inclusive social units that depersonalise the self-concept, where "I" becomes "We" (Brewer, 1991). Prior research in sport has reported the pronoun use of "we" to describe the actions of a sport team, thus projecting their membership as a fan of the team (Cialdini et al., 1976; Sloan, 1989). Abrams and Hogg (1990) explain that when group identity is meaningful, the group becomes a part of the individual concept of self.

Personal identities are similar to traits or individual differences that are volitionally used to define self-concept. Personal identities include traits that a person already possesses and traits the person aspires to possess (Fleming & Petty, 1997). Personal identity serves to define the person in terms of self-descriptions of personal attributes such as personality, physical, and intellectual traits (Turner & Oakes, 1989). Mahony, Madrigal, and Howard (1999) suggest that the San Francisco Giants fans are "tough" because the team plays in gusty and often frigid conditions. Flamboyant players such as David Beckham, aggressive players such as Wayne Rooney, and hardworking athletes such as Tiger Woods attract individuals who desire to posses similar traits in their own self-concept. The selection of a participatory sport (e.g., triathlon) can provide individuals with a desire to expresses characteristics and traits such as physically fit, disciplined, and competitive.

The adoption of a sport identity includes both group and personal identities (Heere & James, 2007; Kolbe & James, 2002). Self-concept represents the social category in which individuals claim group membership and the personal meaning associated with that category (e.g., what being a Real Madrid supporter means to the individual personally). Self-concept suggests a reciprocal relationship exists between individuals and their social world (Deaux, 1996). The story of Alex at the beginning of the chapter illustrates he no longer merely prefers the Lions. Instead Alex has made the team a part of himself and the team has become an extension of him. For Alex, he can choose to enter social situations that promote the expression of a desired self-concept (self-reflection of being a Brisbane Lions fan) that will satisfy needs and accrue benefits. Box 7.3 Lists four general categories of self-concept.

Box 7.3 Self-concept

Individuals hold certain beliefs about themselves that create four general self-concepts:

(1) how we view ourselves (own view)
(2) images of how we think others view us (perceived self)
(3) images of how we would like to be viewed (desired or ideal self)
(4) how references groups view us (group self)

Attachment Processing

Attachment inputs influence the type of cognitive, affective and behavioural processing that occurs within attachment processing. Funk and James (2006) define attachment as the emotional, functional, and symbolic meaning assigned to a sport object by an individual. This meaning of this outcome occurs when an evaluation of a sport object elicits responses that enhance the link between the object and the individual's values and self-concept (Funk & James, 2001). Attachment processing represents a dynamic and emotionally complex internal evaluation process.

Internal processes within attachment continue to include motivation, perception, learning, and memory that each influences the evaluation process. These general processes are important, but specific attitudinal processing takes on more prominent roles. The extrinsic influence of situational factors is reduced but continues to serve as primers for activation of nodes and associative links (e.g., mere exposure, classical conditioning, operant conditioning and observational learning processes, mood state congruence.) This type of processing describes how attitudes become congruent with fundamental values and self-concept developed from life and consumption experiences (Kahle et al., 2001).

A complex cognitive–affective evaluation prevails and the individual attempts to obtain consistency between feelings and beliefs about the sport object. An example of cognitive–affective consistency for a person could be; "I know smoking is bad for me (cognitive)-but give me a cigarette (affective)" Or in sport, Alex believes the Brisbane Lions have no chance of winning the premiership this year, but he still supports them. Discrepancy between beliefs and feelings is important as it shapes the evaluation of the sport object as well as behavioural processing. The internal goal of evaluation is to reduce dissonance and restore consistency to the internal and external meaning of the psychological connection. The motivation process in Chapter 2 discusses how internal tension results from the discrepancy between the present state and the ideal state. The cognitive–affective evaluation process attempts to reduce or eliminate an unpleasant state and restore balance. This creates a psychological connection based on cognitive complexity.

Cognitive Complexity

In sport attachment, the sport experience is an emotional experience and motivates behaviour. This motivation is driven by cognitive and memory functions. Attitudinal processing of this nature can be referred to as "cognitive complexity." Cognitive complexity provides an individual with the evaluative ability to process external and internal forces. This level of complexity influences the integration of personal, psychological, and environmental forces into a larger, more complex network that involves self-concept and important values. Hence, the sport object becomes embedded within the schema that increases in complexity from the attraction stage. The cognitive–affective evaluation process reduces discrepancy between one's initial position and conflicting information to stabilise attitude formation and subsequent behaviour (Pritchard, Havitz, & Howard, 1999). Attachment processing differs from attraction processing in terms of the cognitive complexity that contributes to the strength of the psychological connection.

Attachment Processing

Attachment processing accounts for movement from the attraction stage to attachment stage (see Figure 3.3 for a review of this processing). Funk and James (2006) draw upon a number of literatures (e.g., attachment theory, Bowlby, 1999; personal values, Kahle, et al., 1986; identification, Tajfel & Turner, 1986; attitude formation and change, Petty & Cacioppo, 1986) to inform attachment processing. Attachment explains a wide variety of social behaviours within adults including the meaningful relationships that develop between an individual and an object.

Within the PCM, movement from the attraction stage to the attachment stage indicates a fundamental change to the psychological connection. For example, peer groups and subcultures are influential environmental forces of attachment in the early stages of the PCM. However, the connection changes because the internal meaning of the experience becomes based on the collective meaning of psychological, personal, and environmental forces. The collective integration and strengthening of these forces occurs through attachment processing.

Attachment processing is unique in that the sequence of inputs, internal processes, and outputs collectively bond to form attachment outcomes. To help understand this sequence, it is beneficial to explore a process of connecting objects together through soldering. Soldering is the process through which two metal objects are joined together by means of an alloy. The alloy consists of a homogeneous mixture of elements. This alloy has a relatively low melting point and forms the bond between the two metal objects without damaging the objects. Soldering represents the internal connection process through which attachment outcomes occur. For the PCM framework, this process is analogous to an internal bonding procedure that connects psychological, personal, and environmental inputs and creates different outputs.

Attachment processing employs soldering. Associations linked to a sport object represent the metal objects, or in this case discrete mental association links. In other words, each association represents a thin piece of metal linked to the sport object (e.g., 5 pieces of metal). For example, *speed* motives of socialisation, performance, entertainment, excitement, and diversion represent five mental links. Compare Figure 3.4 with Figure 7.2. In Figure 7.2 the dark grey areas represent the connective alloy. When an alloy is heated, it melts and spreads among the various mental links (i.e., mental associations). As the alloy cools, it creates a bond between two or more mental links. The outcome of this process is that individual mental links are bonded together. The previous discrete associations are now interconnected. In addition, the melting of the alloy does not damage the mental links, but they now exist in an integrated bonded structure. The collective bonding of associations linked to a sport experience produce a psychological connection with a more stable structure.

As previously discussed, attachment processing involves the evaluation of inputs to produce outcomes. Inputs stem from prior attraction outcomes consisting of beliefs, feelings, and behaviour and environmental forces. However, the enhanced connection activates internal forces such as personal values, self-concept, and trust to shape the evaluation process. These internal forces represent the alloy within the soldering process. In other words, personal values, self-concept and trust are the elements of the alloy mixture that forms the "mental" alloy. The melting of the

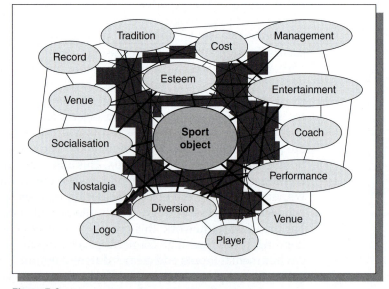

Figure 7.2
Attachment processing: Soldering of attraction outcomes.

alloy results from attitudinal processing. For example, cognitive–affective processing activity heats the mental alloy that bonds the associations into a collective internal meaning. The heat from the attitudinal process (i.e., internal mental soldering) melts the alloy creating the attachment bond of mental links when it cools. As the attachment processing occurs multiple times, the resulting connective bond between mental links produces adequate strength and conductivity to shape attitudes and behaviours.

Attachment processing involves a mental soldering process of associations linked to a sport object. This internalisation creates an integrated psychological connection to a sport object within the attachment stage. Internalisation accounts for the internal bonding of discrete mental associations linked to a sport object into a collective integrated structure. Attachment processing describes why Alex now places emotional, functional, and symbolic meaning on various needs and benefits provided by the Lions (attachment stage outcomes).

Attachment Stage Outcomes

The complexity and intensity of the cognitive–affective activity within attachment processing creates psychological and behavioural outcomes. Psychological and behavioural engagement increase in complexity as the type of actions performed and its frequency are linked to emotional, functional, and symbolic meaning. Behaviour becomes self-expressive related to self-developmental tasks and integration with others. Behaviours may still fluctuate but generally conform to expectancies and uncertainty is resolved in correct behaviour to produce authenticity of the perceived outcomes.

Psychological Outcomes

Attachment represents the strength of the attitude formation toward the sport object or experience. Recent evidence suggests sport attitudes possess several properties such as valence, importance, extremity, certainty, intensity, knowledge, direct experience, and personal relevance (Funk & Pastore, 2000). Pritchard and Funk (2007) argue that these properties can be structured to reflect formation, function, and effects. Attitude formation represents the quality and internal nature of the psychological connection (i.e., complex, consistent, rigid). The formation of the attitude strength occurs when attitude properties of attitude consistency, complexity, and conviction create a platform for the evaluation.

Consistency represents the degree of consistency between feeling and beliefs. Complexity represents prior knowledge and direct experience derived from an individual's evaluation from memory. Conviction represents the structure's rigidity, extremity and certainty, or polarisation of the attitude. Complexity relies more on objective data gained from prior information gathered and direct personal experience, whereas cognitive–affective consistency introduces an emotive or subjective element to evaluation. For example, you may know a great deal about a sport team and have attended or watched a number of games on television, but still not have favourable feelings toward the team.

Attitude function represents the level of processing that determines an attitude's immediacy in retrieval from memory and its propinquity to the self. In other words, the attitude is accessible and centrally located within the cognitive structure (i.e., schema). As level of consistency and conviction increase, attitude towards the team becomes psychologically important, personally relevant and centrally aligned with salient values and self-concept. Likewise, as complexity and consistency increase, ease of retrieval from memory increases. The processes of centrality and accessibility determine the attitude's proximity in two different ways; by determining how close to top-of-mind the attitude is, and its availability as a vehicle for self-representation (propinquity to self).

Attitude effects depict the consequences of strong attitude in terms of its ability to endure and influence. Attitudes centrally positioned and linked to important values and self-expression have a greater capacity to process information. Accessibility, on the other hand, produces a different effect as it governs the attitude's responsiveness during information processing and evaluation. The process of retrieving (accessing) relevant data from complex schema determines sensitivity toward new or competing information. Attachment processing creates a connection with a sport object that evokes passion and strength. In other words, attachment processing creates the heat to solder the association links together.

A stronger connection forms as the individual internalises thoughts, ideas, and behaviour into collective personal meaning. The connection represents an output including self-developmental tasks of individuation (i.e., differentiation of self from others), integration (i.e., integration of self with others), and temporal orientation (i.e., self-changes from situation to situation) (Schultz et al., 1989). For example, Gibson, Willming, and Holdnak (2002) reveal a collegiate football team provides an opportunity to express an identity (individuation) and a sense of belongingness (integration) on football Saturdays throughout the season (temporal orientation).

Personal Meaning

Attachment represents the emotional, functional, and symbolic meaning an individual places on a sport object and this meaning is both situational and enduring. The story of Alex at the beginning of the chapter illustrates how functional meaning refers to the amount of attitude-relevant knowledge and direct experience that accompanies an individual's attitude related to a sport team. The individual also internalises a number of events, interpreting and assigning value and meaning to actions. An individual can now construct value judgments regarding situations and people, integrating a variety of elements of the activity to learn roles (e.g., team, player, venue). Functional meaning is built from affiliation with in-group members and enhances distinction from non-members, adopts the core values of the subculture group, and interacts with fellow spectators via mutual experience (Holt, 1995).

Emotional meaning represents a person's perception of the psychological significance and value of the sport object. Emotion represents the type of affective reaction or potency of feeling that an individual has toward a particular sport object. In the case of Alex, his attitude toward the Lions continues to form as the identity within the subculture becomes salient and accessible (Kaplan & Fishbein, 1969; Tversky & Kahneman, 1973). In other words, Alex internalises the sport team into his self-concept. As the perceived value and benefits derived from the sport identity become salient, accessible and desirable, the individual's attitude crystallises and subsequently increases in importance (Funk et al., 2000). The construction and reconfirmation perspective suggests that the expression of an identity would fluctuate within a given situation. However, the repeated activation of a particular identity to receive desired outcomes would lend stability, duration, and permanence to its basic structure (Deaux, 1996).

Symbolic meaning is the implicit repercussion that purchases, product use, or participation that is freely engaged in and projected to others conveys about the person (e.g., identification as a fan of the team or sport). For Alex, he no longer merely prefers the team, but by making it a part of self, the team becomes an extension of him. The internalisation of the sport subculture's beliefs, customs, and practices is reinforced through confirmation and mastery of the identity and crystallises the attitude importance characteristic. The individual demonstrates the appropriate roles (refines self-presentation) and is recognised by established members of the group (Donnelly & Young, 1988; Schouten & McAlexander, 1995). Identity confirmation and mastery are established when the values and behaviour of the individual conform to the subculture expectancies. The perceived emotional, functional, and symbolic meaning of the sport team can fluctuate given the situation or remain constant across situations based upon activity type and time of consumption.

The perceived meaning attached to the team occurs as personal, psychological, and environmental inputs become embedded within a larger, more complex network that contribute to one's self-concept. Such an evaluation is derived from the formation, function, and effects of the attitude structure that creates a collective strengthening of various inputs linking the team to other important attitude, beliefs, and values. In this context, attachment is thought to reflect not only preference (i.e., volition), but also stability towards an object with a motivation level capable of resisting alternative choices. This creates importance.

Essentially, importance serves to strengthen emotional linkages between the sport object and an individual's self-interest, values, and social identification resulting in a strong psychological connection between the individual and the sport object. However, rather than simply attachment to a sport object such as a professional team, an individual may be attached to a variety of aspects of the sport team, including the actual sport and focal community (Robinson & Trail, 2005) as well as the organisation (Gladden & Funk, 2002). When internal forces are complemented by external forces such as service quality and customer service an element of trust is created and linked to the sport object.

Sport Object Trust

The notion of brand trust is prominent in the marketing literature, but remains underdeveloped in sport consumer behaviour. Morgan and Hunt (1994) believe that the development of brand trust is important in the development of brand loyalty. Brand trust represents a cognitive process that creates confidence in a brand's reliability and integrity (Chatterjee & Chaudhuri, 2005; Chaudhuri & Holbrook, 2001). With the purchase of any product, there is an element of risk and the amount of personal meaning attached to a sport object within attachment is applicable (Funk, Ridinger, & Moorman, 2004). As a result, sport consumers within the attachment stage place a level of trust on the organisation to acquire personal, psychological, and environmental needs and benefits.

Business research suggests that brand trust can develop through a number of different factors. Delgado-Ballester and Munera-Aleman (2001) indicate overall satisfaction with a product or service leads to brand trust. Satisfaction stems from the actual performance of the product or service in terms of matching or exceeding prior expectations. Satisfaction can take the form of positive cognitive responses in terms of brand characteristics such as brand predictability, brand competence and brand reputation (Lau & Lee, 1999). This creates the feeling of brand trustworthiness that impacts brand choice (Erdem & Swait, 2004) and creates a positive relationship with the brand (Chatterjee & Chaudhuri, 2005). The notion of brand trust suggests an individual who has confidence in the organisation that delivers the sport product or service is more likely to invest emotional, functional, and symbolic meaning in a sport object. The level of trustworthiness also reflects the individual values and self-concept within the attachment process.

Behavioural Outcomes

Attachment behaviour increases in complexity, frequency and becomes linked to emotional, functional, and symbolic meaning. Behaviour becomes standard and repetitive creating opportunities for self-expression that can form the basis of behaviour related to self-developmental tasks, and integration with others within the subculture. For example, Holt (1995) highlights the notion of assimilating, producing and personalising behaviour in professional baseball. Assimilating occurs as an individual learns the roles of a sport culture and begins to operate in a unique social world of baseball. Producing is the fantasy of managing, making predictions, establishing relationships, bonding with player, coach, team, emailing the owner, and collecting autographs and paraphernalia. Personalising represents the individuality of an individual's relationship with a professional team through relevant dress, signs, and comments.

The complexity and frequency of behaviours may still fluctuate based on situation and temporal considerations (i.e., situational involvement) but generally conform to expectancies and uncertainty is resolved in correct behaviour to produce authenticity of the perceived outcomes. Spectator research indicates ongoing behavioural responses can include attendance, TV viewing, reading magazines, and using the Internet, buying licensed merchandise associated with the product "sport" and brand "team" level that occur over the length of a season. For example, a baseball enthusiast's interest in the game certainly provokes ongoing responses such as attendance or the use of media sources to acquire information about baseball. However, that same baseball enthusiast would not respond to the same degree, with heightened levels of grief or joy as the play develops and to a game's outcome. In addition, screaming, crying, and clapping behaviour can emerge in short-term situation specific contexts at the event.

Behavioural engagement increases in complexity as the type of actions performed and their frequency are linked to emotional, functional, and symbolic meaning. Behaviour becomes standard and repetitive creating opportunities for self-expression that can form the basis for behaviour related to self-developmental tasks, and integration with others within the subculture. In the story of Alex, he attends a game every week during the season, buys and wears Lions clothing to work and out socially year round, and subscribes to the Fan newsletter. Alex's work computer has a home page set to the Lion Internet site, follows management decisions in the off-season, and participates in charity events involving the club.

The psychological transition from attraction to attachment is one of the least understood areas of research in the sport literature (Funk & James, 2006). In addition, limited marketing research has been devoted to fostering attachment. The next section provides some marketing approaches to move the individual from attraction to attachment.

Attachment and Sport Marketing Action

Sport Marketing Action

Strategic use of marketing mix
Select key target markets
Study and evaluate market
Select information systems

Sport marketing action within the attachment stage involves personalisation. Personalisation basically involves customising the marketing mix to push and pull selected target markets up to the attachment stage. Sport marketers can employ a number of strategies to increase personal meaning of the sport product or service. In fact, the majority of customer loyalty and affinity marketing programs currently being employed in sport marketing are designed to move an individual from attraction to the attachment stage. The following sections provide some useful activities.

Personalisation

Sport marketing action designed for attachment should be considered dynamic and responsive. The positioning of the marketing mix should rely on information obtained through research to employ relationship building techniques. The key to successful positioning lies in the sport marketer's ability to differentiate the product offering from segment competitors. Funk and James (2001) suggest marketing levers developed through relationship marketing (e.g., financial bonding, social bonding, customisation bonding and structural bonding, Zeithaml & Bittner, 2000) can be used to create personal bonding and foster movement. Sport events can implement personal bonding strategies to foster camaraderie, cause, and competency.

Financial and social bonding activities used in attraction stage marketing activities remain useful to overcome fiscal constraints and augment social opportunities. Personalisation attempts to utilise a more holistic approach to social bonding to foster movement from attraction to attachment. Social and interpersonal bonds can help the consumer feel important and make the sport object personally relevant. This can easily be done using operations and player personnel activities. Activities designed to learn peoples' names, engage with them on a one on one basis, acknowledge them through special services, invite them to team and event functions, and provide opportunities to communicate with players, owners, and coaches are beneficial. Personalising the sport object can enhance the emotional, functional, and symbolic meaning of the sport object through activation of value-laden and self-concept evaluations.

Self-concept Bonding

One form of personal bonding attempts to foster sport fan identification (Sutton, McDonald, Milne, & Cimperman, 1997). Sutton et al. (1997) propose increasing team/player accessibility to the public, increasing community involvement activities, and reinforcing the team's history and tradition are good strategies. Fan festivals and supporting events can be personalised to provide fans the opportunity for selective celebratory community components. European and Asian football marketers have long relied upon activities tailored to membership clubs to create opportunities for individuation and integration (i.e., expression of a unique identity and membership as part of a group). Membership clubs provide a strategic resource to reach out and connect with the fans. The idea of personal bonding is equally beneficial for participant sport events.

Value Bonding

Marketing activities can leverage camaraderie, competency, and cause to foster personal meaning of the sport event. A sport marketer can adopt five strategies to build a personalised community (communitatas) through events: enabling sociability; creating event-related social events; facilitating informal social opportunities; producing ancillary events; and theming (Chalip, 2006; Filo, Funk, & O'Brien, in press). Marketers can develop embedded events to create a broader camaraderie bonding window that facilitates informal and formal opportunities at pre-event and post-event parties where friends and family of participants are encouraged to attend. The promotion of discounts at the sport events host hotel can create a situation where individuals stay at the same place thus facilitating informal social opportunities. Strategies can be employed to augment competency through the provision of training programs and personal trainers to maximise participants' physical achievement through the event. Year-round social events can be held for participants to maintain camaraderie and competency, allowing participants to meet, socialise and celebrate their sense of community outside of the event.

Cause-Related Bonding

Cause-related bonding represents an emerging sport marketing action. Cause embodies the inspiration and instrumental goals of involvement that can be activated through corporate social responsibility (CSR) activities. CSR activities generally include cause-related marketing and are an effective means for influencing communities through positive social contributions (Smith & Westerbeek, 2007). The Lance Armstrong Foundation provides cause-related bonding through individuals being part of a group that supports lobbying efforts directed at government to listen to the needs of cancer patients and increase funding for cancer research. Cause-related bonding inspires individuals to become more involved beyond the fundraising initiated through their participation toward achievement of more specific targets or goals.

The notion of corporate citizenship and responsibility are suggested as means to garner brand trust from consumers (Brady, 2003; Willmott, 2003). Sport events that link with charitable causes can enhance participants' perceptions of event sponsors as a result of their involvement with the event. Events like the Lance Armstrong LIVESTRONG Challenge can use art exhibits featuring the works of cancer survivors/participants providing a further opportunity to celebrate survivorship and selective participant socialisation. The wearing of a yellow LIVESTRONG wristband symbolises a unique story of survivorship for the person who wears the wristband or a relative or friend.

Personalisation in the form of self-concept and value bonding provide marketing levers to foster attachment. These bonding strategies strengthen the connection with the sport object by linking it with important external, internal, and goal-specific values making the sport object part of the self-concept and a central anchor within a person's daily life. Personal bonding can also be used in conjunction with Customise bonding.

Customise Bonding

Customisation strategies should be used to personalise the service. First, segmentation strategies should employ the PCM staging tool to identify individuals and then cross reference this information with demographics and benefits. This targeted segmentation approach allows for the opportunity to customise attributes and benefits to enhance personal meaning of the sport object. In other words, customise the unique personal, psychological and environmental needs and benefits individuals find important. This information can then be used to strengthen the psychological connection moving the individual from attraction to attachment. Customisation focuses on tailoring the experience to the individual by considering his or her unique characteristics and situation. In a sport team context, marketers determine how needs and benefits can be personalised and work to provide those opportunities. For example, the Brisbane Lions have a number of membership levels with various attributes and benefits that allow fans to become more involved with the organisation. Flexible ticketing packages and broadcast access can also be offered. Customise bonding can also employ service bonding techniques.

Service Bonding

The role of customer service and satisfaction is important for developing trust and a strong relationship between the consumer and the sport object (Hiscock, 2001). Delgado-Ballester and Munera-Aleman (2001) proposed that overall satisfaction with the product or service is an important factor in the development of brand trust. Filo, Funk, and Alexandris (2008) suggest that brand trust contributes to the emotional, functional, and symbolic meaning that interacts with one's values and self-concept within the attachment process. Research has shown that building on service quality is one of the main strategies to develop customer satisfaction (Alexandris et al., 2004; Zeithaml, Berry, & Parasuraman, 1996).

Service for a marathon starts the moment a runner registers for the event and continues through online announcements, pre-race running programs, parking the car, starting and running the race, spending time in the hospitality tent, going home and checking online for results. This approach requires attention to a large number of details related to the tangible service aspects of the experience including food choices at the venue, accessibility of parking, cleanliness of the venue, crowd control, and safety. As the host, the sport marketer should make the fan or participant guest feel "special" and "unique" as well as part of the collective group. There a number of useful operational schemes such as incrementally moving a person toward a better seat location, premium club seating, access to hospitality events, fan appreciation events, preferential start times for running events and golf, shorter lines at ski lifts, etc. Sport marketing action can also utilise technology to make services and the experience more important and relevant.

Management could also focus on the predictability, competence, and reputation of the services in order to create trust (Lau & Lee, 1999). Sport marketing actions should move beyond simply satisfying consumer needs but personalise the services and show integrity (Chatterjee & Chaudhuri, 2005). Filo and colleagues (2008) suggest trust can be developed through sound corporate responsibility strategies discussed in cause-related bonding. Other means may involve a money back guarantee to reduce the potential risk of purchasing expensive ticket packages or other related merchandise and services during the event. The creation and implementation of 5-star service training programs for volunteers and event day personnel is advisable to build a stronger relationship. Issues related to employees' knowledge, behaviour, and attitudes are important ones and can contribute to the development of brand trust. Reliability requires the delivery of services with consistency; furthermore, reliability relates to management keeping the promises and avoiding over-promising in an organisation's external communication (e.g., advertising). A relationship built upon trust creates greater advertising efficiency (Chatterjee & Chaudhuri, 2005; Erdem & Swait, 2004).

Advertisement-based marketing communication that explicitly informs interested consumers of the superior entertainment experience offered is advisable (Hill & Green, 2000).

Communication Bonding

Individuals with a clear interest in a sport object will exert greater mental effort processing the marketing communication than uninterested individuals. This type of processing results in more self-generated responses that support or counter arguments to engage in some form of consumption (Burkrant & Unnava, 1995). The general market place is filled with various entertainment alternatives but attracted sport consumers will devote mental effort toward processing appeals related to the sport object (Funk & Pritchard, 2006). As a result, the message must be clear and contain strong arguments (Petty & Cacioppo, 1986). A persuasive appeal should convey the fulfilment of important values as well as unique attributes and benefits for consumers in order for them differentiate the entertainment offered by the sporting event from competitors (Gladden & Funk, 2002).

Marketing communication should focus on the primary message argument (e.g., credibility and trustworthiness of source) as well as technical information to induce positive evaluative responses that induce greater formation to affective and cognitive attitudinal processing. The most effective promotional design would likely combine peripheral cues to create positive emotional responses with explicit arguments (e.g., teams benefit to the community) and foster greater message processing. This may include the provision of maximum technical or personal support for the service or product's use, and reinforcing the wisdom of the purchase choice. For example, marketing content advertising a marathon should utilise race-specific information that include detailed race information including characteristics of the race course, climate conditions and technical aspects of the timing systems utilised for the event (Funk & Bruun, 2007).

Internet Bonding

Sport marketing Internet action should capitalise on the interactive components of connectedness and customisation to foster movement to attachment. Web-based forums are beneficial for returning or exchanging tickets throughout the season, receiving input on new logos and mascots, and purchasing personalised team merchandise. The convenience, near instantaneous communication, specificity and accessibility of the Internet provides a unique opportunity to create online communities and sport related forums (Pitta & Fowler, 2005). The forum provides a means through which in-group status can be achieved among users and information is exchanged. Hagel and Armstrong (1997) suggests consumer join and participate in an online community because of shared interest, relationship building, and transaction. Online communities and forums allow marketers access to data on consumer satisfaction, feedback for personalising and customising benefits and services, and tracking change in consumer attitudes.

This approach offers four main forms of communication: one-way communication from marketer to consumer, one-way communication from consumer to marketer, two-way communication from consumer to consumer, and two-way communication from consumer to marketer (Pitta & Fowler, 2005). Online forums provide consumers with a voice, foster discussion regarding management practices, and enhance social interaction among members long after the sport event is over. Web sites such as Cricinfo were developed to provide firsthand accounts, running commentary, and opinions for just about any cricket match of significance to cricket fans worldwide, whose access to the match may have been limited by geography or time. In the early stages, this commentary and information was generally provided by cricket supporters who volunteered their time, energy, effort, and opinions to contribute to the site. Cricinfo is now considered the world's favourite web site dedicated to a single sport, boasting over 20 million users (Shilbury, Westerbeek, Quick, & Funk, 2009).

Fantasy sports leagues and competitions represent another means to enhance personal bonding opportunities. Sport codes across the globe offer competitions. In Australia, foxsports.com.au has approximately 35,000 users and in 2007 an estimated 19.5 million fantasy sports users participated in leagues in the United States and Canada. The majority of these users are 18 to 34 year old males, who each spend around $175 each year on fantasy sports amenities such as leagues fees, information sources including magazines and trade publications, and live-stat-tracking programs (Fantasy Sports Trade Association, 2007).

Sport marketer action within attachment should capitalise on the interactivity of the Internet to augment personalisation. Interactivity has five components: user control, responsiveness, real time interactions, connectedness, and customisation Shilbury et al., 2009). User control is the ability of an individual to vary the content, timing and sequence of the communication. Responsiveness is the ability of the communication to respond to requests of the end user. Real time interactions refer to the response time or speed of the communication. Connectedness relates to the ability of the communication to link an individual to other users or related topics (e.g. fan forums, web logs and hyperlinks). The final component, personalisation/customisation, is the ability to utilise information either supplied by the user or collected by the sender to tailor the communication to the individual (e.g. profiling filters, features such as web sites and footage focussed on and tracking fans favourite athletes).

Sponsorship Bonding

Sport marketing actions can utilise corporate sponsors to move interested consumers toward attachment. Sport events can use sponsorship as a vehicle to integrate products and services such as cars, banks, mobile phones, and restaurants into the meaning placed on the team. This integration can be personalised allowing individuals to use a sport team credit card, ringtones on the mobile, home page for Internet access, VIP special events card at local restaurants. Sponsorship often provides the resources to employ bonding techniques previously discussed. The integration and personalisation through sponsorship strengthens the individual's connection with the sport object by linking the sport object with products and services central to a person's daily life. This creates a stronger integrated cognitive structure that results from the soldering processed depicted in Figure 7.2. In other words, there are more links to be bonded increasing the complexity of the cognitive network.

Summary

This chapter provides a unique understanding of attachment and provides marketing recommendations to help activate this process. Attachment builds upon the attraction stage by creating a stronger, more subjective connection. The attachment process facilitates movement up the PCM elevator through the creation of a meaningful personal connection with a favourite object and enhances the liking of the object as it assumes a deeper significance. Attachment processing involves evaluating external forces, prior attraction outcomes and new internal forces. This type of processing accounts for the internal bonding of discrete mental associations into a collective integrated structure. Attachment processing employs an internal soldering process to create internalisation. The internalisation of a sport object creates a psychological connection that is emotional, functional, and symbolic.

Sport marketing action within the attachment stage involves personalisation. Personalisation involves using the marketing mix to create a stronger bond between the individual consumer and sport object. A number of bonding strategies were discussed including self-concept, values, cause related, customisation, service, communication, Internet, and sponsorship.

References

Abrams, D., & Hogg, M.A. (1990). An introduction to the social identity approach. In D. Abrams, & M.A. Hogg (Eds.), *Social Identity Theory: Constructive and Critical Advances* (pp. 1–9). New York: Springer-Verlag.

Alexandris, K., Zahariadis, P., Tsorbatzoudis, C., & Grouios, G. (2004). An empirical investigation of the relationships among service quality, customer satisfaction and psychological commitment in a health club context. *European Sport Management Quarterly*, *4*, 36–52.

Baker, J., Grewal, D., & Parasuraman, A. (1994). The influence of store environment on quality inferences and store image. *Journal of the Academy of Marketing Science*, *22*, 328–339.

Bloch, P.H., & Richins, M.L. (1983). A theoretical model for the study of product importance perceptions. *Journal of Marketing*, *47*, 69–81.

Bowlby, J. (1999). Attachment and Loss (2nd Ed., Vol. I, pp. xvi–xvii, 172–173.) Basic Books.

Brady, A.K.O. (2003). How to generate sustainable brand value from responsibility. *Journal of Brand Management*, *10*(4/5), 279–289.

Brewer, M.B. (1991). The social self: On being the same and different at the same time. *Personality and Social Psychology Bulleting*, *17*, 475–482.

Burkrant, R.E., & Unnava, H.R. (1995). Effects of self-referencing on persuasion. *Journal of Consumer Research*, *22*, 17–26.

Chalip, L. (2006). Towards social leverage of sport events. *Journal of Sport and Tourism*, *11*(2), 1–19.

Chatterjee, S.C., & Chaudhuri, A. (2005). Are trusted brands important? *Marketing Management Journal*, *15*(1), 1–16.

Chaudhuri, A., & Holbrook, M.B. (2001). The chain of effects from brand trust and brand affect to brand performance: The role of brand loyalty. *Journal of Marketing*, *65*(2), 81–93.

Cialdini, R.B., Thorne, A., Walker, M.R., Freeman, S., & Sloan, L.R. (1976). Basking in reflected glory: Three (football) field studies. *Journal of Personality and Social Psychology*, *34*(3), 366–375.

Deaux, K. (1996). Social identification. In E.T. Higgins, & A.W. Kruglanski (Eds.), *Social Psychology: Handbook of Basic Principles*. New York: Guilford Press.

Delgado-Ballester, E., & Munera-Aleman, J.L. (2001). Brand trust in the context of consumer loyalty. *European Journal of Marketing*, 35(11/12), 1238–1258.

Donnelly, P., & Young, K. (1988). The construction and confirmation of identity in sport subcultures. *Sociology of Sport Journal*, 5, 223–240.

Erdem, T., & Swait, J. (2004). Brand credibility, brand consideration, and choice. *Journal of Consumer Research*, 31, 191–198.

Fantasy Sports Trade Association (2007). The voice of the fantasy sports industry since 1999. Retrieved October 19, 2007 from http://www.fsta.org/index.php

Filo, K., Funk, D.C., & Alexandris, K. (2008). Exploring the impact of brand trust on the relationship between brand associations and brand loyalty in sport and fitness. *International Journal of Sport Management and Marketing*, 3, 39–57.

Filo, K., Funk, D.C., & O'Brien, D. (in press). The Meaning Behind Attachment: Exploring Camaraderie, Cause, and Competency at a Charity Sport Event. *Journal of Sport Management*.

Filo, K., Funk, D.C., & O'Brien, D. (in press). It's really not about the bike: Exploring attraction and attachment to the events of the Lance Armstrong Foundation. *Journal of Sport Management*.

Fleming, M.A., & Petty, R.E. (1997). Identity and persuasion: An elaboration likelihood approach. In D.J. Terry, & M.A. Hogg (Eds.), *Attitudes, Behavior, and Social Context: The Role of Norms and Group Membership* (pp. 171–200). Mahwah, NJ: Lawrence Erlbaum Associates.

Funk, D.C., & Bruun, T. (2007). The role of socio-psychological and culture-education motives in marketing international sport tourism: A cross-cultural perspective. *Tourism Management*, 28, 806–819.

Funk, D.C., & James, J.D. (2001). The Psychological Continuum Model (PCM): A conceptual framework for understanding an individual's psychological connection to sport. *Sport Management Review*, 4, 119–150.

Funk, D.C., & James, J.D. (2004). The Fan Attitude Network (FAN) Model: Propositions for Exploring Identity and Attitude Formation among Sport Consumers. *Sport Management Review*, 7, 1–26.

Funk, D.C., & James, J. (2006). Consumer loyalty: The meaning of attachment in the development of sport team allegiance. *Journal of Sport Management*, 20, 189–217.

Funk, D.C., & Pastore, D.L. (2000). Equating attitudes to allegiance: The usefulness of selected attitudinal information in segmenting loyalty to professional sports teams. *Sport Marketing Quarterly, 9,* 175–184.

Funk, D.C., & Pritchard, M. (2006). Responses to publicity in sports: Commitment's moderation of message effects. *Journal of Business Research, 59,* 613–621.

Funk, D.C., Haugtvedt, C.P., & Howard, D.R. (2000). Contemporary attitude theory in sport: Theoretical considerations and implications. *Sport Management Review, 3,* 124–144.

Funk, D.C., Ridinger, L.L., & Moorman, A.M. (2004). Exploring the origins of involvement: Understanding the relationship between consumer motives and involvement with professional sport teams. *Leisure Sciences, 26,* 35–61.

Gibson, H., Willming, C., & Holdnak, A. (2002). We're gators … Not just gator fans: Serious leisure and University of Florida football. *Journal of Leisure Research, 34,* 397–425.

Gladden, J.M., & Funk, D.C. (2002). Developing and understanding of brand association in team sport: Empirical evidence from professional sport consumers. *Journal of Sport Management, 16,* 54–81.

Hagel, J., & Armstrong, A.G. (1997). *Net Gain: Expanding Markets through Virtual Communities.* Boston, MA: Harvard Business School.

Heere, B., & James, J. (2007). Sport teams and their communities: Examining the influence of external group identities on team identity. *Journal of Sport Management, 21,* 319–337.

Hightower, R., Brady, M.K., & Baker, T.L. (2002). Investigating the role of physical environment in hedonic service consumption: an exploratory study of sporting events. *Journal of Business Research, 55,* 697–707.

Hill, B., & Green, B.C. (2000). Repeat attendance as a function of involvement, loyalty, and the sportscape across three football contexts. *Sport Management Review, 3,* 145–162.

Hiscock, J. (2001). Most trusted brands. *Marketing,* March 1, 32–33.

Holt, D.B. (1995). How consumers consume: A typology of consumption practices. *Journal of Consumer Research, 22,* 1–16.

Homer, P.M., & Kahle, L.R. (1988). A structural equation analysis of the value-attitude-behavior hierarchy. *Journal of Personality and Social Psychology, 54*(4), 638–646.

Kahle, L.R. (1985). Social values in the eighties: A special issue. *Psychology and Marketing, 2*(4), 231–237.

Kahle, L.R., & Kennedy, P. (1989). Using the list of values (LOV) to understand consumers. *The Journal of Consumer Marketing, 6*(3), 5–12.

Kahle, L.R., Beatty, S.E., & Homer, P. (1986). Alternative measurement approaches to consumer values: The list of values (LOV) and values and life style (VALS). *Journal of Consumer Research*, *13*(3), 405–409.

Kahle, L., Duncan, M., Dalakas, V., & Aiken, D. (2001). The social values of fans for men's versus women's university basketball. *Sport Marketing Quarterly*, *10*(2), 156–162.

Kaplan, K.G., & Fishbein, M. (1969). The source of beliefs, their saliency, and prediction of attitude. *Journal of Social Psychology*, *78*, 63–74.

Kelley, S.W., & Turley, L.W. (2001). Consumer perceptions of service quality attributes at sporting events. *Journal of Business Research*, *54*, 161–166.

Kolbe, R.H., & James, J.D. (2002). The internalization process among team followers: Implications for team loyalty. *International Journal of Sport Management*, *4*, 25–43.

Lau, G.T., & Lee, S.H. (1999). Consumers' trust in a brand and the link to brand loyalty. *Journal of Market-Focused Management*, *4*(4), 341–370.

Mahony, D.F., Madrigal, R., & Howard, D.R. (1999). The effect of individual levels of self-monitoring on loyalty to professional football teams. *International Journal of Sports Marketing and Sponsorship*, *1*, 146–167.

Morgan, R.M., & Hunt, S.D. (1994). The commitment-trust theory of relationship marketing. *Journal of Marketing*, *58*, 20–38.

Perkins, W.S., & Reynolds, T.J. (1988). The explanatory power of values in preference judgments: Validation of the means-end perspective. *Advances in Consumer Research*, *15*, 122–126.

Petty, R.E., & Cacioppo, J.T. (1986). The elaboration likelihood model of persuasion. In L. Berkowitz (Ed.), *Advances in Experimental Social Psychology* (Vol. 19, pp. 123–205). San Diego, CA: Academic Press.

Pitta, D.A., & Fowler, D. (2005). Internet community forums: An untapped resource for consumer marketers. *Journal of Consumer Marketing*, *22*(5), 265–274.

Pritchard, M.P., & Funk, D.C. (2007). Examining attitude strength in team attachment: Form, and effect. In D. Sharma, & S. Borna (Eds.), *Developments in Marketing Science* (Vol. 30, pp. 16–21). Coral Gables, FL: Sports Marketing Track, Academy of Marketing Science Conference.

Pritchard, M.P., Havitz, D.R., & Howard, D.R. (1999). Analyzing the commitment-loyalty link in service contexts. *Academy of Marketing Science*, *27*, 333–348.

Robinson, M.J., & Trail, G.J. (2005). Relationships among spectator, gender, motives, points of attachment, and sport preference. *Journal of Sport Management*, *19*, 58–80.

Rokeach, M. (1973). *The Nature of Human Values*. New York: Free Press.

Schouten, J.W., & McAlexander, J.H. (1995). Subcultures of consumption: An ethnography of the new bikers. *Journal of Consumer Research, 22,* 43–61.

Schultz, S.E., Kleine, R.E., & Kernan, J.B. (1989). "These are a few of my favorite things" toward and explication of attachment as a consumer behavior construct. *Advances in Consumer Research, 16,* 359–366.

Schwartz, S.H., & Bilsky, W. (1987). Toward a universal psychological structure of human values. *Journal of Personality and Social Psychology, 53*(3), 550–562.

Shilbury, D., Westerbeek, H., Quick, S., & Funk, D.C. (2009). *Strategic Sport Marketing* (3rd Ed.). Crows Nest NSW: Allen & Unwin.

Sloan, L.R. (1989). In J.D. Goldstein (Ed.), *Sports, Games, and Play: Social and Psychology Viewpoints* (2nd Ed., pp. 175–240). Hillsdale, NJ: Lawrence Erlbaum Associates.

Smith, A.C.T., & Westerbeek, H.M. (2007). Sport as a vehicle for deploying corporate social responsibility. *The Journal of Corporate Citizenship, 25,* 43–54.

Sutton, W.A., McDonald, M.A., Milne, G.R., & Cimperman, J. (1997). Creating and fostering fan identification in professional sports. *Sport Marketing Quarterly, 6,* 15–22.

Tajfel, H., & Turner, J.C. (1986). An integrative theory of intergroup conflict. In S. Worchel, & W. Austin (Eds.), *Psychology of Intergroup Relations* (pp. 2–24). Chicago: Nelson-Hall.

Turner, J.C., & Oakes, P.J. (1989). Self-categorization theory and social influence. In P.B. Paulus (Ed.), *Psychology of Group Influence* (2nd Ed., pp. 147–192). Hillsdale, NJ: Hove and London: Lawrence Erlbaum Associates.

Tversky, A., & Kahneman, D. (1973). Availability: A heuristic for judging frequency and probability. *Cognitive Psychology, 5,* 207–232.

Wakefield, K.L., & Sloan, H.J. (1995). The effects of team loyalty and selected stadium factors on spectator attendance. *Journal of Sport Management, 9,* 153–172.

Willmott, M. (2003). Citizen brands: Corporate citizenship, trust and branding. *Journal of Brand Management, 10*(4/5), 362–369.

Zeithaml, V.A., & Bitner, M.J. (2003). *Services Marketing: Integrating Customer Focus Across the Firm*. New York: McGraw-Hill.

Zeithaml, V., Berry, L., & Parasuraman, A. (1996). The behavioural consequences of service quality. *Journal of Marketing, 60,* 31–46.

CHAPTER 8

Consumer Allegiance to Sport and Events

It's something that's a big part of my life. A major event for me, my family and the community. You look toward the calendar, like when you were in college and you had your 21st birthday, you had a date; like when you moved out of the dorms; and when finals started. Now it's when the LIVESTRONG Challenge is. Yes; I live for this event. It's on my calendar every year along with Thanksgiving, Christmas, and my son's birthday. I know what I'm doing the first weekend of October every year. Period! End of story!! And I know what I need to do to get there the other eleven months out of the year.

Kevin,
LIVESTRONG Challenge
3rd year participant

The above story illustrates Kevin's allegiance to a sport event, the Lance Armstrong Foundation (LAF) LIVESTRONG Challenge. The LIVESTRONG challenge is cycling and running event held every October in Austin, Texas. The personal meaning of this sport event for Kevin reveals a psychological connection that is durable and impacts behaviour. For Kevin the LIVESTRONG still has emotional, functional, and symbolic meaning found in the Attachment stage. However, somehow the event's meaning has strengthened internally and became embedded centrally in his daily life. Allegiance represents the strongest connection within the Psychological Continuum Model (PCM) framework.

Allegiance Stage

Kevin's position within the PCM framework in Figure 8.1 suggests external and internal forces have influenced his upward movement to the Allegiance stage. Funk and James (2001) describe allegiance as loyalty or devotion to some object, group, or cause. Allegiance within the sport consumer behaviour literature is commonly known as loyalty, which includes the core elements of commitment and continuance. Allegiance stage outcomes differ from Attachment stage outcomes in term of the extent to which the internal collective meaning contributes to a stable psychological connection with a sport object and consistent behaviour. As this opening story illustrates, the meaning of the sport event is woven into the everyday fabric of Kevin's life.

Allegiance builds upon the Attachment stage by creating a durable and impactful meaningful connection to the sport object. Chapter 7's discussion of attachment processing describes the internalisation of the sport object that introduces a collective strengthening of mental associations linked to important attitudes, values and self-concept. This strengthening increases the level of behavioural

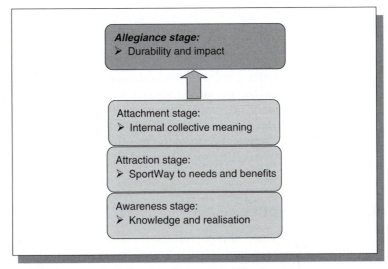

Figure 8.1
PCM framework.

Box 8.1 Attachment processing

Inputs
- External forces
- Attachment outcomes
- Internal forces

Processes
- Affective-cognitive evaluation
- Coalescence

Outputs
- Persistence and resistance
- Cognitive bias
- Consistent and enduring behaviour

---

complexity. Attachment processing continues within the Allegiance stage and facilitates movement up the PCM elevator through both increased psychological and behavioural engagement. This developmental progression marks the transition from "I am a golfer" to "I live to golf" based upon the influence of psychological, personal and, to a lesser degree, environmental factors. Box 8.1 illustrates the attachment processing for the Allegiance stage.

The attachment processing sequence involves the evaluation of personal, psychological, and environmental external forces to shape attitudes and behaviours. Within the Allegiance stage, attachment processing draws primarily upon affective-cognitive evaluation processes and coalescence. The output of these processes is the personal meaning of the sport object becomes more persistent, resistant, influences cognition and is consistent with behaviour. This chapter offers a comprehensive understanding of the attachment processing for Allegiance stage outcomes and provides marketing recommendations to help activate this process.

Allegiance Inputs

Allegiance inputs represent external forces, prior attachment outcomes and internal forces. Environmental forces are informational, experiential and represent the various socialising agents and marketing actions by sport organisations. Environmental considerations such as service quality and customer service continue to operate as inputs. The functional and technical elements of the sport experience underscore the key role environment plays in managing the experience surrounding sport events (Hightower et al., 2002). Environmental forces develop from characteristics of the consumer and the product (person $\times$ situation) and illustrate how individuals can be oriented to different parts of the sport event experience (Robinson & Trail, 2005).

Attachment outcomes represent elevated levels of psychological and behavioural engagement. Psychological engagement is the level of attitude formation in terms of the emotional, functional, and symbolic meaning placed on the sport object. This attitude is based on the collective integration of personal, psychological and environmental forces that produce a sophisticated and complex network that involves self-concept, important values and perceived trust. Behavioural engagement represents the stable level of frequent and expressive behaviour. These attachment outcomes also influence the evaluation of internal forces.

Internal forces are values, self-concept, and trust. Personal values can be categorised as external, internal, and goal specific; an include self-respect, security, warm relationships with others, sense of accomplishment, self-fulfilment, sense of belonging, being well respected, fun and enjoyment in life, and excitement (Homer & Kahle, 1988). Sport event values are Camaraderie, Competency, and Cause (Filo, Funk, & O'Brien, in press). Self-concept represents the personal identities that are volitionally adopted to define ones-self (Funk & James, 2004). An individual can choose to enter social situations that promote the expression of a desired self-concept that will satisfy how she views herself (own view), how she thinks others view her (perceived self), how she would like to be viewed (desired or ideal self), how references groups view her (group self). Kolbe and James (2002) propose that adopting a sport identity is an important component in developing loyalty to a sport team. Trust suggests an individual has confidence in the organisation to deliver needs and benefits through the sport product or service. This creates a level of trustworthiness in that the organisation provides the experience that matches or exceeds expectations.

The inputs for attachment processing within the Allegiance stage are similar to those found in the Attachment stage. The one notable difference is the element of trust that emerges. With regard to developing allegiance, it has been suggested that trust is necessary, but not wholly sufficient, and that affect must also be in place to create brand loyalty (Ringberg & Gupta, 2003). The main difference between Allegiance and Attachment stage outcomes is the processing and evaluation of inputs. Allegiance differs from attachment based on the extent to which various cognitive components (e.g., attitudes, values, self-concept, trust) contribute to an internally complex, stable, consistent and impactful evaluation of a relationship with a team. The next section provides a discussion of attachment processing that creates Allegiance stage outcomes.

Attachment Processing

Attachment processing is unique in that the sequence of inputs, internal processes and outputs create both attachment and allegiance. See Figure 3.5 for a depiction. A beneficial approach to help understand the differences between attachment processing within the Attachment stage vs. Allegiance stage is to examine the process of connecting objects together. Namely soldering and welding. Soldering was discussed in Chapter 7 and represents the internal connection process through which attachment outcomes occur. In contrast, welding represents the internal connection process through which allegiance outcomes occur. For the PCM framework, these processes are analogous to different internal bonding procedures that connect psychological, personal and environmental inputs and create different outputs.

Attachment processing for the Attachment stage employs the soldering process. Figure 7.2 illustrates this process with the dark areas representing the connective alloy. As previously discussed, attachment processing involves the evaluation of inputs using cognitive-affective processes. These inputs represent the alloy within the soldering process. In other words, personal values, self-concept and trust are the elements of the alloy mixture that forms the "mental" alloy. The melting of the alloy results from attitudinal processing. For example, cognitive-affective processing activity heats the mental alloy that bonds the inputs into a collective internal meaning. The attachment process (i.e., internal mental soldering) melts the alloy creating the attachment bond of mental links when it cools. The resulting connective bond between the mental links is not as strong as the original mental link but has adequate strength and conductivity to shape attitudes and behaviours.

The welding process that creates Allegiance stage outcomes differs from the soldering process that creates Attachment stage outcomes. Soldering has a lower-melting point requiring less heat to liquefy the alloy and produce the bond. In contrast, welding requires more heat and pressure to melt the alloy and bond two or more pieces of material. Another difference is welding often damages or alters the shape of the pieces in the bonding process. As a result, welding joins material together through coalescence. Hence, attachment processing that creates Allegiance is similar to coalescence.

Coalescence

Coalescence is the process by which two or more particles forge during contact. For example, when two drops of water touch they forge together to create a single drop. Think of a drop of water on a kitchen counter. If another drop of water falls onto the counter and touches the first drop, the two drops forge creating a single drop. In welding, coalescence produces a bond between two objects. Bonding occurs from pressure and heat to liquify a filler material to form a pool of molten material. The molten material creates the weld pool. Two pieces of metal are forged when the liquid pool cools and two pieces of metal have become one continuous solid. The two metal pieces are also altered during the welding process due to the heat and pressure to create the weld pool.

This welding analogy illustrates how the attachment process creates Allegiance stage outcomes. This process describes how heat and pressure applied to the alloy within the integrated structure of mental associations forges a stronger continuous bond than that found in the Attachment stage. The evaluative process that evaluates the meaning of the sport object creates the heat and pressure applied to the alloy. The alloy mixture consisting of personal values, self-concept and trust continue to provide the filler material and forges the psychological connection. The internal evaluation relies upon enhanced processing to fuse the integrated individual meanings of the sport object (i.e., mental links) together creating a more solid permanent connection that is more persistent, resistant, and impacts cognition and behaviour. Figure 8.2 illustrates the coalescence process for attachment outcomes, values, trust, SPEED, and self-concept. Compare Figures 8.2 and 7.2.

The attachment process within the PCM framework elevator has two distinct sequences. Box 8.2 provides a description of the two types of attachment processing sequences. The first is an internalisation sequence that creates an integrated psychological connection to a sport object within the Attachment stage (i.e., internal soldering of associations). Internalisation accounts for the internal bonding of discrete mental associations linked to a sport object into a collective integrated structure. The second

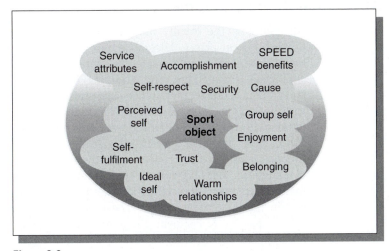

Figure 8.2
Attachment processing: Coalescence of attachment outcomes.

Box 8.2 Attachment process sequences

- *Attachment stage*: Internalisation sequence that creates a integrated psychological connection to a sport object
- *Allegiance stage*: Coalescence sequence that creates a continuous psychological connection to a sport object

is a coalescence sequence that creates a continuous psychological connection to a sport object within the Allegiance stage (i.e., internal welding of integrated structure). Coalescence accounts for the internal fusion of the integrated structure created within the Attachment stage into a continuous permanent structure. Taken together, the attachment process describes why Alex from Chapter 7 places emotional, functional, and symbolic meaning on various needs and benefits provided by the Lions (i.e., Attachment stage outcomes). As more heat and pressure are applied (i.e., mental welding), the psychological connection will continue to strengthen becoming more durable and impactful as the Lions become woven into the fabric of everyday life. The Allegiance stage outcomes represent the strongest possible connection between an individual and sport object. If Alex progresses to Allegiance, then he may finally get that team tattoo he continually talks about.

Allegiance Stage Outcomes

Allegiance is the loyalty and devotion an individual expresses toward a sport object. Allegiance represents the strongest psychological connection and creates the most enhanced level of psychological engagement and complex behavioural engagement. Psychological engagement reflects the strength of the attitude structure that stabilises the connection. Allegiance represents the differentiation within the level of attitude strength from attachment (Dick & Basu, 1994). In other words, allegiance stabilises the emotional, functional, and symbolic meaning of the sport object. This perspective suggests that allegiance is the continuation of the attitude formation and change process that created the meaningful connection within the Attachment stage. The connection is characterised as salient (Kaplan & Fishbein, 1969), readily accessible from memory (Tversky & Kahneman, 1973), and creates an enduring personal disposition toward a sport experience that guides and directs behaviours. Behavioural engagement increases in complexity as the behavioural actions that occur in attachment continue but increase in terms of breadth, depth and frequency. Behavioural engagement forms the basis of continuance, which represents behavioural consistency in terms of complex actions that is enduring and consistent.

Psychological Outcomes

Psychological outcomes in allegiance fall within two main attitude strength outcomes: durability and impact (Funk & James, 2004).

The psychological connection to a sport object strengthens within the allegiance stage to become durable and impactful (Funk & James, 2006). Durability reflects the stability of the connection in terms of persistence and resistance. Impact reflects the role of the connection in terms of influencing cognition and behaviour. Together, these strength outcomes create a connection that is continuous and permanent.

Durability: Persistence

Persistence is the durability of the psychological connection. Persistence represents the degree to which an individual's attitude toward a sport object remains unchanged over a period of time. Persistence represents the activation frequency and duration of the connection (i.e., related cognitive activity in normal daily life: daily, weekly, monthly, over 10 years). For example, a loyal sport fan will constantly think about her team year round. Persistence of thought remains unchanged and stable over an extended period of time regardless of any type of information being encountered (Petty et al., 1995). For example, Kevin has marked the calendar and continually thinks about the LIVESTRONG challenge and what it takes to get there. However, when an individual encounters information contrary to meaning of the sport object, the degree to which the connection remains unchanged reflects a resistance quality.

Durability: Resistance

Resistance reflects the durability of the complexity in the psychological connection. Resistance is the ability of the attitude to withstand personal, psychological, and environmental threats. Resistance to change is thought to be the general underlying factor contributing to consumer commitment (Crosby & Taylor, 1983; Dick & Basu, 1994). Commitment to a sport object is a key difference between allegiance and attachment stages. Commitment's stability results from greater knowledge, certainty in one's opinion, degree of consistency between feelings and beliefs, and personal relevance of information related to evaluating decisions to participate in a leisure activity (Iwasaki & Havitz, 1998). Commitment suggests stability has formed within the cognitive structure developed from an Attachment stage.

Cognitive complexity can reduce discrepancy between one's initial position and conflicting information to stabilize decision-making and subsequent behaviour. Pritchard et al. (1999) suggest that information complexity, level of involvement and volitional choice contribute to patrons' psychological commitment to a recreation activity. Funk and Pastore (2000) suggest loyalty to a professional baseball team is supported by highly formed attitude characteristics that help a person resist changing affiliation to a new club. Resistance to change is key internal mechanism that influences the impact of new environmental inputs.

Impact: Cognitive Processing

Impact is the second attitude strength outcome and influences cognitive processing. Cognitive processing depends upon dispositional, motivational, or situational cues that influence information retrieval and determine how certain judgments and decisions are rendered (Petty et al., 1995). In general, the psychological connection with a sport object may fluctuate over time depending upon the type of thoughts produced at a given moment (interaction of person $\times$ situation). However, a strong and complex connection allows the individual to refute or block against persuasive communication that conveys negative information about the sport object or information about competing alternatives. A strong attitude can bias the types of thoughts a person has about a sport object and the evaluation of information regarding that object. Funk and Pritchard (2006) report a person's level of commitment moderates the impact of newspaper editorials on beliefs and feelings about sport teams. This research revealed committed readers were not affected by the opinion advocated by the columnist, whereas changes in feelings and beliefs occurred for those who did not demonstrate commitment.

Funk and Pritchard (2006) also examined the nature of message evaluation and elaboration following editorial exposure. They observed committed readers had different cognitive responses, such as recalling more facts embedded in the editorials and generating more thoughts associated with positive publicity. In contrast, less committed respondents recalled more facts and generate more thoughts from negative publicity. The authors suggest that when confronted with statements consistent with previous attitude toward a sport object, individuals tend to assimilate the information, perceiving it to be closer to their own attitude. Statements not consistent with previous attitude toward a sport object are contrasted and are perceived as further from their own attitude. This research suggests that committed readers hold wider latitudes-of-rejection that enable connection to the team to endure despite conflicting information. This research indicates that commitment acts as a defensive cognitive processing mechanism to maintain or restore consistency. Individuals will exert considerable cognitive effort to process and re-evaluate information in order to restore internal consistency (Heider, 1958).

Allegiance is an internally stable and complex psychological connection that controls internal processes. The connection serves as a cognitive mechanism activated when a person is confronted with personal, psychological and environmental inputs (positive and negative, new and old information). The individual can choose to ignore or suppress conflicting information by recalling fewer facts, or alternatively can refute the message by generating more counter arguments, or generating more favourable thoughts. This mechanism helps reduce tension and restore internal consistency if information conflicts with current beliefs and feelings. Funk and Pritchard (2006) suggest allegiance reflects an involuntary mechanism whereby inconsistent information is automatically refuted, or processed in a biased manner. In contrast, information that is consistent is easily accepted without much consideration. The cognitive process mechanism is also an important feature that influences behaviour.

Impact: Behaviour

Behavioural allegiance is expressed by a biased, behavioural response, expressed over time, made by the individual, with respect to one or more alternatives out of a set of such opportunities, and is a function of cognitive processes. In other words, a psychological connection that is persistent, resistant and impacts cognitive processing guides behavioural engagement. Behavioural engagement increases in terms of the breadth, depth and frequency of intent and actual behaviour. Behavioural intent consists of an individual's readiness to engage in a specific activity. Intent increases the likelihood that an individual will engage in some form of behaviour (e.g., attend, read, watch, listen, purchase) related to the sport object.

Actual behaviour involves two key elements. The first is the behaviour itself (e.g., attendance at or participation in at a sport event). The second is that the behaviour is expressed with some duration in a situational context. Funk et al. (2000) argue behaviour can be provided more accurately when four elements are considered: (a) *the action* performed, (b) *the target* at which the action was performed, (c) *the context* in which the action took place and (d) *the time* when the action was performed (e.g., watching Real Madrid on TV Sunday afternoon). Actual behaviour forms the basis of continuance and represents behavioural consistency in terms of complex actions that are enduring and consistent. For example, an avid golfer has high level of media use, merchandise use, expenditure on golf products, active participation, and length of time participating. These types of behaviours are enduring and become routine.

Allegiance represents a personal enduring disposition from which an evaluation tendency remains stable over time, resists counter persuasive information or alternative forms of entertainment, influences the type of thoughts and judgments rendered and guides behaviour. Hence, allegiance reflects the extent to which an attitude is persistent, resistant, and influences cognition and behaviour. These four strength-related consequences of an attitude are thought to represent causal indicators of a strong, stable and continuous relationship with an athletic team and are viewed as determinants of loyalty (Funk et al., 2000). From this perspective, one can conceptually elaborate upon previous definitions by partitioning the attitudinal component of loyalty into three independent yet related components: persistence, resistance, and cognitive processes. Box 8.3 provides a brief description of Allegiance stage strength-related outcomes.

The strength-related outcomes help clarify the multi-dimensional nature of allegiance. Backman and Crompton (1991) propose consumers have high and spurious allegiance profiles. These profiles represent the relationship between an individual's behaviour and psychological connection. For example, a spectator with a high allegiance profile would demonstrate all four strength-related outcomes. In contrast, a spectator with spurious allegiance would demonstrate one strength-related outcome of repeat consumption, but have weak or ambivalent levels with respect to the other three (Funk & James, 2006). For example, Sarah goes to every Manchester United match during a season and watches away games on TV. However, Sarah admits that she does not really care about ManU and only attends and watches matches to spend time with her friends.

The strength-related approach utilised by the PCM framework to understand the Allegiance stage provides a more in-depth understanding of how attitudes and behaviours may fluctuate. This approach allows for the differentiation between Allegiance stage and Attachment stage outcomes. The main difference between the two stages is the degree of durability and impact of the four strength-related outcomes listed in Box 8.3. The approach is also useful in developing marketing action for Allegiance.

Box 8.3 Strength-related allegiance stage outcomes

Persistence

● Activation frequency and duration of the psychological connection
  – cognitive activity that occurs daily, weekly, monthly, yearly, lifetime
  – cognitive activity increases in a specific situation in response to information being encountered

Resistance

● Stability in the complexity of the psychological connection
  – Commitment: resist changing affiliation when confronted with personal, psychological and environmental inputs.
  – Rigid internal attitude structure with highly formed characteristics of knowledge, direct experience, extremity, certainty, intensity, cognitive-affective consistency, volitional choice.
  – Speed of retrieval from memory, personal relevance, and important to self.

Cognitive processing

● Cognitive mechanism activated by the psychological connection
  – Creates information processing bias to ignore or suppress conflicting information by recalling fewer facts, refuting message by generating counter arguments and favourable thoughts
  – Increases mental elaboration to evaluate and re-evaluate information to restore internal consistency and reduce tension if information conflicts with current beliefs and feelings

Behaviour

● Behavioural intent and actual behaviour activated by the psychological connection
  – Biased, behavioural response, expressed over time
  – Behavioural complexity in terms of breadth, depth and frequency
  – Behavioural consistency in terms of complex actions that endure

Sport Marketing Action

Allegiance represents one of the greatest consumer profiles a sport marketer can have. Allegiance contributes to a sport marketer's ability to charge premium prices for licensed merchandise, tickets and registration, seating and amenities, compete for market share, acquire corporate sponsors, and establish barriers to entry (e.g., Aaker, 1996; Buchanan & Simmons, 1999; Randall & Ulrich, 1998). Allegiance allows a sport organisation to resist competition for consumer dollars from entertainment alternatives and launch new products and services (Jacoby, 1971). Allegiance as a competitive advantage enhances repeat customers and allows for less spending on attracting new customers (Rentshler et al., 2002). Oliver (1999) suggests that depending upon the industry, the net present value increase in profit that results from a 5% increase in customer retention varies between 25% and 95%.

Sport marketing action

Strategic use of marketing mix
Select key target markets
Study and evaluate market
Select information systems

Chapter 1 illustrates the substantial consumer base from which sport organisations can draw. However, this chapter also points out that most countries are experiencing a decline in active sport participation (Van Sluijs et al., 2005), while the demand for spectator sport fluctuates and fragments (Andreff & Szymanski, 2006). Sport marketers continue to face the "leaky bucket syndrome," which is the loss of existing customers. There is also a diverse and ever-expanding range of options in the sport and entertainment marketplace. Rosenberg and Czepiel (1983) suggest that keeping an existing customer is six times less expensive than attracting a new customer. For example, a fitness facility can lose up to 40% of its entire customer annually (Sawyer & Smith, 1999). Managed professional sport teams can also experience significant losses in membership, sponsorship, and ticket sales when performance suffers (Gladden & Funk, 2002). Sport events and recreational sport programs continually face challenges in retaining participants (Alexandris et al., 2004; Kelly & Warnick, 1999).

Loyalty Lifecycle

Chapter 4 revealed how socialising agents as environmental inputs introduce or draw individuals to sports as participants and spectators. Common socialising agents in sport are parents, peer groups, siblings, relatives, and coaches that shape preferences for sports, teams and recreational activities. Allegiant consumers acting as socialising agents have the ability to combat the leaky bucket syndrome as well as expand the consumer base by creating awareness. The committed consumer also has a profound impact on creating attraction. Whether generating word of mouth or using formal marketing channels, sport marketing activities must capitalise on the allegiant consumer profile. In addition, the loyal consumer can also jump starting the developmental progression of the next generation. For example, an allegiant fan may pass down season tickets to his children. Likewise, a golfer can transfer his or her club membership to a sibling. Other industries such as hotels and airlines do not allow for this type of loyalty transference. Season ticket holders have children and relatives that may be the next generation of allegiant consumer. The role of socialising agents is important for the loyalty lifecycle. These agents are critical for the sport marketer as the loyal consumer helps introduce the next fan or participant to the product or service. In other words, allegiant consumers shape the attitude and behaviour of the next loyal consumer.

You Don't Change the Jockey During the Race

The owner of a thoroughbred racehorse running in the Melbourne Cup is not likely to stop the horse during the race to replace the jockey. Hence, the sport marketer operating the PCM elevator to build allegiance should not stop providing the sport marketing action that originally helped move the individual to the Attachment stage. The sport marketer should keep doing what was successful in fostering attachment. Sport marketers can keep the marketing actions focused on why the individual became attached in the first place and revisit the key reasons why the passion and heat developed in the first place. In other words, do not stop servicing the client.

Sport marketing action within the Allegiance stage should focus exclusively on servicing the attached client. This entails continuing a "service" orientation approach-keep doing what you are doing. This approach attempts to continue business with existing attached customers, reducing the loss of this segment, and looking for ways to increase the level of businesses. There exists a number of customer loyalty and affinity marketing programs that can serve to increase both attachment and build allegiance. Some possible changes would be to sharpen the focus of current attachment strategies and introduce new strategies. For example, threshold limits used in customer loyalty programs could be adjusted to reward not only the frequency of consumption (i.e., depth), but also the complexity and diversity of consumption activities (i.e., breadth). Sport marketing action for allegiance is about sustaining and reinforcing attachment strategies that over time create an enduring disposition that is stable, resists counter persuasive information or alternative forms of entertainment, influences the type of thoughts elicited and judgments rendered, and guides behaviour.

Chapter 7 provided a number of strategies for personalisation. Allegiance marketing activities should strive to refine and sustain the bonding strategies. This approach utilised a number of bonding techniques to increase the emotional, functional, and symbolic meaning of the sport object and experience. Self-concept bonding attempts to foster identification with the sport object. Value-bonding leverages camaraderie, competency and cause opportunities. Customise bonding targets specific needs and benefits to personalise the experience. Service bonding focuses on the predictability, competence and reputation of customer service and satisfaction to create trust. Communication bonding involves developing appropriate promotional content that conveys and informs the individual about the various bonding opportunities. Internet bonding is related to communication bonding, but capitalises on interactivity components of connectedness and content. Finally, sponsorship bonding utilises corporate sponsors to link the sport object with products and services central to a person's daily life. In summary, don't weaken or remove the bond; make it stronger by applying more heat and pressure.

Passion vs. Commitment

The passion and heat created in the Attachment stage may fluctuate but commitment within the Allegiance stage endures. As in any relationship, whether it is between an individual and a sport object or between two individuals in a relationship, the passion and heat of attachment is not likely to be sustained. However, the level of commitment and well-being found within a long-term stable relationship is sustainable. The sport marketer must continually help the allegiant individual revisit why he or she is passionate about the product or service. Attending or participating in a sport event is like preparing and taking a romantic holiday to rekindle the passion in this committed relationship. For example, a committed recreational runner can renew her passion for running while preparing for a marathon event. A die hard football fan can renew his passion for a team as it plays in the UEFA cup tournament. The emotional, functional, and symbolic meaning is also rekindled while watching or participating in the actual event (marathon or UEFA cup final).

The sport marketers must continue to utilise and understand sport consumer behaviour to keep abreast of participation patterns, influences to buy or consume, and levels of satisfaction with various aspects of the sport experience. The use of the PCM staging tool can help identify allegiant individuals and further study how their personal, psychological, and environmental needs and benefits shift over time. The sport marketer can look for innovative solutions to reposition the attachment strategies for this segment. However, such decision must consider marketing objectives in relation to the organisation overall.

Marketing and the Organisation

The Allegiance stage will necessitate the use of a comprehensive information system. In fact, sport marketing action within allegiance will require the integration of marketing within the overall sport organisation (e.g., finance, operations, human resources). Allegiance strategies must be consistent with the overall mission of the sport organisation as marketing is just one respective department. The use of bonding strategies will require involvement from the entire organisation in the development and dissemination of quality services, programs and products. Most industries stop servicing the client when marketing objectives change. The focus is more on attracting new customers versus retaining existing ones. The level of service drops as the efforts are redirected toward new markets. For example, the focus on a new Asian market may shift the focus from a previous Hispanic market.

Summary

This chapter offers a discussion of the attachment processing for Allegiance stage outcomes and provides marketing recommendations. Attachment processing facilitates movement up the PCM elevator through increasing both psychological and behavioural engagement. Attachment processing represents a coalescence sequence that fuses and strengthens the connection created within the Attachment stage. Allegiance builds upon the attachment by creating a more permanent and continuous connection between the individual and the sport object. An Allegiance stage connection differs from an Attachment stage connection based on the extent to which affective processing contributes to the connection's durability in terms of resistance, persistence and impact on cognitive processing and behaviour.

Sport marketing action for allegiance should strive to sustain attachment bonding strategies. The loyalty lifecycle should consider the role of loyal consumers as socialising agents to introduce the next fan or participant to the product or service. The sport marketer should keep doing what was successful in creating the heat and passion of attachment in the first place. Marketing activities should strive to sustain the bonding strategies with a specific focus on personalisation and service to create commitment. Finally, sport marketing actions should be consistent with the overall mission of sport organisation.

References

Aaker, D.A. (1996). Building strong brands. *Academy of Marketing Science Journal*, *25*, 260–261.

Alexandris, K., Zahariadis, P., Tsorbatzoudis, C., & Grouios, G. (2004). An empirical investigation of the relationships among service quality, customer satisfaction and psychological commitmentin a health club context. *European Sport Management Quarterly*, *4*, 36–52.

Andreff, W., & Szymanski, S. (2006). *Handbook on the Economic of Sport*. North Hampton, MA: Edward Elgar Publishing.

Backman, S.J., & Crompton, J.L. (1991). Using loyalty matrix to differentiate between high, spurious, latent and loyal participants in two leisure services. *Journal of Park and Recreation Administration*, *9*(1), 1–17.

Buchanan, L., & Simmons, C.J. (1999). Brand equity dilution: Retailer display and context brand effects. *Journal of Marketing Research*, *36*, 345–355.

Crosby, L.A., & Taylor, J.R. (1983). Psychological commitment and its effects on post-decision evaluation and preference stability among voters. *Journal of Consumer Research*, *9*, 413–431.

Dick, A.S., & Basu, K. (1994). Customer Loyalty: Toward an integrated conceptual framework. *Journal of Academy of Marketing Science*, *22*, 99–113.

Filo, K., Funk, D.C., & O'Brien, D. (in press). The meaning behind attachment: Exploring camaraderie, cause, and competency at a charity sport event.

Funk, D.C., & James, J.D. (2001). The Psychological Continuum Model (PCM): A conceptual framework for understanding an individual's psychological connection to sport. *Sport Management Review*, *4*, 119–150.

Funk, D.C., & James, J.D. (2004). The Fan Attitude Network (FAN) Model: Propositions for exploring identity and attitude formation among sport consumers. *Sport Management Review*, *7*, 1–26.

Funk, D.C., & James, J. (2006). Consumer loyalty: The meaning of attachment in the development of sport team allegiance. *Journal of Sport Management, 20*, 189–217.

Funk, D.C., & Pastore, D.L. (2000). Equating attitudes to allegiance: The usefulness of selected attitudinal information in segmenting loyalty to professional sports teams. *Sport Marketing Quarterly, 9*, 175–184.

Funk, D.C., & Pritchard, M. (2006). Responses to publicity in sports: Commitment's moderation of message effects. *Journal of Business Research, 59*, 613–621.

Funk, D.C., Haugtvedt, C.P., & Howard, D.R. (2000). Contemporary attitude theory in sport: Theoretical considerations and implications. *Sport Management Review, 3*, 124–144.

Gladden, J.M., & Funk, D.C. (2002). Developing and understanding of brand association in team sport: Empirical evidence from professional sport consumers. *Journal of Sport Management, 16*, 54–81.

Heider, F. (1958). *The Psychology of Interpersonal Relations*. New York: Wiley.

Hightower, R., Brady, M.K., & Baker, T.L. (2002). Investigating the role of physical environment in hedonic service consumption: an exploratory study of sporting events. *Journal of Business Research, 55*, 697–707.

Homer, P.M., & Kahle, L.R. (1988). A structural equation analysis of the value-attitude-behavior hierarchy. *Journal of Personality and Social Psychology, 54*(4), 638–646.

Iwasaki, Y., & Havitz, M.E. (1998). A path analytic model of the relationships between involvement, psychological commitment, and loyalty. *Journal of Leisure Research, 30*, 256–280.

Jacoby, J. (1971). A model of multi-brand loyalty. *Journal of Advertising Research, 9*, 29–35.

Kaplan, K.G., & Fishbein, M. (1969). The source of beliefs, their saliency, and prediction of attitude. *Journal of Social Psychology, 78*, 63–74.

Kelly, J., & Warnick, R. (1999). *Recreation Trends and Markets: The 21st Century*. Champaign, IL: Sagamore Publishing.

Kolbe, R.H., & James, J.D. (2002). The internalization process among team followers: Implications for team loyalty. *International Journal of Sport Management, 4*, 25–43.

Oliver, R. (1999). Whence consumer loyalty? *Journal of Marketing, 63*, 33–44.

Petty, R.E., Haugtvedt, C.P., & Smith, S.M. (1995). Elaboration as a determinant of attitude strength: Creating attitudes that are persistent, resistant, and predictive of behaviour. In R.E. Petty, & J.A. Krosnick (Eds.), *Attitude Strength: Antecedents and Consequences* (pp. 93–130). Mahwah, NJ: Lawrence Erlbaum Associates.

Pritchard, M.P., Havitz, D.R., & Howard, D.R. (1999). Analyzing the commitment-loyalty link in service contexts. *Academy of Marketing Science, 27*, 333–348.

Randall, T., & Ulrich, K. (1998). Brand equity and vertical product line extent. *Marketing Science, 17*, 356–380.

Rentshler, R., Radbourne, J., Carr, R., & Rickard, J. (2002). Relationship marketing, audience retention and performing arts organisation viability. *International Journal of Nonprofit and Voluntary Sector Marketing, 7*, 118–130.

Ringberg, T., & Gupta, S.F. (2003). The importance of understanding the symbolic world of customers in asymmetric business-to-business relationships. *The Journal of Business and Industrial Marketing, 18*(6/7), 607–626.

Rosenberg, L., & Czepiel, J. (1983). A marketing approach for consumer retention. *Journal of Consumer Marketing, 1*, 45–51.

Robinson, M.J., & Trail, G.J. (2005). Relationships among spectator, gender, motives, points of attachment, and sport preference. *Journal of Sport Management, 19*, 58–80.

Sawyer, S., & Smith, O. (1999). *The Management of Clubs, Recreation and Sport: Concepts and Applications*. Champaign, IL: Sagamore.

Tversky, A., & Kahneman, D. (1973). Availability: A heuristic for judging frequency and probability. *Cognitive Psychology, 5*, 207–232.

Van Sluijs, E.M.F., Van Poppel, M.N.M., Twisk, J.W.R., Brug, J., & Van Mechelen, W. (2005). The positive effect on determinants of physical activity of a tailored, general practice-based physical activity intervention. *Health Education Research, 20*, 345–356.

CHAPTER 9

Constraints to Sport and Event Consumption

Makoto is a Reds fan. The Urawa Reds play in the Japanese Football League (J. League) and have been Makoto's favourite team since childhood. For 15 years he was a premier club member and attended every home match and watched away matches on TV. However, after the birth of his first child Makoto rarely attends matches. When his friends asked why he no longer attends, Makoto says he does not have time due to family obligations and his new job requires long hours. The cost of tickets also makes it difficult for Makoto to take his family. As a result, Makoto and his family often watch the Reds on TV or follow the team via the Internet.

The primary focus of previous chapters has been on understanding how personal, psychological, and environmental factors increase an individual's connection with a sport object within the psychological continuum model (PCM) framework. In other words, what external and internal factors push and pull an individual from awareness, to attraction, to attachment, and to allegiance. This information illustrates how a person's involvement with sport object progressively develops. The progression is depicted in Figure 3.6 as occurring in a linear fashion with corresponding levels of psychological engagement (minimal to enhanced) and stages of behavioural engagements (simple to complex). However, the example of Makoto illustrates how individuals encounter barriers that can alter or prohibit behavioural engagement. In other words, how life can present obstacles that inhibit or alter the progression.

Makoto remains an Urawa Red's fan, but he now perceives family, work and costs as reasons why he cannot attend Red's games. To overcome these barriers, Makoto and his family watch the matches on TV. The perception of a barrier or constraint is an important element in the PCM's developmental framework. The integration of leisure constraint theory and substitution can provide sport consumer behaviourists with a holistic understanding of sport consumption activity. This information is particularly useful for marketers in helping consumers overcome perceived or actual constraints. A sport marketer can provide solutions to help individuals negotiate constraints in order to engage in a consumption activity. This chapter provides a discussion of the personal, psychological, and environmental constraints that influence behavioural engagement.

Figure 9.1 depicts the PCM framework with the addition of traffic signals (e.g., black, light grey and dark grey lights) between

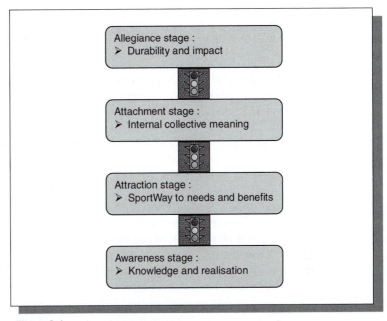

Figure 9.1
PCM framework and constraints.

the four floors. The traffic signal represents the outcome from processing personal, psychological, and environmental inputs. This processing occurs within the three formative processes of awareness, attraction, and attachment previously discussed. Hence, the outcome of processing illuminates the specific signal indicator black, light grey, or dark grey and leads to the level of psychological and behavioural engagement. The black light indicates a person's willingness to move upward to the next psychological stage with an increased level of behavioural engagement. The black light also indicates a person is willing to engage in the corresponding level of behaviour (i.e., frequency and complexity) within that stage. The light grey light suggests a person is cautious and uncertain about moving upward to the next psychological stage. In addition, light grey indicates inconsistency exists between the forms of engagement as behaviour is constrained or altered. The dark grey light suggests a person is not willing to move upward to the next psychological stage and will not engage in the corresponding level of behavioural engagement.

The traffic signals placed within the PCM framework illustrate how perceived constraints can limit, alter, or prohibit both motivation and goal directed behaviour. As previously discussed in Chapter 2, sport motivation reflects desires to satisfy internal needs or receive positive benefits through sport consumption activities (e.g., Iso-Ahola, 1982; MacInnis, Moorman, & Jaworski, 1991). The realisation of needs and benefits help facilitate psychological movement upward within the PCM framework. However, a person's psychological connection to a sport object does not always lead to the corresponding level of behaviour (Funk & James, 2006). In addition, individuals may exhibit behaviours not consistent with their level of psychological engagement. These inconsistencies are illustrated by the dark grey and light grey shaded areas in Figure 9.2.

As previously discussed, human behaviour is complex and may not follow such a simplified linear pattern as illustrated by the grey boxes in Figure 9.2. Most often, behavioural engagement does not match the level of psychological engagement due to perceived constraints. The dark grey shaded areas in Figure 9.2 represent this occurrence and indicate that psychological engagement is enhanced but behaviour is simple. For example, Makoto is at the Allegiance stage with respect to the Urawa Reds, but does not exhibit typical behaviours associated with allegiance. Makoto's behaviour may appear infrequent and more representative

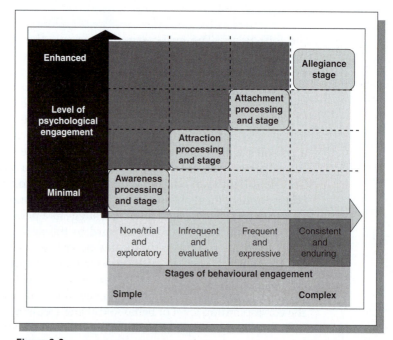

Figure 9.2
Constraint regions within PCM framework.

of Awareness and Attraction stages. The dark grey shaded areas indicated the presence of a latent loyal individual. In contrast, the light grey shaded areas indicate a spurious loyal individual and occur when the level of behavioural engagement is frequent and complex, but the level of psychological engagement is minimal. This mainly occurs when a person engages frequently in sport consumption activities for other reasons than his or her psychological connection with the focal object. For example, a person may attend every Reds football match but does not care about the team and only attends to socialise with friends and family. Another example would be if a person exercises for health reasons but does not enjoy the activity.

The potential inconsistencies illustrated in Figure 9.2 indicate that some personal, psychological, or environmental force intervenes to alter or prohibit the type and frequency of sport consumption activity. In other words, something constrains a person's motivation to engage in goal directed behaviour. Motivation is an important aspect of the developmental progression within the PCM framework. The other equally important part is the perception of barriers that constrain or inhibit behaviour or alter motivation. In other words, motivation and perceived constraints can be thought of as two sides of the same developmental coin. Pritchard, Funk, and Alexandras (in press) echo this sentiment suggesting both motives and constraints are important when understanding how to build and sustain volume among a sport consumer base.

Motivation vs. Constraints

Whereas motivation facilitates intentions and behaviour, constraints prevent or dampen it. Sport consumer behaviourists continue to consider the "why" in terms of the psychological motives behind sport consumption activity. Motivation research seeks to answer, "Why do people buy?" however, it does not address "Why do people stop buying?"; "Why do people buy less?"; or "Why do people buy something else?" Some research suggests that the link between motivation and product behaviour is ambiguous and some external force must intervene to prevent the motivated consumer from acting consistently (Assael, 1995; Bagozzi, 1993). Bagozzi (1993) insight remains informative today as accurate predictions of behaviour from intentions will remain elusive until attention is directed at how internal mechanisms mediate between intentions and behaviour. Unfortunately, understanding how these obstacles influence intention to engage in sport consumption activities remains scarce (Oliver, 1999). Even in higher stages of involvement such as attachment and allegiance, obstacles can alter or discontinue behaviour as well as influence the individual to substitute different behaviours.

Current theory and writing suggest that constraints play a formative role in the decision-making process through volition (Pritchard et al., in press). Pritchard and colleagues suggest customers who perceive barriers as inhibiting their sport consumption activity feel less free to continue their behaviour. This perspective runs parallel with Bagozzi (1993) who suggests motivation's ability to explain consumer behaviour would improve when volition's role in the sequence was considered (i.e., motivation→volition→behaviour). As previously discussed in Chapter 6, volitional choice represents the perception of free will or freedom to choose. Individuals believe their decision to act is unhindered and is a central component of movement from awareness to attraction. According to Pritchard, Havitz, and Howard (1999) a strong sense of volition is present in individuals who want to continue their support of a brand and resist change to alternative brands. In this sense, volition operates within the decision-making process making people feel *free to act* without the presence of perceived constraints. As a result, the bulk of research attempts to understand how external factors create the perception of constraints and take away a person's volition.

Perceived Constraints

Perceived constraints are reasons individuals have for not participating in some form of sport consumption activity. Constraints are factors perceived or experienced by individuals that limit the formation of leisure preferences and inhibit or prohibit participation in leisure activities (Jackson, 1991). In other words, a constraint can emerge from direct experience through participating in a sport activity or a perception of what it takes to participate (e.g., risk). The same holds true for the purchase of a sport product or service. The perception of a constraint influences the developmental progression within the PCM framework, but more importantly may limit, alter or prohibit behaviour. Prior research indicates that constraints can reduce the frequency of participation (Alexandris & Carroll, 1997; Raedeke & Burton, 1997). Constraints represent barriers to participation and can interact with other personal, psychological, and environmental factors to direct behaviour (e.g., no participation, less participation, substitution of activity).

A number of constraints have been uncovered in the literature. Box 9.1 provides a list of notable leisure constraints that can

Box 9.1 Leisure constraints

- Lack of accessibility
- Lack of facilities
- Lack of financial means
- Lack of interest
- Lack of partner/friend
- Lack of prior knowledge
- Safety and security
- Lack of time

account for why people may not start participation, may not continue participation or may alter the form of sport consumption activity (Alexandris & Carroll, 1997). Lack of accessibility refers to a person's ability to access a sport product or service. The geographic location of a golf course, fitness facility or sport event along with the element of travel, and climate are relevant. The type of facility is also important in terms of enhancing the experience with appropriate venues and equipment. Playing football on a pitch that is not well maintained can diminish the experience. Financial constraints deal with the cost of the consumption activity. For example, a San Francisco 49ers game in the NFL cost $59.00 to $94.00 for a ticket with $25.00 for parking, $8.00 per beer and $4.25 for a hot dog (USD). Lack of interest is simply the lack of motivation. Lack of partner refers to an inability to find someone to participate with and diminishes opportunities for socialisation. Lack of prior knowledge indicates a person has limited functional knowledge, physical ability and skills, and possible little direct experience. For example, prior knowledge is often a constraint for playing golf. Safety and security refers to the environment and atmosphere in which the consumption activity takes place. Some individual may dislike large crowds at sport events or feel threatened if travelling alone. Security is an important concern whether attending a live sport event or using the Internet. Lack of time often stems from other obligations such as family, work, and lifestyle obligations.

Individuals at different levels of activity involvement may perceive different types of constraints. For example, individuals at the Awareness stage of the PCM may perceive a lack of prior knowledge as a barrier. Individuals at the Attraction stage may find lack of partner or safety and security to be a constraint. Individuals at Attachment or Allegiance stages may find lack of finances, time or accessibility to be a constraint. Research is needed to understand the relationship between the type of constraint and the level of involvement. This information is critical for providers of sport products and services to better understand which constraints may prohibit consumption activity and how to best help the consumer in the decision-making process.

In the area of sport spectator research, negative elements of the sport experience have been identified as constraints. External factors such as the weather, ticket pricing, and the nature of the competition (e.g., close game, rival team) negatively influence or constrain US attendance at football games (Welki & Zlatoper, 1999). Owen and Weatherston (2004) report that external factors such as weather, competition, lack of player quality, and rain on match day can reduce attendance within the Super 14 Rugby Union league. Similarly, Schofield (1983) observed spectator attendance at cricket matches in the United Kingdom were less attractive due to bad weather and financial cost. Pritchard et al. (in press) report similar external constraints along with media consumption can impede live attendance at sport events.

Mainstream marketing researchers have also identified similar constraints. Lepisto and Hannaford (1980) identified five types of barriers: (1) *marketing constraints* is the failed fit between product and consumer and is the type of constraint most easily controlled, (2) *cultural constraints* are prevailing cultural norms and values that might restrain behaviour, (3) *social constraints* are the influence of reference groups and social expectations on actions, (4) *personal constraints* represent a consumer's lifestyle or pattern of living, and (5) *structural constraints* restrict behaviour due to certain physical, temporal, or spatial challenges.

The research on constraints has provided a number of factors that inhibit or alter consumption. Constraints are generally viewed as negative factors and originate from either internal or external sources. As a result, marketers feel understanding the negative factors can provide strategic insight into developing marketing recommendations to help individuals overcome constraints. The role of marketing in relation to perceived constraints is to help individuals overcome barriers to consumption by negotiating negative factors. The next section provides a discussion of how marketers can help sport consumers negotiate constraints.

Sport Marketing Action

Sport marketing action attempts to build and sustain volume. To achieve these goals, marketers can attract new customers, do more business with existing customers or reduce the loss of existing customers. Marketing action that incorporates an understanding of perceived constraints can increase the likelihood of building and sustaining volume by assisting the consumer in negotiating through perceived obstacles. Simply put, marketing action helps the customer overcome perceived or actual barriers, thus facilitating the negotiation process as part of decision-making.

Sport marketing action

Strategic use of marketing mix
Select key target markets
Study and evaluate market
Select information systems

Strategic Use of the Marketing Mix

Strategic use of the marketing mix allows the sport marketer to facilitate the negotiation of constraints. As discussed in Chapter 4, this marketing action involves manipulating the marketing mix elements to develop a marketing approach to meet the needs and wants of current and potential consumers. The most common method is to position the marketing approach by incorporating the 4 P's of the marketing mix. For example, modifying the product or service such as 5-players a side competing on a smaller field in recreational football, Twenty20 cricket matches, various membership levels, flexible ticketing packages, and broadcast access. These strategies help the individual overcome constraints such as time, number of players needed, and cost.

Helping the individual negotiate constraints can also employ service and promotional strategies. The management of product characteristics and situational effects should address negative customer service experiences and enhance service quality. Whether it is a fitness facility, stadium or running event, providing quality service amenities can assist with making sure the experience is a good one (Shilbury, Westerbeek, Quick, & Funk, 2008). When service elements fail to perform at an event, negative experiences result creating perceived barriers. Research on marketing constraints reveals service failures in terms of service provider interactions influence discontinuance (Keaveney, 1995). The strategic use of promotion should allow individuals to overcome constraints. For example, Internet studies reveal constraints to on-line consumption stem from financial cost, product performance, time, and convenience costs (Forsythe & Shi, 2003).

The overriding goal is to strategically manipulate products and services to respond to changes in interest and demand. However, in order to accomplish this goal, modification decisions should concentrate on differences that exist with key target markets.

Select Key Target Markets

The second action of the SMA procedure involves selecting key segments on which to focus the marketing approach. Individuals with different demographic and psychographic profiles may perceive constraints differently (e.g., gender, age, geography, SPEED motives). Individuals at different levels of activity involvement may face a unique set of constraints. For example, individuals at the Awareness stage of the PCM may perceive a lack of prior knowledge as a barrier. Individuals at the Attraction stage may find lack of partner or safety and security to be a constraint. Individuals at Attachment or Allegiance stages may find lack of finances, time, or accessibility to be a constraint. Customisation strategies can help consumers in key target markets negotiate constraints through bundling attributes and benefits and tailoring the experience. In general, highly motivated patrons should be more willing to negotiate and resist the impact of constraints.

Unfortunately, there is limited information regarding the relationship between the type of constraint and the level of involvement. This information is critical for providers of sport products and services to understand which constraints may prohibit consumption activity within key target markets. This leads to the final sport marketing action to help the consumer in the negotiation process.

Study and Evaluate the Markets

The evaluation of key target markets as well as the immediate environment in which the service exchange takes place allows decisions regarding the marketing approach for key markets. However, questions remain as to which constraints are most potent. Research on customisation strategies should employ the PCM staging tool along with demographics and benefits to identify key constraints for selected target markets. In addition, research should address the relative impact of internal vs. external constraints.

There are two general categories of perceived constraints: external and internal. External constraints block behaviour due to a lack of partner, lack of accessibility, lack of finances, lack of facilities, service quality, and safety and security, and work and family commitments. Internal constraints are interpersonal and intrapersonal and include lack of interest, lack of knowledge, lack of fitness and skill, lack of self-esteem. Crawford, Jackson, and Godbey (1991) propose external constraints are the most powerful predictors of behaviour, while structural constraints are the least powerful ones. The majority of studies support the important role of internal constraints in limiting an individual's participation in leisure activities. However, external constraints are certainly present, but these may require less effort to negotiate (Jackson, Crawford, & Godbey, 1993). Ganesh, Arnold, and Reynolds (2000) suggest that extrinsic factors such as service quality and customer service are important for repeat consumption. It may also be advantageous to consider the constraint's locus of origination in terms of whether the perception originates from internal or external sources.

Enquiry into the role of internal and external constraints along with the role of motivation collectively remains an important issue to study and evaluate by sport marketers. The constraint negotiation process is a complex inter-relationship between motivation, constraints, and negotiation. How the individual balances motivation and constraints is critical for understanding the negotiation strategies employed by individuals and key target markets. The integration of this balance proposition within the PCM framework provides the opportunity to address the interaction between constraints and motivation.

This information can assist developing more tailored marketing strategies for current and potential consumers. It is important to remember that the perception of a constraint does not necessarily mean non-participation or non-consumption. An individual may choose to substitute behaviour with an alternate behaviour. The concept of substitution suggests individuals will interchange activities to satisfy motives, needs, and preferences. A psychological decision is made to substitute an originally intended consumption activity with another that has acceptable equivalent outcomes (Brunson & Shelby, 1993). This can occur by varying the means of gaining access, the timing of the experience, and/or the setting and the consumption activity. In other words, consumers when faced with a constraint will apply strategies and resources to overcome the constraints through a "negotiation" process. The negotiation process may direct some individuals to choose alternative consumption activities. For example, a person may substitute attending a live sport event by watching the event on-line, via television at a pub or attending an organised watch party. In other words, some individuals may substitute behaviour with a variety of related consumption activities. As a result, marketers can offer alternative or substitutive products and services to allow different opportunities to engage in sport consumption activities.

Substitution

When faced with a constraint, an individual may engage in an alternate sport consumption activity to provide the opportunity to satisfy needs and receive equivalent benefits.

Summary

This chapter provides a discussion of the personal, psychological, and environmental constraints that prohibit the developmental progression outlined within the PCM framework. Specific attention was given to behavioural engagement since perceived or actual constraints often alter or inhibit sport related consumption activity. A variety of constraints were discussed to illustrate the opportunities and challenges sport marketers face. Understanding constraints provide sport marketers with valuable information to develop marketing actions designed to help consumers overcome obstacles. A sport marketer can provide solutions to help individuals negotiate constraints or find acceptable substitute behaviours.

References

Alexandris, K., & Carroll, B. (1997). An analysis of leisure constraints based on different recreational sport participation levels: Results from a study in Greece. *Leisure Sciences, 19*(1), 15.

Assael, H. (1995). *Consumer Behaviour and Marketing Action* (5th Ed.). Cincinnati, OH: South-Western College Publishing.

Bagozzi, R.P. (1993). On the neglect of volition in consumer research: A critique and proposal. *Psychology & Marketing, 10*, 215–237.

Brunson, M., & Shelby, B. (1993). Recreation substitutability: A research agenda. *Leisure Sciences, 15*, 67–74.

Crawford, D.W., Jackson, E.L., & Godbey, G. (1991). A hierarchical model of leisure constraints. *Leisure Sciences, 13*, 309–320.

Forsythe, S.M., & Shi, B. (2003). Consumer patronage and risk perceptions in internet shopping. *Journal of Business Research, 56*, 867–875.

Funk, D.C., & James, J. (2006). Consumer loyalty: The meaning of attachment in the development of sport team allegiance. *Journal of Sport Management, 20*, 189–217.

Ganesh, J., Arnold, M.J., & Reynolds, K.E. (2000). Understanding the customer base of service providers: An examination of the differences between switchers and stayers. *Journal of Marketing, 64*, 65–87.

Iso-Ahola, S.E. (1982). Toward a social psychological theory of tourism motivation: A rejoinder. *Annals of Tourism Research, 9*, 256–262.

Jackson, E. (1991). Leisure constraints/constrained leisure: Special issue introduction. *Journal of Leisure Research, 23*, 279–285.

Jackson, E.L., Crawford, D.W., & Godbey, G. (1993). Negotiation of leisure constraints. *Leisure Sciences, 15*, 1–11.

Keaveney, S.M. (1995). Customer switching behaviour in service industries: An exploratory study. *Journal of Marketing, 59*, 71–82.

Lepisto, L.R., & Hannaford, W.J. (1980). Purchase constraint analysis: An alternative perspective for marketers. *Journal of the Academy of Marketing Science, 8*, 12–25.

MacInnis, D.J., Moorman, C., & Jaworski, B.J. (1991). Enhancing and measuring consumers' motivation, opportunity, and ability to process brand information from ads. *Journal of Marketing, 55*, 32–53.

Oliver, R. (1999). Whence consumer loyalty? *Journal of Marketing, 63*, 33–44.

Owen, P.D., & Weatherston, C.R. (2004). Uncertainty of outcome, player quality and attendance at national provincial championship rugby union matches: An evaluation in light of the competition review. *Economic Papers, 23*, 301–324.

Pritchard, M., Funk, D.C., & Alexandris, A. (in press). Barriers to pepeat patronage: The impact of spectator constraints. *European Journal of Marketing.*

Pritchard, M.P., Havitz, D.R., & Howard, D.R. (1999). Analyzing the commitment-loyalty link in service contexts. *Academy of Marketing Science, 27*, 333–348.

Raedeke, T.D., & Burton, D. (1997). Personal investment perspective on leisure-time physical activity participation: Role of incentives, program compatibility, and constraints. *Leisure Sciences, 19*, 201–228.

Schofield, J.A. (1983). The demand for cricket: The case of the John Player League. *Applied Economics, 15*, 283–297.

Shilbury, D., Westerbeek, H., Quick, S., & Funk, D.C. (2008). *Strategic Sport Marketing* (3rd Ed.). Crows Nest, NSW: Allen & Unwin.

Welki, A.M., & Zlatoper, T.J. (1999). U.S. professional football game-day attendance. *Atlantic Economic Journal, 27*, 285–298.

PART 3

Provides an "Event Management Checklist: A Functional Guide to Preparation and Success" to help understand marketing actions related to the development, promotion and delivery of a sport event.

Event Management Checklist: A Functional Guide to Preparation and Success.

If you plan it, they will come

An important factor in conducting any event is the advance planning accomplished by the managing organisation weeks, months, and years prior to the event. The purpose of the Event Management Checklist: A Functional Guide to Preparation and Success is to provide a comprehensive understanding of marketing actions related to the development, promotion, and delivery of an event. This checklist is a generic tool for planning various types of events and divided into three areas: (1) *Administrative Services*, (2) *Facilities and Support Services*, and (3) *Special Events and Services.* The checklist should be used in concert with the four steps of the Sport Marketing Action process from Chapter 4: Strategic Use of the Marketing Mix, Select Key Target Markets, Study and Evaluate the Market and Selection Information System. Although some components covered in the checklist will not apply to all events, it is hoped that the scope of the checklist is broad enough to touch on many of the areas that will need to be considered. Hence, the checklist covers a number of topics from A to Z to provide assistance in preparing your next event. I would like to acknowledge the work and inspiration of Dave Griner for this checklist.

Administrative Services

A. Administration and Management

1. Policy Development

   (a) Formulate the idea of the event by answering the questions why, what, how, where, and for whom?
   (b) Conduct a feasibility study by discussing the questions in more depth. If the aims of the event can be feasibly met within the group's budget:
      (i) announce the decision to hold the event
      (ii) state the nature and aims of the event in writing
      (iii) form an administrative committee to manage the event
      (iv) appoint an event director.
   (c) When developing policy, be sure that the organisation's policies are in agreement with local, regional and state policies and regulations.

2. Event Director

   (a) The event director is the key person; the person who knows generally what is going on with every facet of the event.
   (b) Responsibilities will include:
      (i) monitoring and controlling the progress of the event
      (ii) designating staff and delegating responsibility
      (iii) maintaining open lines of communication to all staff
      (iv) major decision making.
   (c) The event director is a key person in determining the success of the event; therefore, selection of the event director should be made with care.
   (d) On the day of the event, the event director should not have specific responsibilities, but should be free to deal with problems that may occur during the course of the event.

3. Administrative Staff

   (a) The administrative staff are the core group responsible for the event.
   (b) Responsibilities will include:
      (i) handling the majority of preliminary paperwork
      (ii) developing organisational tables, flowcharts, and plans (see A5)
      (iii) in conjunction with the event director, dividing the event into manageable tasks and assigning a coordinator to each task
      (iv) bookkeeping.

4. Office Facilities
   (a) Ideally, there should be a centralised office or headquarters from which the administrative staff works.
   (b) This office should minimally contain:
       (i) a telephone, Internet access and web resources, mobile phones, laptop or desktop
       (ii) a filing system for copies of all pertinent paperwork and all correspondence
       (iii) any office equipment which the administrative staff might need
       (iv) adequate workspace for at least the event director, the publicity coordinator, and the financial coordinator.
5. Table of Organisation
   It is important to agree on the precise roles, responsibilities, and tasks.
   (a) Organisational tables should be developed to avoid ambiguous ties and provide a visual picture of the responsibility areas.
   (b) All workers need to know to whom they are responsible, who is responsible to them, whom they are working with, and the exact function of the organisation.
   (c) Organisational tables should be written down and distributed to all workers to ensure smooth communication.
   (d) When developing tables of organisation, strive to optimise the amount of responsibility assigned to each worker.
6. Site Selection
   (a) Strive to find a neutral site where many people will feel comfortable.
   (b) Strive to find a site that is central to the population that the event is trying to attract.
   (c) Examine the logistics of the site:
       (i) transportation and parking
       (ii) available utilities
       (iii) cost of the site
       (iv) weather and the availability of an alternate site
       (v) size of site in relation to expected attendance
       (vi) appropriateness of the site for the event.
   (d) Determine when the site is available.
7. Date Selection
   (a) It is advantageous to establish a specific, recurring date so that people will plan their calendars around the event.
   (b) If the event is an outdoor event, strive to choose a date when weather conditions are usually pleasant.
   (c) Research what other events are going on and try to minimise conflicts within the community.

(d) Whatever happens, do not change the date midway through the planning stage.
(e) For outdoor events, select a backup date in case of bad weather.

B. Community Relationship

(a) Approach all community groups in a professional manner that will guarantee the organisation upholds a good image.
(b) Involve the organisation in community activities.
(c) Include all appropriate community organisations on the event guest list.
(d) Send out invitations that are creative and unusual so that people will remember the event.
(e) Always provide a contingency plan for potential problems that may affect the event and the invited guests.
(f) Send thank you notes to all offices that assisted with the event setup as well as to all involved in the event itself.
(g) If possible, provide all event participants with a remembrance of the event (e.g., certificates of participation, mementos, prizes, trophies, etc.).
(h) If the event is a long one, provide breaks or intermissions during the activity as well as the opportunity to obtain refreshments.

C. Computer Systems

1. Registration
   (a) Decide what registration information to input into the computer system.
   (b) A computer system used for registration will provide invaluable lists for the rest of the event by sorting the information. For example, lists based on demographics could be generated from a large sport festival that includes a marathon event and shorter distance races.
2. Event Support
   (a) A computing system can also be used for other aspects of the event, such as ticketing, accounting, and inventory.
   (b) Event information should be stored on a central hard drive and a backup external system to ensure the safety of records.
3. Results
   (a) Computing event results on the computer provides for consistency in computation and presentation.

4. Guidelines
   (a) If the organisation does not have access to a computer, consider leasing or borrowing one from a school/ university, private source, large company, computer store, library, state agency, etc.
   (b) Ensure that the programs/software will perform the tasks that need to be accomplished.
   (c) Remember that "garbage in is garbage out." The computer cannot distinguish between good and bad data.
   (d) If no one in the organisation is really familiar with computing systems, do not use one because it will only cause problems.
   (e) Run backup copies of all records on external drives, USB/ memories sticks, and have a backup computer in case of emergency.

5. Contracts
   (a) Determine if a formal contract is necessary or if a letter of agreement will be suitable.
   (b) It is possible to negotiate anything, but make sure all conditions agreed upon appear on the final contract.
   (c) Consult with a lawyer or office that knows about contracts to make sure the contract is legal and binding, and does not create liability concerns for the organisation.
   (d) If a contract is more appropriate, make sure it:
      (i) specifies all parties involved
      (ii) specifies the time, date, day, and location of the event
      (iii) contains duplicate copies
      (iv) provides a place for both parties to sign
      (v) specifies a time by which the contract needs to be signed and returned
      (vi) discusses any special considerations.

D. Financial Considerations

1. Budget and Resource Planning
   (a) For best results, appoint a budget coordinator to control the financial aspects of the event.
   (b) Strive to balance event costs with the estimated income of the event.
   (c) Evaluate every area of the budget and research costs as much as possible to determine cost estimates for each event item.
   (d) Create budget targets (both expenditure limits and income targets) early in the planning stage and inform all coordinators of these targets.

(e) Consider a short-term loan if cash flow is a problem in the planning stage.

2. Merchandising and Concessions

   (a) Independent concessionaires

      (i) request participation well in advance

      (ii) maintain contact during the planning stages to establish the needs of the concessionaire (electricity, tables, chairs, etc.)

      (iii) check inventory

      (iv) establish a commission (10–15%) to be collected daily

      (v) if food is involved, check with the local health authorities.

   (b) Using staff members to sell event merchandise

      (i) inventory all merchandise to be sold

      (ii) brief salespeople on duties and supply them with event information because they will be asked many questions

      (iii) assign a group of people to set up and take down each day

      (iv) keep a file of good and reliable salespeople.

   (c) Physical arrangements

      (i) place concessions in an area big enough to accommodate a large flow of traffic

      (ii) place concessions in a noticeable location that will not interfere with the event

      (iii) if the event is an outdoor one, consider a covered area for concessions

      (iv) if the event is an indoor one, utilise large rooms with more than one door or large hallways

      (v) provide storage for merchandise each night in a secured area; equipment needs will include: cash box, receipts, pens, tape, cord, markers, rubber bands, staples, hammer and nails, change aprons, appropriate change, etc.

      (vi) consult with the Fire authorities to insure that arrangements pass fire codes

      (vii) provide security for concessionaires and salespeople located on the periphery of the event or group vendors together.

   (d) Post-event financial report

      (i) include a complete report on gross sales and net profits in the final event report

      (ii) if selling merchandise for other people, return unsold merchandise and settle sales account.

3. Admissions
    (a) The organisation should not rely totally on admissions, but should have a reserve fund to pay participants and any staff.
    (b) The best method to secure admissions is to sell tickets in advance.
    (c) If selling advance tickets, implement a strong publicity campaign and an aggressive sales campaign.
    (d) The necessary added security to prohibit gate crashers needs to be considered when deciding whether or not to charge admission.
    (e) When determining the admission price, consider the event costs, the attendance estimate and the prices charged for similar events by other organisations.
4. On-Site Cost Obligations
    (a) Be aware of the cost of services (i.e., setup, custodial, security, etc.) as well as rental costs. These extra costs will all need to be added into facility costs.

E. Fundraising

1. Corporate Sponsorship
    (a) Strive to find corporations that have interests aligned with the event.
    (b) Choose corporations where it is possible to deal personally with the management.
    (c) Be well-prepared with a specific, detailed budget, and a full understanding of the event.
    (d) If other similar events occur throughout the year, consider selling sponsors to all events as a series.
    (e) It is easier to sell one sponsorship package than many individual tickets.
    (f) Begin sponsorship sales early.

F. Post-Event Evaluation

Only by evaluating can success be determined and a better plan developed for the next event.
1. Evaluation should not be overlooked or considered an unimportant step in the event plan.

2. Discuss and assess preparation; organisational structure; the event itself; feedback from spectators; press; participants; and staff.
3. Define possible solutions to problems for future activities or events.
4. Evaluate the projected audience (demographics) vs. the actual audience.
5. Discuss the methods of publicity used (include samples) and their effects on the event.
6. Solicit feedback from the different groups of people involved, either verbally or through a written document (i.e., survey, focus group, questionnaire, and interview).
7. Ask key personnel to write out "how to" reports on their individual assignments to be included in the event records.
8. Most importantly, compile all event information and evaluation information in an event file and retain for future event planning.

G. Human Resources

1. International Services
   (a) The committee may wish to liaison with language services (see Facilities and Support Services) to discuss interpreters and translators for each international delegation.
   (b) Provide a host/hostess for each international delegation who can acquaint all guests with the community and handle problems which may arise in registration, housing, etc. Hosts should be available throughout the event to handle questions and provide appropriate assistance.
2. Protocol
   (a) Protocol will involve familiarising the organisation with the customs, beliefs, manners, likes/dislikes, religion, etc. of all the event participants.
   (b) When all this information has been obtained, utilise it when planning seating at banquets, assigning housing, developing menus, etc. to eliminate embarrassing situations and hostilities.
3. Hospitality
   (a) If possible, for long events, arrange an area that will contain foreign newspapers and translated copies of event information.
   (b) Liaison with international groups within the community to provide a feeling of "home" for international delegates.
   (c) Provide special events that incorporate international themes.

4. Nerve Centre
   (a) Establish a base of operations at the event site where the event director can be reached at all times.
   (b) If the event is a large one, include other key personnel at the event headquarters (security, emergency services, etc.).
   (c) Link headquarters with all event areas through some form of communication (hand radios, telephone, mobile, and pager system).
   (d) One person at headquarters should be in charge of communication so that conflicting information will not be dispersed.
   (e) Periphery areas should channel all communications through headquarters so that key personnel can handle all problems quickly and efficiently with as little disturbance to the event as possible.
   (f) Emphasise to all personnel that the means of communication is only as effective as the people using it; therefore, be concise and to the point.
5. Personnel
   (a) Key personnel for the event will include all event committees.
   (b) The people appointed to key positions should be trusted to produce a successful event. They will include:
      (i) personnel with special skills
      (ii) personnel with previous event experience
      (iii) personnel with special interests.
   (c) Key personnel must link with the event director and be able to delegate responsibility to those working for them.
   (d) Committee coordinators must provide the event director with up-to-date reports of project status on a regular basis.
   (e) Committee coordinators should have all requests authorised by the event director or administrative staff.
6. Trained Volunteers (*see also I*)
   (a) Volunteers will provide the organisation with the many hands it needs to accomplish all the tasks necessary for a successful event.
   (b) Volunteers are only as effective as the training they have been given by the event's key personnel.
   (c) Although the importance of volunteers cannot be stressed enough, the essential tasks should be carried out by organisational personnel who have a higher degree of commitment to the event and whose presence can be guaranteed.
7. Public Relations

"As much assistance as possible should be generated from professionals in the media and community who are willing to serve as volunteers (e.g., local radio, TV and press staff, university public information staff as well as independent public relations firm's staff members, civic and cultural group leaders, etc.) to maintain a highly professional image for the event."

(a) Media relations

   (i) It is important to establish friendly relations with the media from the start of the event planning.

   (ii) Compile a list of media sources and database to establish the contact person for each source. If possible, find someone at each source that is sincerely interested in the event and will channel information to its proper destination.

   (iii) Give the media sources the information they need in order to best cover the event. Remember who, what, where, when, why, and how.
- be accurate
- be brief
- one page of information
- short sentences
- include name, date, place, time, sponsors, and highlights.

   (iv) Make sure you list names and telephone numbers of contact persons.

   (v) Keep it simple.

   (vi) All communications should be in writing.

   (vii) Submit releases in advance of deadlines:
- daily newspapers 1 week to 10 days
- weekly newspapers 2 to 3 weeks
- magazines 2 to 3 months
- radio 10 days to 2 weeks
- television 2 weeks.

   (viii) Appoint a contact person from the organisation who will act as media liaison. This ensures consistency of communications. This contact person should be easy to reach at all times.

   (ix) Invite all media to attend the opening day of the event at least 1 week in advance. Provide all those who accepted the invitation with a complimentary pass and a press kit. Arrange parking for camera crews, if necessary.

   (x) Consider "news availability" and establish an announced time and place for a representative of the organisation to meet with media.

   (xi) Provide flexibility for reporters to obtain a one-on-one interview that is important for radio and television news broadcasts.

   (xii) After the event, thank all the media sources that were helpful and provide them with follow-up information on the event.

(xiii) Maintain contact with the media so that they will be familiar with the organisation when the next activity is planned.

8. Event Promotions

   (a) Know the likes and dislikes, collective habits, interests, etc. of the expected audience to determine what direction the promotions campaign is going to take.

   (b) Promotions happen on two levels: mass media (advertising, media, and community relations) and word of mouth (individuals talking to other individuals).

   (c) Promoting on the individual level requires organisation, good coordination, dedicated volunteers, and creativity.

   (d) Cost effectiveness should be an objective of the promotion campaign. Promotion is not free, but it can be done inexpensively with forethought and creativity.

   (e) Seek commercial sponsorship to underwrite advertising costs.

   (f) Include the event in newsletters that are targeted at specific audiences.

   (g) Place the event on the calendar of local publications.

   (h) Display posters and fliers in prominent locations in high traffic areas. Include the name of the event, dates, times, and location.

   (i) Distribute brochures locally where the target audience will see them.

   (j) Secure billboards and bus signs to advertise the event.

   (k) Place advertisements for the event with all media sources.

   (l) Investigate media co-sponsors (radio, TV, Internet, and newspaper) for the event. Secure in-kind service sponsorship agreements.

   (m) Begin promotions campaign well in advance to ensure that printed materials will be completed in time for advance distribution.

   (n) Send press releases to media sources from the beginning of the planning stage until the event happens. Releases will be infrequent and general in the early stages, but as the event approaches, send special, and descriptive releases about the event.

   (o) Develop a promotions chart working backwards chronologically from the date of event.

9. Programmes

   (a) Programmes serve not only as an excellent source of information, but also as revenue sources and souvenirs.

   (b) Decide on the format of the programme

    (c) Informational content

    (d) Use of advertising

    (e) Presentation of information

    (f) Price

    (g) If using advertising in the programme, schedule ample time to solicit the advertisements and the copy from interested persons.

    (h) Include the information those attending the event will want to know as well as information that is important to the event itself (behaviour guidelines, location guide, schedule of events, etc.).

    (i) If selling programmes, decide on a price that will help defray programme costs but is not so prohibitive that people will not buy programmes.

    (j) Place programme sellers in prominent locations and inform them of the selling strategy.

    (k) Investigate potential print sponsors for in-kind sponsorship agreements.

10. Press Guide

    (a) The press guide will contain in-depth information about the event and the event participants that cannot be found in the programme (background information on the participants and key event personnel, home addresses of participants, telephone numbers for key personnel, etc.).

11. Media Centre

    (a) Establish one or more locations accessible to the event for the use of the media services.

    (b) These media centres should include chairs, tables, telephone lines, and typewriters, computers with Internet connection, copying machines, supplies, refreshments, etc. or easy access to the aforementioned items.

    (c) A separate location should be provided for individual interviews.

    (d) Security should be provided at each media centre to check press credentials and prohibit unprivileged access.

12. Celebrities

    (a) Provide each celebrity with a schedule of the event well in advance.

    (b) Obtain a list of needs from each celebrity at least 1 week in advance of the event, so that arrangements can be completed on time.

    (c) Compile a celebrity benefit package which might include; VIP credentials, reserved seat passes or access, information about special transportation and reserved parking, invitations to meals, receptions, etc.

    (d) Arrange a celebrity parking area and inform police or security of celebrity license numbers.

    (e) Assign a host to each celebrity to ensure that all needs are met.

    (f) Implement special security precautions, if necessary, for the protection of the celebrities.

    (g) Allow adequate time for celebrities to check equipment and to make special arrangements with technical services.

    (h) If inviting local celebrities to attend the event, be aware of the community social circles when deciding whom to invite. It may be necessary to seek information from community organisations and corporations.

13. Registration

    (a) Pre-event materials

      (i) If adequate advance work and communications are provided, it will ensure a smooth registration process.

      (ii) Initial communications with participants should include:
- confirmation of previous arrangements (date, location, and fees involved)
- information about the nature and intent of the event, information about other event participants, a signed contract (in duplicate), and a participant information sheet
- a cover letter welcoming the participant and explaining the enclosed information.

      (iii) Two weeks prior to the event, another mailing would include:
- information on housing, food, security, registration
- an event schedule
- a map of the event site
- information on parking
- any reimbursement information.

      (iv) Remain in constant contact with all participants and double-check the information received from them so that the majority of their needs will be anticipated.

      (v) For record keeping purposes, create a file for each participant with copies of all correspondence received.

      (vi) Refer to the Event Information Template for Internet content provided in Chapter 6.

    (b) One-stop service

      (i) The goal is for registration to be a quick, painless process for all participants.

      (ii) Have enough people to handle all registration stations plus a few extra people to fill in or run errands.

      (iii) Organise the registration procedure in a logical, linear fashion with many signs to inform participants of the procedure.

    (iv) If possible, conduct a practice registration session with all personnel to test the system and ensure that all involved understand their duties.

(c) Locator service

    (i)   During the registration process, ascertain from each participant where he or she will be staying (or double-check this information if it is already available) in order to develop a list for locating people in case of emergency.

(d) Event information

    (i) Upon registering, participants should receive another packet containing all the information they will need for the event.

    (ii) event badge or pass

    (iii) copies of event schedule

    (iv) map of event site

    (v) program book

    (vi) meal schedule and tickets

    (vii) special information about the site

    (viii) complimentary tickets (if applicable)

    (ix) event agenda.

H. Schedule

1. Time Span

(a) When planning an event for the first time, one of the most common errors is to start planning too late.

(b) Use the method of backward planning: start with the event day and plan backwards to determine the important deadlines that need to be met.

(c) Post deadlines and emphasise the importance of meeting these deadlines.

(d) Each committee should devise its own timetable for accomplishing its goals and submit it to the event director for approval.

(e) As the event approaches, timetables should become more and more specific until event day, when timetables might be broken down into units of minutes and seconds, if necessary.

(f) During the event, keep a time log that can be used as a pattern for next year's event.

(g) In evaluating the event, discuss timetables and make necessary changes where predicted times did not match with actual time.

(h) If the event should fall behind schedule, inform all participants who will be affected and attempt to make adjustments to return to schedule (by shortening performances, warm-up periods, introductions, etc.).

2. Event Space
   (a) Make reservations as early as possible. Some sites must be reserved at least 1 year in advance.
   (b) Make reservations through the proper office and complete any required paperwork as fully as possible.
   (c) Reservations should be made by the organisation's officers.
   (d) Discuss payment for event site (if applicable) when making the reservation.
   (e) Discuss policies that must be adhered to, which would include facility as well as local policies, when making the reservation.
   (f) Comply with any contractual agreements entered into with the facility management.
   (g) Notification of cancellation of the event should be made at least 2 weeks prior to the scheduled date of the event.

3. Setup
   (a) It may be necessary to measure the event site to determine exactly what will fit on the site and the best configuration of the equipment.
   (b) The setup coordinator should have a timetable for setup and designated responsibilities for each crew member.
   (c) Provide for traffic patterns that do not overlap excessively to avoid spectator traffic interfering with staff or participant traffic.
   (d) If there are areas set aside for certain purposes, mark these areas clearly.
   (e) If possible, anticipate all equipment necessary so that there will be no last minute emergencies.
   (f) When setting up, make sure that equipment works and that the workers who will be running the equipment know how to do it properly and quickly.
   (g) Take photographs or compile drawings of the setup so that next year there will be plans to refer to.
   (h) At the end of the event, evaluate the setup and note any changes or improvements that should be considered.

4. Restoration
   (a) If possible, have the same people who set up to perform the breakdown.
   (b) The breakdown coordinator should have a timetable for breakdown and designated responsibilities for each crew member.

(c) If equipment was borrowed or rented from various agencies, know when and where to return it. Assign the responsibility of returning equipment to crew members. Strive to return equipment as promptly as possible and obtain a receipt for the event records.

(d) If items belong to the organisation and are reusable, compile a list of where items are stored.

(e) Provide plenty of trash cans and bags.

(f) Assist participants with any equipment or needs they may have.

(g) If a contract for use of the site has been signed, be sure to comply with all the stipulations. Otherwise, strive to return the site to its original condition.

(h) A tour of the site with the site owner or maintenance supervisor is necessary before leaving the site to discuss any possible damages.

I. Volunteers

1. Assign one person the job of compiling the volunteer needs for each coordinator, recruiting the volunteers and assigning them to a coordinator or have coordinators recruit their own volunteers.

2. Create a volunteer database.

3. Notify all volunteers in writing what their duties are and where and when to report.

4. Indicate what special privileges their volunteer status entitles them to.

5. Indicate whom volunteers are to report to, who will be reporting to them and whom they will be working with.

6. Keep in constant communication with all volunteer staff throughout the planning of the event and the event itself. Communication is "essential to keep people motivated, involved and committed, in addition to keeping abreast of information. So often those in the firing line are ill-informed."

7. If special training is required of the volunteers, do it at least 1 week in advance of the event.

8. Brief volunteers of their duties on the day of the event and answer any last-minute questions they may have.

9. Do not limit the volunteer pool – use all community members who may be interested:

   (a) Organisations

      (i) organisations will often volunteer as a group to work one specific area of the event

      (ii) this is a favourable situation because the people know one another and may often do their own scheduling

      (iii) establish a contact person within each organisation

      (iv) it may be useful to "contract" the organisation for specific duties individual.

  (b) Recruit through word of mouth, posters, fliers, etc.

  (c) Attempt to reach a large geographic area.

  (d) Use individuals as supplementary volunteers for groups in case specialists do not show up at the event.

  (e) Recruit specific people for specialised duties such as off-duty police for security, a hand radio club for communications, and media specialists to assist with promotions.

  (f) It may be useful to contract with the specialists for specific duties.

10. Thank all volunteers for their services at the close of the event (verbally, in writing, with a banquet or get-together, with a token of appreciation).

11. Request that coordinators evaluate volunteers in order to develop a core group who will work the event from year to year.

12. Solicit feedback from volunteers concerning event improvements.

Facilities and Support Services

J. Communications

A network linking all aspects of the event is critical to the flow of internal and external information.

1. Telecommunication Services
   (a) Provide telephone/mobile/internet service both in the planning stages of the event and during the event.
   (b) Do not rely solely on wireless service and have at least one dedicated land line.
   (c) The more available, the better, especially where the media is concerned.
   (d) In the planning stages, it is suggested to have a dedicated website to handle queries and at least one line hooked up to an answering machine so that participants, media advertisers, staff, and anyone else related to the event can leave messages at any time.
   (e) For a large event, it may be necessary to hire people whose sole responsibility is answering the phone, emails, and routing queries to the proper destination.
   (f) If these operators are given the information necessary to answer the common questions people have, the public will be pleased with the efficient service and key personnel will have time for more important matters.
   (g) For an extensive telephone system, publish a listing of important numbers.
   (h) Establish a message centre where people can obtain their messages.
2. Radio Network
   (a) For best results, establish a separate committee for the radio operators.
   (b) Strive to find a special interest group in the community that will be willing to work the event.
   (c) After explaining event needs, this group will govern themselves well.
   (d) Radio operators can provide emergency radio support as well as regular transmissions.
3. Data
   (a) If a majority of the event information is on-line or on a computer, the ability to send data from one location to another will be essential. This will require the installation of computer telephone lines and wireless devices.

K. Equipment

1. Determine all the equipment that will be needed for the event.
2. Check the event site to validate what equipment is already available and what will need to be obtained from outside sources.
3. A secure storage area close to the event site should be available for equipment storage. Best results are obtained by assigning a small group of people to this area to implement a check-in and check-out system. This will familiarise the workers with the equipment and the people handling it.
4. If equipment needs to be reserved, rented or purchased, begin early so that it will be available and arrive on time. Check with other groups that put on events to see what equipment they use and where they obtain it.
5. Acquire adequate vehicles and assign many people to help move equipment. Develop a detailed schedule for setup, breakdown, and daily moves.
6. Maintain an inventory of all equipment and its condition.
7. At the close of the event, see that all equipment is returned to its owners or properly stored.
8. Record what equipment worked well and jot down any ideas for changes or improvements.

L. Facilities

1. Event Venue Sites
   (a) In choosing event sites, ensure that the site chosen is appropriate for the event that is going to take place.
   (b) Coordinate with those working on equipment and construction to ensure that the site will be ready for the event.
   (c) Determine the staffing needs for each site and relay this information to the appropriate personnel.
   (d) See that the site is maintained in good condition throughout the event.
   (e) Comply with all existing policies and regulations.
   (f) Communicate with event headquarters any changes in schedule so that the information will be disseminated to the appropriate services.
2. Service Support Facilities
   (a) All venues should include service support areas such as restrooms, storage space, parking, lost and found, etc.

(b) Estimate how many people will be attending the event and ensure that each venue meets the expected minimum and maximum seating capacities.

(c) Service support facilities should be well-marked.

3. Special Support Facilities

(a) Special support facilities include those areas unique to the event and may include workrooms, locker rooms, training rooms, meeting rooms, dressing rooms, VIP lounges, etc. It will be necessary to decide what support areas will be needed before looking for a site.

(b) Special support facilities should also be well-marked, with special attention paid to access.

4. Special Sites

(a) If the event involves a special site that is not readily available in the community, planning should begin very early because special construction may be needed.

(b) Speak with other groups that have sponsored the event to determine how they planned for the special site.

(c) Speak to those who will use the special site for guidance on construction.

5. On-Site Facility Control

(a) "Careless issue of credentials can result in significant losses of ticket revenue."

(b) A system of credentials and passes will need to be implemented to control facility access.

(c) Create distinct passes and be sure those workers checking credentials are aware of the privileges and restrictions associated with each pass.

(d) Inform those persons who have been issued credentials of the privileges associated with the credential. This will aid in avoiding embarrassment and disappointment.

(e) Credentials should be cancelled when participants leave to ensure that unauthorised persons will not obtain special privileges.

(f) On-site security should also be ample enough to eliminate or minimise gate crashing. Allowing gate crashers easy access to the event is not fair to those who bought tickets and may cause security problems in the long run in addition to loss of ticket revenue.

6. Site Liaison

(a) There needs to be one person responsible for coordinating the event at each site. Each site liaison should be in communication with the event headquarters to discuss progress and problems.

7. Backup Sites
   (a) If it is possible, establish a backup site for the event. Do so well in advance of the event so that reservation will not be difficult.
   (b) Having a backup site necessitates planning the event twice, if the use of the backup site is going to be a success. All those involved with the event need to know their responsibilities at either site and must be able to perform them equally well in both locations.
   (c) If setup is involved, it will have to be done in both locations to ensure that the event starts on time.
   (d) If conditions necessitate the use of the backup site, establish a time and place to make this announcement so that everyone involved with the event will receive the same information at the same time.
8. Facility Restoration (see L4)

M. Food Service

1. Capacity/Time Requirements
   (a) The food service requirements will vary greatly depending on the size and focus of the event.
   (b) If an alcohol permit needs to be obtained, begin the process well in advance of the event with the appropriate state and local authorities. It will also be necessary to consult security policies to ensure compliance.
   (c) The majority of food service specialists require a meal figure at least 48 hours in advance and some may require it 3 to 5 days prior to the event. A minimum number of orders are also required.
   (d) Attempt to determine how many participants will be requiring food service through advance correspondence.
   (e) It is better to order too much food than too little. In most circumstances, the extra food will be consumed by staff personnel.
   (f) If possible, begin the food service requirements at the same time the facility reservation is made.
   (g) Even though professional food service may cost a little more, in the long run it is the most convenient method to use.
   (h) Provide food service in an appropriate area (sanitary with excellent ventilation).
2. Menu
   (a) Strive to accurately predict special dietary requirements (diabetic, sodium free, vegetarian, and kosher) through

advance correspondence with event participants and convey this information to the food service personnel.

(b) Establish a menu of well-balanced meals that meet a wide variety of nutritional needs with a varied selection of dishes to accommodate different tastes.

(c) If many events are occurring at different times throughout the day, provide a box lunch option for event participants.

3. Refreshments/Water on Site

(a) If housing many people, provide food service accessible to the housing sites for a minimum of breakfast and a night snack and provide lunch and dinner at the event site.

(b) Snacks should be available at the housing site and also on the event site in a special "participant only" area.

(c) Refreshments should also be provided at the event headquarters, medical areas, media centre, staff rest area, and other all-day areas.

(d) Water and other beverages should be available in unlimited supply at the same locations listed above.

4. Corporate Donations

(a) Request donations of beverages (soda, wine for a banquet, and coffee), snacks and other popular food items from area merchants and companies.

N. Geographic Relationship between Event Sites

1. For multi-site events, it is important to optimise the distance between sites. If the sites are too close, they may interfere with each other (e.g., stages at a music festival). Yet, sites that are too far apart may discourage spectators and participants from enjoying the entire event and may require the added expense of transportation between sites and additional security.

O. Housing

1. VIP Housing

(a) When housing VIPs, special security measures will need to be taken to ensure that only those people authorised to have contact with the VIPs are allowed access.

(b) Special care should be taken to provide the best housing facilities for VIPs and to see that all their needs are met.

2. Officials

(a) Due to the nature of the job, it is wise to also provide officials with a high degree of security.

(b) It may be necessary to provide an escort for officials from the housing site to the event site and back.

3. Participants
   (a) It is suggested that people of similar interest, teams, sports, age, etc. be housed together.
4. Families
   (a) Provide some housing for those participants travelling with family. It would be wise to group the family housing together, especially if small children are involved, so as not to disturb the other participants.
5. Media
   (a) Often, the organisation must pay for media services housing. Realising it is important to treat the media well, strive to find adequate housing close to the event site for a reasonable price.
6. General Housing Guidelines
   (a) House similar groups together.
   (b) Decide on how many individuals per room and then assign as many rooms as possible in advance.
   (c) Welcome all participants, inform them of the housing guidelines and answer any questions they may have.
   (d) Staff each housing site from early morning until after the last event is over. Staff members should be on hand to assist participants, check credentials, answer the telephone, and relay messages.
   (e) Security should be available night and day both within the housing site and patrolling between sites.
   (f) Telephones should be available in all housing sites for both incoming and outgoing calls.
   (g) Expect the unexpected and use good judgment in placing the extra people who may show up.
   (h) Walk through the housing site and determine where directional and informational signs should be placed.
   (i) It may be necessary to check with the health, sanitation, and fire authorities to ensure that housing meets local standards and codes.
7. General Condition
   (a) Look for housing with modest, comfortable rooms, and a quiet atmosphere.
   (b) If the event is a lengthy one, provisions should be made for cleaning the rooms or cleaning supplies should be made available if a cleaning staff would present security risks.
   (c) Common areas should be cleaned daily.
   (d) A system of trash collection and removal is essential. This may include the availability of large trash containers or bags to all participants in order to keep rooms trash free.

(e) If large trash bags are distributed to each room prior to the end of the event with instructions requesting that all trash be placed in the bag and left in a specified location, this will aid in the general clean-up when the event is over.

8. Geographic Location
   (a) The housing site should be close enough to the event site that walking to the site is a viable option, yet not so close that participants are not able to obtain any privacy.
   (b) No matter how close housing is to the event site, it is recommended that a vehicle be on hand for emergencies or for the elderly or disabled.

9. Negotiating with the Site Owner
   (a) Establish a rapport with the housing owner.
   (b) Discuss all housing policies, including cost, form of payment, liability coverage, security and insurance, use of alcohol, late evening parties, off-limit areas, bedding, clean-up responsibilities. These policies may be included in a contract with the housing management.
   (c) When the event is over, make an appointment to walk through the site with the owner to discuss possible damages.

P. Signage/Decorations

1. Requests from each task force detailed information on signage needs (i.e., content, quantity, date needed, etc.).
2. Attempt to standardise signs in size, colour and style and coordinate the signs with any decorations.
3. If decorations are required or desired, solicit help from those in the community with artistic talents.
4. Ensure that all decorations are tastefully done and placed in locations that will not interfere with the event, but will add to the total effect of the event.

Q. Language Services

1. Availability of Interpreter
   (a) If the event involves groups of different nationalities or individuals who are hearing impaired, interpreters/signers should be made available so that no person involved with the event is inconvenienced in any way because of an inability to communicate.

(b) It is wise to anticipate needs in this area so that services can be secured well in advance of the event.

(c) If the materials to be interpreted are going to be available in advance, provide the interpreter/signer with the materials so that there will be ample opportunity to prepare.

(d) Use all multi-lingual persons at the disposal of the organisation. These would include international students and professors, language students and professors, and community members.

2. Capabilities to Translate Materials

(a) All information that needs to be translated should be prepared well in advance so that the work will be completed in time to mail the information out.

(b) Capable translators should be utilised so that the intent of the information is not lost in the translation.

R. Maintenance/Construction/Capital Improvements

1. Early in the planning stages, determine the construction/improvements that need to be made so that ample time will be provided to complete these projects.

(a) If work is to be handled by an outside organisation, provide a work order that specifies all the work to be done.

(b) If construction is going to be handled by an outsider contractor, obtain prices from several different sources.

(c) Review the progress of the construction/improvements on a regular basis and see that the time schedule is adhered to as closely as possible. If the major projects are finished well in advance of the event date, last minute changes, and requests can be handled efficiently.

S. Medical

"Everyone must know their responsibility during an injury situation."

1. Site Support

(a) Become familiar with the healthcare systems available in the community.

(b) Provide a clearly marked first aid area with qualified individuals (e.g., nurses, paramedics, and Red Cross certified persons) available to handle minor problems.

(c) Rely on professionals for major medical care.

      (d) Implement an accident reporting system indicating the nature of the injury and the action taken for accountability purposes.

2. Emergency Medical Service (EMS)

      (a) Decide if it is necessary to have an EMS team at the event.

      (b) If so, determine where they will be stationed so that there will be no traffic obstacles to contend with.

      (c) If not, make sure that the number is publicised to all workers and posted on all phones and communication devices.

      (d) Implement a communication system so that messages are relayed rapidly and accurately to event headquarters where a member of the team is stationed or a key administrator is available to contact the EMS team.

3. Medical Transportation

      (a) Be sure to have enough transportation available to handle a number of emergencies. This may mean having several emergency vehicles on site and several more on call.

      (b) If life flight is available in the community, it would be reasonable to contact this service about the event and establish a crisis plan for life-threatening emergencies.

4. Hospital Liaison

      (a) Establish a working rapport with the area hospitals and keep them informed about the event (nature of the event, number of people involved, dates, etc.).

5. Professional Staff

      (a) Arrange a roster of hospitals and doctors available to respond to emergency medical situations.

      (b) Attempt to have at least one doctor on the event site at all times.

T. Safety and Security

1. Internal Communications

      (a) Communication must follow the chain-of-command in each security force so that workers will not be overstepping their duties.

      (b) Provide for a rapid means of communication between periphery forces, the security force supervisors, and the event director. This will most likely involve establishing a command post (see T10).

      (c) Communication will involve a walkie-talkie, radio or pager system, or a combination of systems.

      (d) Consider the use of earphones for loud events.

(e) Communications should be clear and concise and should not include profanity or derogatory comments.

(f) Develop a code system to communicate critical information concerning situations such as fire, bomb threat, weather, medical emergency, engineering emergency, etc.

2. Police

(a) Contact the police department early in the planning stages of the event and acquaint them with the goals of the event.

(b) Use the police department to control traffic coming to and leaving the event.

(c) If possible, use off-duty police in uniform at the event to add an atmosphere of authority and control.

(d) Use police to escort any personnel who may be in danger from the crowd (VIPs, officials, performers, etc.).

(e) The number of police needed will be determined by the nature of the event and the anticipated behaviour of the spectators.

(f) The event security force will inform the organisation of how many security officers will be needed at the event.

(g) Approximately one police officer per 1,000 spectators will be required.

(h) Do not neglect to express gratitude for the services of the police when the event is concluded.

3. Fire

(a) Develop a good relationship with the Fire Marshal as he/she had the power to stop your event.

(b) Be sure to comply with all fire codes and have the event sites inspected before the start of the event.

(c) Develop a reporting system for fires and inform all workers of the system in their training.

(d) Establish communication with the local fire departments and link with them throughout the event so that at least one department is available to service the event at all times. Inform all workers of the location of on-site fire-fighting equipment and instruct them on how to use it properly.

4. Transportation

(a) Ensure that security and safety vehicles are available to handle both emergencies and rule violators.

(b) Provide an unobstructed parking area for all safety and security vehicles.

5. Traffic

(a) Determine the geographic service area in which the event will impact on and provide traffic control throughout that service area.

      (b) Let the police control incoming and outgoing traffic.

      (c) Provide plans for servicing all the possible traffic that will attend the event (car, bus, boat, bicycle, helicopter, etc.).

6. Crowd Control

"Good crowd control consists of much preventive planning and organisation long before problems arise."

      (a) Establish an event security staff and distinguish these people with some form of identification (i.e., jackets, T-shirts, hats, arm bands, vests, etc.).

      (b) Inform each worker responsible for crowd control of his/her duties, the area each person is responsible for and who each worker reports to.

      (c) Make all efforts to start the event on time.

      (d) Provide continual surveillance on crowd convenience facilities (restrooms, concessions, drinking fountains, and aisles) as people become irritated when forced to wait in line.

      (e) Encourage people to keep moving and not to loiter in areas not related to the event.

      (f) Do not allow spectators into reserved areas.

      (g) Instruct security staff to be constantly moving through the patrol area or supervising from above.

      (h) Define a plan of action for quietly intercepting individuals or groups causing a disturbance and removing them if necessary.

      (i) If the individual or group becomes abusive, threatening or physical, do not hesitate to call the nearest police officer to handle the problem.

      (j) Make behaviour expectations known through advertising, the event program, announcements, and visible postings.

      (k) Encourage patrons to report threatening and dangerous situations.

      (l) Avoid general admission ticketing and seating whenever possible.

      (m) Develop an emergency evacuation plan.

      (n) If alcohol is allowed at the event, special attention will be needed. If it is not allowed, establish policies for prohibiting its use.

      (o) Ensure that the public address system works and that the volume and clarity are adequate.

      (p) Do not turn the lights off completely.

      (q) Do not exceed the facility seating capacity.

      (r) Devise a plan to prevent intrusion into the event:

          (i) soft plan: appeal to the better judgment of individuals to not invade the event

   (ii) hard plan: show that force will be used to prevent individuals from invading the event.
   (s) Before the end of the event, position security to facilitate the flow of traffic as it leaves. Position security personnel both in front of and behind the crowd.
   (t) Provide surveillance until all spectators have left the premises.
7. Parking
   (a) Use off-duty police or parking staff to regulate the flow of traffic in the parking areas before and after the event. Identify the parking staff by brightly coloured vests, hats, flashlights, etc.
   (b) Do not mix vehicles in the parking areas. Provide separate areas for buses, RVs, automobiles, etc.
   (c) Provide adequate signage to assist in regulating traffic flow and delineate off-limit parking areas.
   (d) Provide unblocked parking areas and routes for emergency vehicles.
   (e) Contract with a wrecker crew in advance of the event and use them during the event to tow parking violators.
   (f) If necessary, devise a system of parking passes to be used at each event site.
8. Emergency Action Plan
   (a) Define any possible emergencies that could occur during the event.
   (b) Devise an action plan to handle each emergency.
   (c) Educate all workers on the implementation of the plan.
   (d) Practice the plan on a regular basis so that the responsibilities will become familiar to all involved in the plan.
   (e) Constantly evaluate the plan in light of the type of event, those involved, changes in layout, etc.
9. Lost and Found
   (a) Establish one area as lost and found and announce the location verbally and/or in the event program book. Provide signage indicating the lost and found area.
   (b) Date and tag items turned into lost and found and develop policies on the fate of the item if it is not claimed within 30 days.
   (c) For a lost person, designate an out-of-the-way area as the meeting place for those groups which have become separated.
10. Command Post
   (a) Establish and maintain a command post for the duration of the event that can handle all communications related to EMS, fire, and security.

      (b) An officer from each special force working at the event should be stationed in the command post or available at all times to handle problems and coordinate with the other forces.

      (c) One of the people in the command post should be assigned the task of media liaison so that if an emergency does arise, those directly involved can deal with the emergency and the liaison can provide the media with accurate, timely information.

11. Credentials

      (a) Decide who will be allowed access to the different areas of the event site.

      (b) Develop a credential system that allows access to different areas.

      (c) Inform individuals what privileges are inherent with their specific credentials.

      (d) Strictly enforce the credential plan to eliminate any breaches in security and provide peace of mind for all involved with the event.

12. Interagency Communication

      (a) If possible, assign separate tasks to the different special forces involved in the event. This will aid in preventing agency rivalries.

      (b) If interagency communication is necessary, this communication should occur in the command post and then be transmitted back through the proper chain of command.

13. VIP Security

      (a) When VIPs are involved in the event, a balance will need to be reached between visibility and security.

      (b) Be very open and inform the VIP of the event security guidelines at the outset.

U. Transportation

1. For an event that will involve people from many distant locations, establish credit or a discount with a travel agency or airline.

2. Make certain what travel arrangements have been made by all participants or offer to make arrangements for them.

3. As information is received, develop a transportation chart that contains all the pertinent information on each participant.

4. If using volunteers as drivers, recruit friendly, courteous people who know the area and own reliable vehicles.

5. Recruit backup drivers for missed, delayed flights, buses, etc.

6. Check with the local automobile dealers for donations of vans for a shuttle service.
7. Coordinate with the local transit authority to provide adequate transportation of the public to the event.
8. On-site transportation
   (a) Depending on the size of the event, a variety of transportation needs, including golf carts, cars and vans, and buses, may be required.
      (i) golf carts
      (ii) convenient for moving supplies and equipment
      (iii) anyone can drive
      (iv) cover short distances quickly
      (v) all-terrain (for most purposes) or people movers.
   (b) Cars and vans
      (i) maintain an inventory of vehicles
      (ii) arrange for fuelling and service of vehicles
      (iii) arrange for appropriate licensing and insurance for all vehicles
      (iv) arrange for parking and storage of vehicles
      (v) if vehicles are assigned to specific individuals, issue appropriate parking permits and instructions concerning the return of the vehicle
      (vi) assign experienced and dedicated drivers to VIPs and other important persons involved in the event
      (vii) establish a schedule if a shuttle service is being provided between sites and/or housing sites and circulate this schedule to all users.
   (c) Buses
      (i) for large events, buses can be used for airport transportation, intra-venue transportation and transportation to "all participant" events
      (ii) devise a schedule to meet the needs of participants and circulate to all users
      (iii) control the use of buses through a credential checking system
      (iv) use properly licensed drivers and equip long-trip buses with radios
      (v) long distance buses should be suitable for long-term riding
      (vi) establish a communication post at the event headquarters for the bus service.
   (d) No matter what form of transportation is being used, make sure all are in excellent condition prior to the event.
   (e) Determine the time between event sites or posts to provide a ballpark idea to participants and personnel.

9. Weather
   (a) Climatic data
       (i) During the event, keep in contact with the National Weather Service to be aware of any special weather conditions not only in the event area, but also in areas that might affect participants and/or spectators.
       (ii) Inclement weather plan.
       (iii) The development of an inclement weather plan should take place well before the event because it may involve reserving alternative sites or special equipment.
       (iv) If the inclement weather plan is going to go into effect, establish policies for announcement of the plan so that all those affected can be informed at the same time and will receive the same information.
       (v) If it has been announced that the inclement weather plan is in effect, stick with that plan and do not change in midstream.
   (b) Shade and shelter
       (i) Shade and shelter should be provided for both the participants and spectators to avoid excess exposure to the elements. This may be one of the considerations when selecting a site.
       (ii) Cover all electrical equipment with plastic to prevent moisture damage. If moisture cannot be avoided, do not continue the event for safety reasons.
   (c) Weather warning/watch plan
       (i) Devise a plan to inform key personnel of possible changes in the weather. The plan may involve coded messages over the public address system or special radio codes.
       (ii) If weather conditions continue to worsen, it may be necessary to inform spectators so that those who desire to leave may do so. The announcement should be made calmly and clearly to avoid panic.
       (iii) If conditions are extremely severe, it will be necessary to implement contingency plans for the safety of all involved until the weather conditions improve.
       (iv) Safety plans should be developed well in advance and all workers should know their responsibilities if the plan is implemented. It may be necessary to review or practice emergency plans before the event to clarify any questions or errors.

CHAPTER 12

Special Events
and Services

V. Awards

1. In conjunction with the event director, determine the number and kind of awards to be presented.
2. Well in advance of the event; shop around for the best price.
3. Have awards properly prepared.
4. Request delivery of the awards in advance of the event so that the award preparation can be checked for accuracy and number.
5. Provide secure storage for the awards until the event.
6. If awards are going to be displayed in advance or during the event, provide proper security.
7. Orchestrate and carry out an awards presentation.
   (a) Furnish a text for the presenter or announcer.
   (b) Select music for the presentation.
   (c) Select VIP and backup presenters.
   (d) Provide a seating area for the presenters.
8. Choose an appropriate area for the awards ceremony and ensure that those receiving the awards (and NOT the presenter) are the centres of attention.

W. Ceremonies

1. Opening Ceremony
   "The Opening Ceremony ... is an event of major significance and should be planned and promoted to be a rewarding experience for the spectators and, more importantly, [those] participating in the [event]. This is a high point in their participation ... and should be made memorable."
   (a) It is recommended that a small core of dedicated persons work on all aspects of this event. Since everything happens at once, and only once, there must be sufficient people with the know-how to take over immediately in case of emergency.
   (b) Secure a site of large enough proportions to accommodate the ceremony.
   (c) Recruit local talent to take part in the opening ceremony in ways deemed appropriate to the program.
   (d) Conduct a dress rehearsal and other rehearsals as required.
   (e) Liaison with other committees (signage, publicity, security, parking, housing, transportation, etc.) and discuss requirements for the opening ceremony.
   (f) Consider the needs of those participating in the ceremony.

Participants may spend a long period of time waiting in the staging area and may require food, beverages, and access to restroom facilities.

2. Closing Ceremony
   (a) Like the opening ceremony, the closing ceremony is also a special event for the participants and spectators and should represent a sense of accomplishment and fulfilment.
   (b) The closing ceremony is the culmination of a "professional experience ... that people will want to buy again."
   (c) The closing ceremony should continue the event theme, but need not duplicate the extravagance of the opening ceremony, especially when many of those people involved with the event will be exhausted.

X. Clinic

1. Recruit clinicians who are experts in their fields.
2. Strive to provide a written guide of the key points that will be discussed in the clinic to all participants so they will not have to frantically take notes.
3. Attempt to register all participants in advance so the clinicians will know how many people to prepare for.
4. Provide all special equipment and secure special technicians.
5. Follow the planning process outlined in this checklist.

Y. Hospitality

"Hospitality begins with the first communication with participants and continues throughout the event until the last participant is homeward bound."

1. Welcome program
   (a) A warm welcome to all participants will set the tone for the event.
   (b) Assign workers to assist participants with luggage and answer any questions.
   (c) Provide all participants with a welcome packet that may include toiletries, snacks and a memento of the event.
   (d) If many groups are involved, assign a host/hostess to each group to coordinate their activities and see that questions and problems are handled promptly.
   (e) Organise either a formal or an informal get-together to officially welcome all participants and give them a chance to get acquainted.

2. VIP hospitality (see also Administrative Services)
3. Contact the VIP to confirm the arrival time and mode of transportation.
4. Ensure that all special needs have been taken care of.
5. Reserve a vehicle for VIP transportation.
6. Arrange a timetable for the VIP and send a copy accompanied by other pertinent event information (programme book, housing arrangements, etc.).
7. Arrange for reserved parking and establish the route the VIP will take to the event.
8. Consult with security and parking concerning any special arrangements.

Z. Special Events

1. Recreational Opportunities
   (a) If a recreational facility needs to be reserved, contact local department.
   (b) Know what equipment must be provided by the organisation.
   (c) Comply with all policies and regulations.
   (d) Follow the planning process outlined in this checklist.
2. Dances (Social Events)
   (a) Comply with all policies and procedures
   (b) Complete a dance agreement and discuss with the appropriate authorities.
   (c) Follow the planning process outlined in this checklist.
   (d) All arrangements must be finalised no later than 2 weeks prior to the event.
3. Victory Banquet
   (a) Special consideration should be given to reservations, food service, parking, and general space requirements.
   (b) Orientation should be given to those who will be speaking at the event.
   (c) Dress guidelines should be provided to all participants, especially any award recipients.
   (d) Provide accurate invitations and programs.
   (e) If the media will be involved, make all necessary arrangements to accommodate them.
4. Demonstrations
   (a) Provide a wide variety of demonstrators who are all qualified in their field.
   (b) Provide adequate work space and materials for each demonstrator.

(c) Depending on the type of demonstration, if merchandise is involved, it will be more convenient to sell it in an area separate from the demonstration and staffed by organisation members.

(d) Provide space for many people to view the demonstration.

(e) Following the planning process outlined in this checklist.

5. Entertainment

(a) Entertainment can be provided in a variety of ways: on-stage performers; rovers (clowns, cartoon characters); photo and autograph booths; movies; games (carnival, video, arcade, quiet, and active).

(b) Safety and security should be a top priority if entertainers and spectators will be mingling.

(c) Request all special equipment and secure special technicians.

(d) Follow the planning process outlined in this checklist.

6. Exhibitions

(a) Discuss logistical concerns such as layout, electricity, etc. with all participants.

(b) Request all special equipment and secure special technicians.

(c) Strive to attract a cross-section of the population to the exhibition through a variety of publicity campaigns.

(d) Follow the planning process outlined in this checklist.

Index

Administrative services for events
  Date Selection 205–206
  Event Director 204
  Office Facilities 205
  Policy Development 204
  Site Selection 205
  Staff 204
  Table of Organisation 205
Affective processing 34, 50, 92, 95, 112,
    115, 119, 145
Affective outcomes 121
Allegiance
  Inputs 170–171
  Outcomes 174–179
    Figure of 179
  Processing 52, 171–174
    Figure of 169, 173
    Sequence 173
  Sport Marketing Action 179–183
    Loyalty Lifecycle 180–181
  Stage 47–48, 168–170
Association network
  Description of 37–38
  Sport Fan Network 37, 120, 128, 139,
    147, 161
Attachment 140
  Inputs 142–145
  Outcomes 149–154
  Processing 46, 51–52, 145–149
    Figure of 141
    Sequence 173
  Sport Marketing Action 154–155
    Marketing Action Bonding 155–161
  Stage 47, 138–142
Attitudinal Processing 34, 40, 48–49, 92,
    119, 140, 148, 171

See also Affective Processing,
    Cognitive Processing, and
    Behavioural Processing
Attitude formation and change 48–49,
    96, 122, 141–142, 146, 149–152, 176
Attraction
  Inputs 112–114
    Table of 119
  Processing 45, 51, 114–122
    Figure of 111, 114
  Outcomes 119–123
  Sport Marketing Action 123–130
    Marketing Action Levers 124–127
  Stage 47, 110–111
  Tools to Measure Attraction 23–25,
    124–127
Awards 238
Awareness
  Inputs 90–92
  Outcomes 95–97
  Processes 92–95
  Processing 45, 50–51, 95–97
    Figure of 92
  Sport Marketing Action 97–100
    Life-Cycle Positioning 98–100
    Table of 100
    Strategies 98
    to Adolescents 102
    to Adults 102
    to Children 100–102
  Stage 46–47, 51, 88–89
Behavioural engagement 49–53, 96,
    115, 121–122, 142, 149, 153–154,
    169–170, 174, 177, 188, 190–191
Behavioural processing 34–50–51, 92,
    94–96, 112, 115, 119–120, 145

Behavioural Outcomes 39–41, 48, 50–51, 95, 121, 153, 174
Camaraderie 143–144, 156, 170, 182
Cause 143–144, 156, 170, 182
Cause-Related Bonding 156–157, 182
Ceremonies
  Closing 239
  Opening 238–239
Charity Inputs 118–119, 127
Clinic 239
Coalescence 172–174
  Figure of 173
Cognitive-Affective Processing 51–52, 115, 146, 148
Cognitive Complexity 121, 146–147, 150, 175
Cognitive Processing 34, 50–51, 92, 94–95, 112, 115, 119, 145, 176
Communication Bonding 159, 182
Commitment 175–176, 182–183
Community Relationship 206
Competency 143–144, 156, 170
Computer Systems for Events
  Event Support 206
  Guidelines 207
  Registration 207
  Results 206
Constraints 102, 188, 191
  Description of 188–189
  Figure of 190
  Leisure, Table of 193
  Marketing barriers 194
  Perceived 192–193
  Sport Marketing Action 194–198
  Within PCM 188–189
Consumer Behaviour, study of 5–6
Contracts for Events 207
Corporate Social Responsibility 127–128, 156
Customise Bonding 155, 157, 182, 196
Decision-Making 30
  See also Sport Decision-Making Sequence
Drive State 18
Durability
  Persistence 175
  Resistance 175–176
Engagement 41, 48–53
  Figure of 49

See also Behavioural & Psychological Engagement; Internal Processing
Environmental Inputs 32, 35, 60, 90–92, 112–116, 124, 142, 147, 170, 180, 188–189, 197
  See also Socialisation, Mass Media, Sport Subculture, Utilitarian Motives
  See Table of 119
Esteem Motive 24
Event Information Template 129, 131
  See also Attraction
Event Management Checklist
  Description of 201
Excitement Motives 24
Experiential Lever 126–127
External Forces 32–33, 194, 197
  See also Environmental Inputs
Facilities
  Backup Sites 225
  Event Venue Sites 223
  Service Support 223–224
  Special Support 224
  Special Sites 224
Facilities and Support Services
  Communications 222–223
  Equipment 223
  On-Site Control 224
  Site Liaison 224
Financial Considerations for Events
  Admission 209
  Budget and Resource
    Planning 207–208
  Merchandising and Concessions 208
Financial Levers 125, 155
Food Service
  Capacity/Time Requirements 225
  Corporate Donations 226
  Menu 225–226
  Refreshments 226
Fundraising for Events
  Corporate Sponsorship 209
Geographic Relationship between Event Sites 226
  See also Housing
Goal Behaviour 20
Hedonic Motives 22–23, 59, 94, 113, 119–120, 138
  See also SPEED motives

Hierarchy of Needs   17
Hospitality   239–240
Housing
  Families   227
  General Condition   227–228
  General Housing Guidelines   227
  Geographic Location   228
  Media   227
  Negotiating with Site Owner   228
  Officials   227
  VIP   227
  Human Resources
  Celebrities   214–215
  Event Promotions   213
  Hospitality   210
  International Services   210
  Media Centre   214
  Nerve Centre   210–211
  Personnel   211
  Press Guide   214
  Programmes   213–214
  Protocol   210
  Public Relations   211–213
  Registration   215–216
  Trained volunteers   211
    See also Volunteers
Impact
  Behaviour   177–178
  Cognitive Processing   176–177
Importance   141, 152
Inputs   31–33, 46, 110, 112, 115–116, 118,
    121, 124, 130, 139–140, 142, 147,
    152, 171, 177, 188–189
  See also Internal and External
    Forces, Awareness, Attraction,
    Attachment & Allegiance, PCM
  Table of   119
Inputs Phase   32–34
  See also Inputs and Attitudinal
    Evaluation
Internal Forces   92–94, 197
  See also Personal and Psychological
    Inputs
Internal Processing   31, 33–50, 92, 97,
    111, 114, 147, 171
  Definition of   33
  Figure of   33
  In Allegiance   52, 171–174
  In Attachment   51–52, 145–149

In Attraction   51, 114–122
In Awareness   50–51, 95–97
  See also Knowledge Acquisition, Sport
    Consumer Decision-Making
    Sequence, PCM Framework
Internalisation   149, 151–152, 173–174
Internet Bonding   159–161, 182
Internet Lever   78, 129–130
Involvement
  Definition of   16, 66
  Facets   66–67
    See also Centrality, Pleasure and
    Sign
  Figure of   67
  Measurement of   67–68, 80–81
  Profiles of   69, 81
    See also PCM Staging Algorithm
  Related to Constraints   193–194, 196
  Table of   66
Knowledge   34–39, 95–97, 112, 120–122,
    175
  Acquisition of   34–39, 95–96, 112
  Definition of   31
  See also Motivation, Perception,
    Learning, Memory, Personality
    and PCM
Language Services
  Capabilities to Translate
    Materials   229
  Interpreter   228
Learning   36
Levers   124–130
  See also Financial, Social, Experiential,
    Cause-Related, Sponsorship,
    Brand, Internet and Event
    Information Template
List of Values   143
Maintenance/Construction/Capital
    Improvements   229
Marketing and the Organisation   183
Marketing Action Questions   8
Marketing Mix   60–64, 75, 97, 99, 154,
    195
Marketing Reports   75–77
Mass Media   90–91, 95, 103, 115
Medical
  Emergency Medical Services
    (EMS)   230
  Hospital Liaison   230

Medical (*continued*)
  Professional Staff   230
  Site Support   229–230
  Transportation   230
Memory   37, 146, 150
Motivation   17–20, 22, 190–191
  See also SPEED, SportWay, Sport and
    Event Consumer Motivation
    Process
  Versus Constraints   191–192
Need Recognition   17–22
Negotiation   195–197
Outputs   95–97
  See also Engagement, Awareness,
    Attraction, Attachment and
    Allegiance
Outputs Phase   39–41
Passion   150, 182–183
Perceived Constraints   192
Performance Motive   24
Perception   36
Personal Inputs   33, 35, 92–94, 112–117,
    124, 147, 170, 188–189
Personal Meaning   138, 151–152, 168, 182
Personalisation   154–155, 182
Personality   38
  See also Inputs
Pleasure Facet   66
Post-Event Evaluation   209–210
Primary Research   74, 76
Processes   92, 146
  Soldering
  Welding
  See also Socialisation, Internal
    Processing, Knowledge
    Acquisition, Awareness,
    Attraction, Attachment and
    Allegiance
Psychological Continuum Model (PCM)
  Description of   42–45
  Engagement, figure of   49
  Figure of   43
  Movement within   45–47
  Processing within   50–53
  Stages within   46–48
  Staging Algorithm   66–73
Psychological Engagement   48–49–53,
    96, 115, 121–122, 140, 142, 149–153,
    169–170, 174, 188, 190–191

Psychological Inputs   33, 35, 94,
    112–113–117, 124, 147, 170, 188–190
Psychological Outcomes   39–40, 48, 120,
    95, 149, 174
Pull Motives   19, 35, 114
Push Motives   19, 35, 114
Safety and Security
  Command Post   233–234
  Credentials   234
  Crowd Control   232–233
  Emergency Action Plan   233
  Fire   231
  Interagency Communication   234
  Internal Communications   230–231
  Lost and Found   233
  Parking   233
  Police   231
  Traffic   231–232
  Transportation   231
  VIP   234
Schedule for Events
  Event Space   217
  Restoration   217–218
  Setup   217
  Time Span   216–217
Secondary Research   74–76
Segmentation   61, 64–65, 76, 99
  See also Staging Algorithm
  Segmentation categories   65
  Selection strategies   64
Self-Concept   93, 142, 144–146, 136, 148,
    151–152, 170–171, 173, 182
  Bonding   155–157, 182
Service Bonding   157–159, 181–182
Service Orientation   58–59, 113–114, 142,
    153, 158, 170, 180, 183, 195, 197
Sign Facet   66
Signage/Decorations for Events   228
Social Impact   4–5
Social Learning Process   90, 94–95, 146,
    151
Social Lever   126, 155
Socialisation   89–92
  Agents   90–91, 98, 100–103, 113, 115,
    126, 147, 170
  Motive   24, 93
  Process   89
Soldering   147–149, 171, 174
  Figure of   148

Special Events
  Dances (Social Events)   240
  Demonstrations   240–241
  Entertainment   241
  Exhibitions   241
  Recreational Opportunities   240
  Victory Banquet   240
Special Event and Services   238
SPEED Motives   30, 32, 35, 41, 45, 47,
      59–60, 73, 94, 101, 118–119, 126,
      148, 196
  Definition of   23–25
  Table of   24
Sponsorship Bonding   161, 182
Sponsorship Lever   127–128
Sport Decision-Making Sequence   8, 90,
      111, 147, 169–171
  Definition of   31–32
  Figure of   30, 31
Sport Exchange Process   58–59
Sport Events   4–5
  Charity   118, 143, 156–157
  Unique aspect of   9–10
Sport and Event Consumer
      Behaviour   4–7
Sport and Event Consumer Motivation
      Process   16–23, 146, 190
  Definition of   16
  Model of   17
Sport Information System   77–78
Sport Marketing Action   8–9, 11, 97, 123
  Description of   58–62
  Figure of   60
  Select Information Systems   77–80
  Select Key Target Markets   64–73, 196
    See also PCM Staging Algorithm
  Strategic Use of Marketing Mix   62–
      64, 195–196
  Study and Evaluate Market   74–76,
      196–198

See also Awareness, Attraction,
      Attachment and Allegiance
Sport Object Trust   148, 152–153, 158,
      170, 173, 182
Sport Subculture   91–92
SportWay   21–22, 30, 34–35, 60
  Definition of   21
  Model of   21
Staging Algorithm   66–73, 99, 101, 125,
      183
  Classification Procedure   70
  Description of   66, 70
  Examples of   71–73
  Involvement Profiles   82
  PCM Staging Score Procedure   80–81
Stimulus-Response   141–142
Substitution   197–198
SWOT   61, 76, 75–76
Tension Reduction   17, 19
Transportation   234
  On-Site   235
Trust   148
Unique Aspects of Sport and Event
      Product   9–10
Utilitarian Motives   22–23, 59, 94, 113,
      118–120, 138
  See also External Inputs
Value Bonding   156–156
Values   94, 138–139, 142–144, 147, 170,
      173
  See also Camaraderie; Competency,
      Cause
  Value bonding   182
Volition   116–118, 120, 152, 170, 175, 192
Volunteers   218–219
Want Pathway   18–21
Weather   236
Welding   172–174